# DOCTOR · WHO

## THE ULTIMATE MONSTER GUIDE

### JUSTIN RICHARDS

**BBC**
**BOOKS**

10 9 8 7 6 5 4 3 2 1

Published in 2009 by BBC Books, an imprint of Ebury Publishing. A Random House Group company.

The Random House Group Limited Reg. No. 954009
Addresses for companies within the Random House Group can be found at www.randomhouse.co.uk
A CIP catalogue record for this book is available from the British Library.

ISBN 978 1 849 90091 1

The Random House Group Limited supports the Forest Stewardship Council (FSC), the leading international forest certification organisation. All our titles that are printed on Greenpeace approved FSC certified paper carry the FSC logo. Our paper procurement policy can be found at www.rbooks.co.uk/environment.

Commissioning Editor: Albert DePetrillo        Cover and interior design: Lee Binding
Project Editor: Steve Tribe                    Production: Antony Heller and Phil Spencer
Creative Consultant: Justin Richards

Printed and bound in China by C&C Offset Printing Co., Ltd

BBC Books would like to thank the following for providing photographs and for permission to reproduce copyright material. While every effort has been made to trace and acknowledge all copyright holders, we would like to apologise should there have been any errors or omissions.

All images copyright © BBC, except:

Page 41 Cassandra artwork and page 190 Lazarus artwork by Russell T Davies
Page 48 (main and bottom left), page 49 (mechanism), page 66 (top left), 103 (bottom left), 304 (bottom right) the Braxiatek Collection
Page 81 (bottom left, middle, right), page 95 (Dalek design sketches) Raymond P. Cusick
Page 82 (bottom middle) Hulton Archive/Getty Images
Page 85 (bottom right) Topham Picture Source
Page 89 (centre) Andrew Beech
Page 94 (bottom left, middle) David Richardson
Page 97 (all except bottom left) Mike Tucker

Page 128 (main), page 152 (bottom left) Miss Susan Moore
Page 186 (bottom left), page 262 (bottom) Charles Lumm
Page 209 Valiant artwork © and courtesy of Peter McKinstry
Page 222 (all), page 248 (main) Mat Irvine
Page 324 (main), page 326 (all except bottom left), page 345 (top right) Tony Cornell
Page 352 (top) – Jonathan Saville
All production designs and storyboards are reproduced courtesy of the Doctor Who Art Department.
Some behind-the-scenes images are courtesy of Millennium FX.
All computer-generated imagery courtesy of The Mill.

All photographic compositions and colourisation by Lee Binding.

With additional thanks to:
James Carter, Mathew Clayton, Will Cohen, Stephen Cole, Stuart Cooper, Paul Cornell, Stuart Crouch, Russell T Davies, Kevin Davis, Ben Dunn, Sarah Emsley, Jacqueline Farrow, Cameron Fitch, Mark Gatiss, Neill Gorton, Ian Grutchfield, Clayton Hickman, David J. Howe, Gwenllian Lloyd, Tom MacRae, Vicki McKay, Peter McKinstry, Isobel McLean, Brian Minchin, Steven Moffat, James North, Marianne Paton, Nicholas Payne, Helen Raynor, Elwen Rowland, Edward Russell, Gary Russell, Jim Sangster, Matthew Savage, Robert Shearman, Tom Spilsbury, Edward Thomas, Mike Tucker, Paul Vanezis, Peter Ware

## ALL THE STRANGE, STRANGE CREATURES...

Since the very first episodes of *Doctor Who*, the Doctor has had his enemies. The first aliens he encountered were the Daleks – the deadliest of all his many intergalactic foes. This book provides a wealth of information about most of the monstrous foes the Doctor has encountered in over 45 years of television time travel. From the Abzorbaloff to the Zygons, it provides background information, story synopses, and behind-the-scenes secrets about monsters and villains, aliens and enemies, and creatures and demons from the current series of *Doctor Who* and from the classic era that ran from 1963 to 1989 on BBC One. It covers the lives of ten Doctors, and features dozens of the friends and companions who have joined him on his journey. A journey that is set to continue with a new Doctor very soon…

Come with us and see the most extraordinary sights and creatures of the universe. Or, as the Doctor himself might say, stay behind – and regret your staying until the day you die…

# THE ABZORBALOFF

The Abzorbaloff comes from Clom, the twin planet of Raxacoricofallapatorius. A hideous, green humanoid creature, it can absorb other life forms just by touching them, in the process gaining all their knowledge and experience. It is desperate to find and absorb the Doctor, believing he will be the ultimate 'meal' and provide him with a wealth of experience.

For a while the victims of the Abzorbaloff are still visible – as faces embedded in its skin. They retain some individuality, and can talk and even read the Abzorbaloff's thoughts. Ultimately, the Abzorbaloff is destroyed by the combined wills of its victims, working together to pull it apart.

Aristocratic tuft of hair

Ornate cane holds the Abzorbaloff's power

Green, saggy, Slitheen-like skin

Faces of the victims it has absorbed still have some life of their own

### ELTON POPE

When he was a child, Elton Pope saw the Doctor one night in his house. That moment is etched in his memory – not least as it was the night Elton's mother died. Years later, Elton tried to track down the Doctor, joining up with others who shared his goal. They became firm friends, but that friendship was poisoned by the arrival of Victor Kennedy – who was actually the Abzorbaloff. All of the group were absorbed, except Elton, who finally got to meet the Doctor properly and learn the truth about his mother's death.

 # LOVE & MONSTERS

Elton Pope meets up with several other people who are trying to find the Doctor, and together they form a group called LINDA. Gradually, they come to spend less time looking for the Doctor and more having fun. Then the mysterious Victor Kennedy arrives and sets himself up as their leader, organising them to renew their search. Elton tracks down Rose's mother, Jackie, but she realises what he is up to and warns Rose.

By the time the Doctor and Rose find Elton, Victor Kennedy has revealed himself to be the Abzorbaloff, and has absorbed all the other members of the group. But together, their faces embedded in the creature's skin, they are able to tear him apart.

Written by
**Russell T Davies**
Featuring
**Elton Pope, with the
Tenth Doctor and Rose**
First broadcast
**17 June 2006
1 episode**

### LINDA

Elton makes up the name LINDA, which stands for London Investigation 'N' Detective Agency. Its members – Mr Skinner, Ursula Blake, Bliss, Bridget and Elton – are trying to discover everything they can about the Doctor, but as they become friends they get distracted. Mr Skinner reads extracts from his novel, Bliss shows off her sculpture, Bridget supplies home-cooked food. They even form a band and perform old ELO hits.

But the arrival of Victor Kennedy refocuses them on finding the Doctor – with disastrous consequences.

### THE HOIX

When Elton, having heard reports of a police box turning up in Woolwich, finds the Doctor and Rose, they are battling against the alien Hoix.

Little is known about the Hoix, although it is partial to pork chops. Elton witnesses the Doctor and Rose trying to calm the Hoix by throwing liquid from a red bucket over it.

The Doctor pauses in his task when he sees – and recognises – Elton. Scared, Elton runs off. Moments later he hears the TARDIS dematerialise – the Hoix, presumably, has been dealt with.

### THE HOWLING HALLS

When the Doctor rescues Elton from the Abzorbaloff, it is the second time he has saved Elton's life. The first was when Elton was a four-year-old child – the night his mother died.

There was a living shadow in the Popes' house, an elemental shade that had escaped from the Howling Halls. The Doctor stopped it, but he was too late to save Elton's mother.

Since that first glimpse of the Doctor, Elton Pope has yearned to discover more about the mysterious wanderer in time and space.

##  MAKING MONSTERS

Neill Gorton's Millennium FX team created both the Abzorbaloff and the hideous Hoix. As with almost all the alien creatures to appear in *Doctor Who*, the Hoix was created to fulfil its role and description in the script. Put together largely from bits and pieces 'left over' from other monsters, it was, nonetheless, an impressive creation by the Millennium FX team.

The Abzorbaloff, however, was devised very differently: it did not spring from the mind of the writer and the pages of the script. It was, in fact, devised by young William Grantham as his entry in a competition to design a *Doctor Who* monster, run by the popular children's BBC television programme *Blue Peter*. The prize was for William to see his creation appear in an episode of *Doctor Who*.

The design that William submitted was turned into a costume by Millennium FX, and sculpted to fit comedian and actor Peter Kay, who played both Kennedy and the Abzorbaloff itself. The faces of the creature's victims were sculpted into the costume – complete

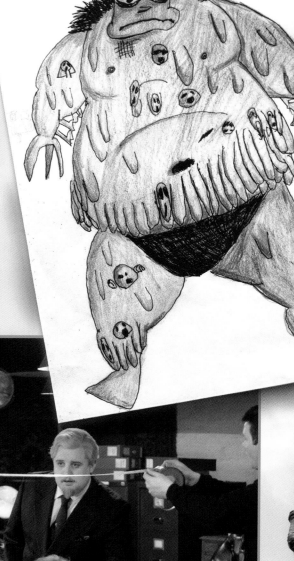

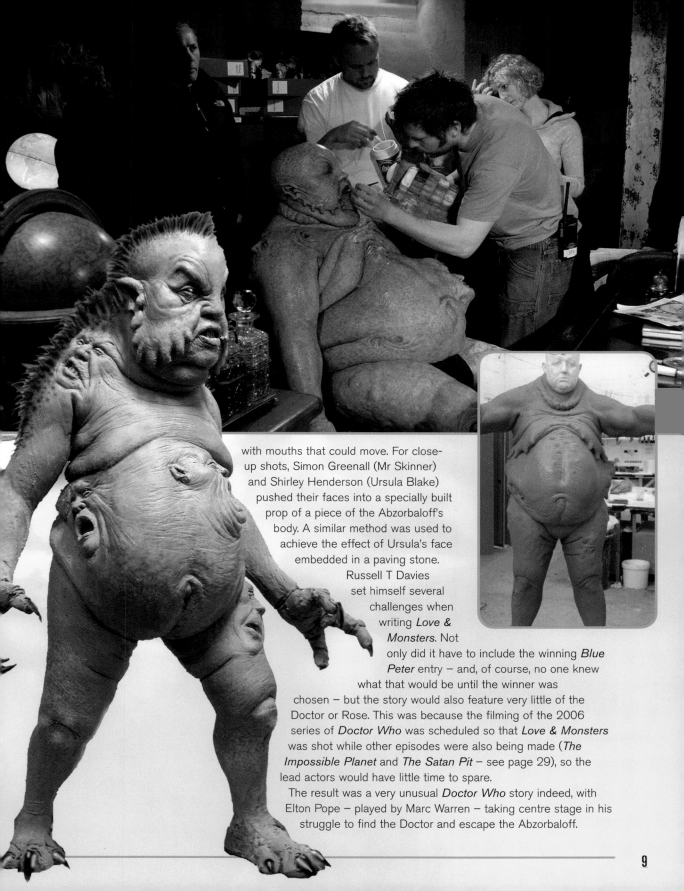

with mouths that could move. For close-up shots, Simon Greenall (Mr Skinner) and Shirley Henderson (Ursula Blake) pushed their faces into a specially built prop of a piece of the Abzorbaloff's body. A similar method was used to achieve the effect of Ursula's face embedded in a paving stone.

Russell T Davies set himself several challenges when writing *Love & Monsters*. Not only did it have to include the winning *Blue Peter* entry – and, of course, no one knew what that would be until the winner was chosen – but the story would also feature very little of the Doctor or Rose. This was because the filming of the 2006 series of *Doctor Who* was scheduled so that *Love & Monsters* was shot while other episodes were also being made (*The Impossible Planet* and *The Satan Pit* – see page 29), so the lead actors would have little time to spare.

The result was a very unusual *Doctor Who* story indeed, with Elton Pope – played by Marc Warren – taking centre stage in his struggle to find the Doctor and escape the Abzorbaloff.

9

# THE ADIPOSE

When their breeding planet was lost, the Adiposian First Family was forced to find another way to give birth to a new generation. Their solution was to create Adipose children on another planet. They chose Earth, knowing that they would have to operate in secret or risk being reported to the Shadow Proclamation for their illegal activities. The Adiposians hired 'Miss Foster' to run the project.

The Adipose children created on Earth are cute-looking creatures made from excess body fat. But the Adipose can also convert bone, organs, hair – turning a whole human body into Adipose material.

Millions of Adipose are created when Miss Foster is forced to activate her programme early because of the intervention of the Doctor and Donna Noble. These Adipose children are picked up from Earth, and eventually taken into care by the Shadow Proclamation.

Single fang made from reconstituted calcium deposits →

Adipose creature is composed entirely out of fat →

## PENNY CARTER

Working as a science correspondent for the *Observer* newspaper, journalist Penny Carter attended a briefing given by Miss Foster at Adipose Industries. But the research Penny had already done led her to believe there was something very wrong at the company. And Miss Foster's answers to Penny's questions did nothing to allay her suspicions.

Penny had already discovered that much of the Adipose research data had been faked. But when she tried to infiltrate Adipose Industries and investigate further, she was captured by Miss Foster – who showed her an actual Adipose creature and explained what was really happening.

Whether or not Penny believed Miss Foster, she was tied to a chair while Miss Foster activated the Inducer that brought on the creation of millions of Adipose from the million customers who had been taking the Adipose capsules.

Spectacles complete the image, and correct any visual defects →

Miss Foster is actually Matron Cofelia →

← Outward appearance of a smart businesswoman

Miss Foster is actually Matron Cofelia of the Five-Straighten Classabindi Nursery Fleet (intergalactic class). Employed by the Adiposian First Family to foster a new generation of Adipose children, she selects Earth as a breeding planet, which is illegal under Galactic Law.

The company seems to offer a miraculous slimming treatment. Simply take a capsule every day, and you will lose exactly one kilogram of fat each night. 'The fat just walks away,' says the company advertising. And it's literally true – the fat is converted into child Adipose creatures. With over a million customers in Greater London, millions of Adipose are created when Matron Cofelia activates the conversion programme.

When the Adiposians arrive to take their children, they kill the one person who can implicate them in the crime – Matron Cofelia. She thinks she is being taken up to the spaceship, but the Adiposians retract their transporter beam, and she falls to her death.

11

 # PARTNERS IN CRIME

Written by
**Russell T Davies**
Featuring
**the Tenth Doctor and Donna with Rose**
First broadcast
**5 April 2008**
**1 episode**

The Doctor and Donna Noble both independently investigate Adipose Industries – which purports to offer a miraculous weight-loss product. In fact, the company, run by the alien Matron Cofelia, is a front for the creation of millions of Adipose children, made out of human body fat.

Realising that the Doctor might alert the Shadow Proclamation to her illegal activities on Earth, Matron Cofelia activates an Inducer, kick-starting the creation of millions of Adipose. The Doctor and Donna stop the Inducer before people lose too much of their bodies and die. The thousands of Adipose already created are taken on board a huge spaceship, and Matron Cofelia is killed by the Adiposians so she cannot incriminate them.

### FINDING DONNA

The Doctor is surprised to find Donna at Adipose Industries. As he is watching Matron Cofelia through her office window, he catches sight of Donna – also watching through the office door.

Dona has in fact been investigating Adipose Industries in the hope of finding the Doctor again. She guessed that he would turn up somewhere that there was something odd going on. Having found him again, Donna is determined not to let the Doctor go! Before long, the two of them are plunged headlong into danger – just like the first time they met.

### CAPSULE

Each Adipose customer is given a pendant made of 18-carat gold, in the shape of an Adipose capsule. At first touch, the capsule immediately bio-tunes itself to its owner. This acts as a focal point for inducing the birth of the Adipose. One creature is 'born' each night from a kilogram of the customer's excess body fat.

Donna brings a new un-tuned capsule into Stacy Campbell's house, causing an unscheduled Adipose birth. Matron Cofelia activates a full parthenogenesis – killing Stacy as her body is completely changed into Adipose creatures.

### ROSE RETURNS

Although she doesn't realise, it is immediately after defeating the threat posed by Matron Cofelia that Donna first meets a young woman who will have a huge impact on her life – Rose Tyler.

With the barriers between worlds and dimensions breaking down, Rose is able to transfer across to our Earth from her own, parallel world.

She knows already that Donna will be important – and acts to save her from the effects of the Time Beetle, one of the Trickster's Brigade, in the episode *Turn Left* (see page 309).

# CREATING THE ADIPOSE

The Adipose creatures were all completely computer generated. For scenes where they interacted with people – like when Matron Cofelia shows an Adipose to Penny Carter – a 'soft toy' version was used, then replaced by The Mill with the computer-generated image.

The scenes featuring hundreds of Adipose were made using a special software tool called Massive, which had been created by Stephen Regelous and used to animate huge armies in the *Lord of the Rings* films. The creatures in the foreground were animated individually, while the crowds behaved according to artificial intelligence rules built into them by the software. Stephen Regelous had been hoping his Massive software would one day be used on *Doctor Who*. He made the trip over to London from his home in New Zealand to program the software himself.

### DADDY'S HERE

The enormous spaceship which arrives to take the Adipose creatures away was created as a computer-generated image by The Mill. The ship was then added to specially shot sequences to show it arriving over London, or passing by Donna's grandfather Wilf as he looks through his telescope in another direction and misses it.

The circular design was inspired by the shape of the alien mothership that appears at the end of the classic Steven Spielberg science fiction film *Close Encounters of the Third Kind*.

On this page, you can see The Mill's design for the Adipose spaceship (above right). Compare this with the final computer-generated image (left) of the ship as it flies over London.

The rays of light which transport the Adipose creatures up to the ship – and which drop Matron Cofelia to her death when they are turned off – were also computer generated.

Helmet hides fact that real astronaut has been replaced

Ambassadors are emitting over 2 million rads of radiation

MICHAELS

The Alien Ambassadors are sent to Earth in the place of human astronauts returning from a mission to Mars – but they, in turn, are kidnapped from the landed space capsule. When they reappear, the 'astronauts' seem to have been infected with a deadly form of radiation – they can kill people merely by touching them.

The Ambassadors had been kidnapped by forces opposed to contact between Earth and the aliens, and are now being forced to kill, to make it seem that they are hostile. But on board their mothership, where the real astronauts are being held, the aliens believe that mankind has imprisoned their ambassadors. If they are not returned, the aliens will destroy the Earth.

Bullets are deflected and flattened by a force field

Ambassadors can kill or disable with an electrical charge from the hand

### THE MARS PROBE MISSIONS

Space Control is the British equivalent of NASA's Mission Control. From here, the Mars Probe missions are launched and monitored. After sending back pictures and messages from Mars, all contact with *Mars Probe 7* is lost. Then, inexplicably, it blasts off and heads back to Earth.

Eight months later, as *Mars Probe 7* nears Earth, *Recovery 7* is sent up on a rescue mission. Astronaut Charles Van Lyden docks with the stranded, silent *Mars Probe 7* capsule and opens the hatch. He expects to find his fellow astronauts, Frank Michaels and Joe Lefee. Instead, his face contorts in terror and an unearthly sound is heard back at Space Control – a sound which the Doctor recognises as an alien message.

# THE AMBASSADORS OF DEATH

Written by
**David Whitaker**
Featuring
**the Third Doctor,
UNIT and Liz**
First broadcast
**21 March–2 May 1970
7 episodes**

On their return to Earth, the astronauts from *Mars Probe 7* and *Recovery 7* are kidnapped – but they are actually Ambassadors sent by an alien race, and they need radiation to survive. General Carrington believes the aliens are evil and has arranged their kidnap, forcing them to commit murder. He plans to unmask one of the them on live television and turn public opinion against the well-intentioned aliens.

But the Doctor – who has visited the alien mothership in another rocket – and his friends from UNIT, find and free the other two Alien Ambassadors. They manage to stop Carrington's broadcast, and the Ambassadors are returned to their mothership.

## THE ALIEN SHIP

The disc-shaped vessel is half a mile in diameter. It gives out radio impulses like those emitted by pulsars, and signals that jam NASA's cameras, so they can't get a picture of it.

The Doctor goes up in a rocket from Space Control to visit the ship. Inside, he finds an environment prepared for him. The interior of the ship is like a glowing orange cave. Here the real astronauts are being held in a mock-up of the reception centre at Space Control. They believe they are back on Earth waiting to be given the all-clear after decontamination.

## ALIEN COMMUNICATION

Because the aliens' form of intelligence is so different from ours, they can only communicate by sending pictographic signals.

Their first communication is a set of instructions, which the Doctor finally manages to decode. These instructions show him how to build a device with which to communicate with the Ambassadors.

General Carrington and his men use a similar device to force the aliens to do what he wants – threatening to withdraw the aliens' access to the radiation they need if they don't cooperate.

## GENERAL CARRINGTON

General Carrington is the head of the newly formed Space Security Department. When he was an astronaut on *Mars Probe 6*, he met the aliens on Mars. His fellow astronaut (Jim Daniels) was killed by the aliens, who did not realise their touch could be fatal to humans. But Carrington blames them for the death and sets a trap for them.

Carrington believes that destroying the aliens is his moral duty, and will go to any lengths to 'save the Earth' – even killing scientist Lennox, and his own superior Sir James Quinlan.

Each Auton is animated and controlled by a portion of the Nestene Consciousness

Faces of shop-window Autons depend on style of other 'real' mannequins

Auton is made entirely from a special plastic that is impervious to bullets

Hand gun – fingers drop away to reveal deadly weapon

While they are not named explicitly in the episode *Rose*, the shop dummies that come to life and menace the Doctor and Rose in the Nestene lair are called Autons. First encountered by the Doctor in his third incarnation, the creatures are blank-faced, plastic humanoids created by the Nestene Consciousness and animated by a tiny portion of its collective being. Each Auton has a gun hidden inside its hand, the fingers dropping away to allow it to fire. Bullets have no effect on the Autons.

## THE NESTENE CONSCIOUSNESS

The Doctor describes the Nestene Consciousness as 'a ruthlessly aggressive intelligent alien life form'. It is, literally, living plastic – able to take on any shape. Since the Last Great Time War, when its food stock planets were destroyed, the Nestene has mutated from a disembodied, mutually telepathic intelligence into a living plastic desperate to find further food stocks from which to renew itself.

#  SPEARHEAD FROM SPACE

Written by
**Robert Holmes**
Featuring
**the Third Doctor,
UNIT and Liz**
First broadcast
**3–24 January 1970
4 episodes**

The TARDIS lands in the middle of a strange meteorite shower, and the Doctor swiftly discovers the Nestene plan to colonise Earth. Killer Autons are collecting the 'meteorites' that contain fragments of the Nestene Consciousness. At the nearby Auto Plastics factory, the Nestene Consciousness creates killer Autons and facsimiles of people.

Recovering from his enforced regeneration, the Doctor works with his old friend Brigadier Lethbridge-Stewart, who is in charge of UNIT, to stop the invasion. Together with Doctor Elizabeth Shaw, he creates a weapon to stop the invaders. But with shop-window dummies and Madame Tussauds' waxworks coming to life, he may already be too late.

### EXILED TO EARTH

After many years of wandering through space and time in the TARDIS, the Doctor was captured by his own people, the Time Lords, and put on trial for interfering in the affairs of other planets. He put up a spirited defence, accusing the Time Lords of complacency and inaction, but nevertheless he was found guilty and sentenced to exile – with a new appearance – on Earth in the late twentieth century.

Earth was chosen as it has always been one of the Doctor's favourite planets and seemed vulnerable to attack.

### UNIT

After his involvement in foiling the plans of the Great Intelligence (see page 344), Colonel Lethbridge-Stewart was promoted and put in charge of a military taskforce – UNIT – set up to deal with otherworldly threats. With a remit to investigate the unusual and the alien, UNIT's first major battle was against the Cybermen (see page 57). Just as the exiled Doctor arrived on Earth, the organisation was pitched against the Nestene threat. Brigadier Lethbridge-Stewart immediately recruited the Doctor to act as UNIT's Scientific Adviser.

### CHANNING

Until the recovery of the Swarm Leader, Channing (above) forms the spearhead of the first invasion attempt. He controls Hibbert, managing director of Auto Plastics, and directs the Autons.

Since they are all essentially part of the same being, Channing can see what any of the Autons or facsimiles sees and can direct them mentally.

When the Doctor destroys the part of the Nestene Consciousness that is on Earth and it withdraws its influence, Channing dies. He is reduced to a faceless mannequin.

# COLONISATION

The Nestene Consciousness is a living plastic, able to create forms for itself on any planet it wishes to colonise – forms ideally suited to conquest. It has been colonising worlds for a thousand million years.

   The Nestene Consciousness can even create perfect plastic copies of politicians, soldiers, and others in strategic positions. During their first attempted invasion, these facsimiles were stored in a display at Madame Tussauds waxworks until activated and sent to take the places of the original people.

# TERROR OF THE AUTONS

Written by
**Robert Holmes**
Featuring
**the Third Doctor,
UNIT and Jo**
First broadcast
**2–23 January 1971
4 episodes**

The Time Lords warn the Doctor that an old enemy of his – the Master – has come to Earth. The Master reactivates an energy unit and creates more Autons. He plans to help the Nestene in another attempt to invade Earth, promising to help them establish a bridgehead and create panic using deadly plastic daffodils.

As UNIT battle against killer Autons disguised in grotesque carnival masks for a supposed plastics promotional tour, the Doctor persuades the Master that the Nestene Consciousness will not honour its agreement with him. Together the two Time Lords manage to send the creature back into deep space.

### FAKE POLICE

Investigating the circus where the Master has hidden his TARDIS (disguised as a horsebox), the Doctor and Jo are attacked by an angry mob. They are saved by two policemen. But the policemen are in fact Autons, as the Doctor realises. He rips the face mask from one of them and, with the help of UNIT, the Doctor and Jo escape. During the battle, Captain Yates drives a car straight at one Auton and knocks it over a cliff. When it tumbles to the bottom, it simply gets to its feet and starts to climb back up.

### DEADLY DAFFODILS

The killer daffodils – or Nestene Autojets, as the Master calls them – have their instructions imprinted on every cell as a program-pattern, which reveals a nose and mouth when converted to 'visual symbols'. Activated by radio signal, the daffodils spray plastic film over the nose and mouth of their victim. This film is then dissolved by the carbon dioxide from the lungs as the victim dies. The Master plans to set off the daffodils with a radio impulse. The Autons have distributed almost half a million daffodils – each designed to kill.

# LIVING PLASTIC

The alien Nestene Consciousness can bring anything made of plastic to life. Nestene plastic has instructions imprinted on every cell as a program-pattern. The Nestene Consciousness can use thought control to activate any plastic to act as its eyes and ears, as well as animate it – often with deadly results.

## KILLER CABLE

Having failed to kill the Doctor with either a booby-trap bomb or the killer Autons, the Master resorts to a more subtle approach. Disguised as a telephone engineer, he gets into UNIT HQ and replaces the flex on the Doctor's telephone with a longer, plastic cord. He then calls the Doctor and transmits an activation signal down the telephone.

Imbued with Nestene intelligence, the phone cable comes to life and attempts to throttle the Doctor, who is only saved by the timely intervention of the Brigadier.

## LIVING DOLL

To kill Mr Farrell, owner of the plastics factory he is using to create Autons and daffodils, the Master uses a grotesque, troll-like doll. Activated by heat, the doll comes to life and kills Farrell.

Trying to uncover the doll's secrets, the Doctor finds out that it is made from solid plastic, but fails to discover what activates it. It again comes to life and attacks Jo when Captain Yates is using the Doctor's Bunsen burner to make cocoa.

The doll is finally destroyed when Yates shoots it to bits.

## FIENDISH FURNITURE

The plastics factory's production manager, McDermott, takes issue with the Master over his plans for the business. The Master invites him to try out a 'new product' – a black plastic armchair. Although initially sceptical, McDermott eventually sits down. At the Master's command, the chair folds in on itself, trapping McDermott inside and suffocating him. The Master exploits the same weakness in human 'design' with plastic daffodils, using considerably less plastic to cause suffocation.

 # ROSE

Written by
**Russell T Davies**
Featuring
**the Ninth Doctor
and Rose**
First broadcast
**26 March 2005
1 episode**

Working in a department store, Rose Tyler is attacked by shop-window dummies in the basement. She is saved by the mysterious Doctor, who tells her he is an alien stopping the attempted invasion of Earth by the Nestene Consciousness and its killer Autons.

Initially sceptical, Rose tries to find out more about the Doctor, but her enquiries lead her and her boyfriend, Mickey, into deadly danger. Mickey is captured by a plastic wheelie-bin, and his Nestene duplicate tries to get Rose to lead it to the Doctor. Eventually, Rose helps the Doctor to find the lair of the Nestene Consciousness. Together, they manage to destroy the creature, and Rose leaves with the Doctor in his TARDIS.

### ROSE

Nineteen-year-old Rose Tyler lives with her mum, Jackie, on the Powell Estate in London. She works in a large department store, where she meets the Doctor for the first time, when he rescues her from attacking Autons, concealed there by the Nestene Consciousness.

Although they part company, the Doctor finds Rose again as he tracks down the Nestene Consciousness. Rose is too curious about the Doctor to let him walk out of her life, and before long she is caught up in his extraordinary adventures.

### THE NESTENE PLAN

The Nestene protein planets have rotted away and the Nestene Consciousness has had its food stocks destroyed in the last great Time War between the Daleks and the Time Lords.

So by the time of this third attempted invasion, the Consciousness sees Earth as a suitable alternative food supply, made attractive by the oil, smoke, toxins and dioxins in the air.

It plans to take over the world, activating Autons concealed in shops using a signal transmitted through the London Eye.

### SHOP DUMMIES

To spearhead its attack on Earth, the Nestene Consciousness once again uses shop-window dummies that come to life and smash their way out of the shops to attack. These are simple Autons with no independent thought. Once they have been activated, they exist only to kill, using their deadly wrist-guns.

As well as 'standard' killer Autons, as used in the first attempted invasion, the Nestene also create 'child' mannequins. The Autons 'model' all manner of designer clothes – even bridal gowns.

# RESURRECTING THE AUTONS

The new-look Autons for the 2005 series of *Doctor Who* were designed by Neill Gorton and Matthew Savage, under the supervision of the production designer, Edward Thomas. The original concept design is shown here.
Writer and executive producer, Russell T Davies, explains:

'I decided to bring back the Autons – although this time, the Doctor never actually uses their name! – because it was important that Rose, in her first adventure, could consider the whole thing to be one big trick. If, in the first five minutes of the episode, she saw a great big tentacled thing, then we don't have too many of those on Planet Earth – she'd know they were aliens! But plastic, even if it's living plastic, can keep her doubting for a long time, while she gets to know the Doctor. Is it radio control? Or clever prosthetics? Smoke and mirrors?

'It was an honour to resurrect the creations of one of the programme's finest writers, the late Robert Holmes – what a genius! If a small spark of his wonderful mind can touch the new series, then we're very lucky indeed. As a writer, I'd like to think this episode is a tribute to him, with love and gratitude.'

### GETTING A CONSCIENCE

In *Spearhead from Space* (above), the tentacles that emerge from the tank containing the Nestene Consciousness were 'physical props' – real tentacles provided by the Visual Effects team. A model of the Consciousness was made and filmed for *Terror of the Autons*, but the final effect was not considered convincing enough, so an electronic glow was substituted. For *Rose*, the Nestene Consciousness was created as a computer-generated image (CGI) and added in post-production.

# RESURRECTING THE AUTONS

The Autons' return gave the new production team the opportunity to enhance one small part of *Doctor Who*'s golden past.

In the final episode of the first Auton serial, *Spearhead from Space*, the shop-window dummies come alive in the shop windows.

As Russell T Davies points out: 'The Autons step forward, they raise their arms, they slice down – and then we see nothing, the picture cuts away, and the audience hears the distant sound of glass smashing. Breakable glass panes were probably too expensive for that wonderful, inventive production team! At last, 35 years later, thanks to the brilliant technicians of BBC Wales, the audience can finally see that glass break. It was worth the wait!'

## SCRIPT EXTRACT

JACKIE looks round.
DUMMIES are stepping down from every window. All sorts of different shapes and sizes. And it's all strangely calm, SHOPPERS just looking, bemused. Jackie turns to see –
THREE CHILD DUMMIES walk out of the doors of Daisy and Tom-type shop. Faces just ovals, no features at all.
CUT TO the far end of the street. CAROLINE's scared, CLIVE steps forward. A DUMMY turns to face him. Enraptured:

CLIVE
It's true. Everything I've read. All those stories. It's all true.

The dummy lifts up its arm to point at him.
The wrist is hinged, its hand swings down. Revealing a metal tube.
And Clive's so sad, because he knows what happens next:
The dummy fires.

Tentacle can whip out and kill

Beautiful humanoid features

Axons transform into monstrous creatures

Axons initially appear benevolent

Axons are made from Axonite – the same material as Axos itself

The Axons are semi-humanoid manifestations of a composite space parasite – Axos – that feeds on the energy of the planets it visits, destroying them in the process. At first the Axons appear to be beautiful, benevolent golden-skinned humanoids (right), but in fact they are terrifying, tentacled monsters in disguise (left and above). The Axons are immune to bullets and can kill at a touch. They absorb energy and transmit it back to Axos – one Axon is able to transfer the entire output of a nuclear reactor.

# THE CLAWS OF AXOS

An organic alien ship lands on Earth, carrying friendly humanoid aliens who offer Axonite as a gift in return for refuge, claiming their planet was destroyed by a solar flare. But the ship, its occupants and the Axonite are all a single creature that plans to feed on Earth's energy. It starts to absorb energy from the reactor of the Nuton National Power Complex.

As the Axons are revealed to be grotesque, tentacled creatures, the Doctor and UNIT are forced into an uneasy alliance with the Master, a renegade Time Lord who has led Axos to Earth. The Doctor offers to give Axos time-travel technology, but tricks it into becoming trapped in a time loop – forever travelling through a never-ending figure-of-eight in time.

Written by
**Bob Baker & Dave Martin**
Featuring
**the Third Doctor, UNIT and Jo**
First broadcast
**13 March–3 April 1971**
**4 episodes**

### AXONITE

Axonite, Axos and the Axons are a single entity. Axonite can absorb, convert, transmit and programme all forms of energy. The Axons describe it as 'a thinking molecule. It uses the energy it absorbs not only to copy but to recreate and restructure any given substance'. Axos offers it as a gift, copying and enlarging a frog to show how Axonite can provide unlimited food and power.

In fact, once distributed around the world, Axonite will absorb the Earth's energy to feed Axos: 'All things must die… Axos merely hastens the process…'

### CREATING THE AXONS

Writers Bob Baker and Dave Martin were invited to write a *Doctor Who* story after submitting a comedy script to the BBC. Their outline, titled *The Gift*, included a creature that was all brain and looked like a giant skull landing in Hyde Park in London. Eventually the story – for a while called *The Vampire from Space* – became less 'epic' and more affordable for the BBC's budget.

The Axons were designed to resemble the interior of Axos, which was organic. Some of the costumes were 'blobby' while others were more tentacled. In fact, the costumes were so organic that costume designer Barbara Lane re-used one, spayed green, as an alien plant, the Krynoid, in the 1976 Fourth Doctor story *The Seeds of Doom*.

# THE BEAST

Horns are an ancient symbol of satanic power

At a time before Time itself even existed, there was the Beast. Feared and deadly, it became the template for every representation of evil that followed, right across the universe. It entered the legends of countless planets – Earth, Draconia, Vel Consadine, Damos, and even Skaro. The same image, same *creature*, informed the devil, the horned beast, the Kaled god of war… But, despite its mighty power, the Beast was defeated and imprisoned on an isolated planet circling a black hole. The ancient people that captured the Beast bound it to the core of the planet. They ensured that the planet would be sucked into the black hole, destroying the Beast, if their ancient prisoner ever escaped.

Beast's anatomy echoes many traits associated with gods and devils

Vicious claws

Manacles bind the Beast to his prison

# THE IMPOSSIBLE PLANET and THE SATAN PIT

The Doctor and Rose arrive on Sanctuary Base 6, on a planet in an impossible orbit around a black hole. The crew and their servants, the Ood, are drilling to find the power source that keeps the planet safe – but the planet is the prison of the Beast, and they have awakened him.

The Beast turns the Ood against the humans, and also possesses archaeologist Toby Zed. It plans to escape from the planet inside Toby's mind (the only way it can leave without being sucked into the black hole).

The Doctor finds the Beast's animalistic body chained up inside the planet, and realises the truth. He plunges the planet into the black hole, and Rose ejects the possessed Toby into space.

Written by
**Matt Jones**
Featuring
**the Tenth Doctor
and Rose**
First broadcast
**3–10 June 2006
2 episodes**

## KROP TOR

The planet that is prison to the Beast now has no name, but in the scriptures of the Veltino – an ancient race that, perhaps, knew of the Beast – it is called Krop Tor, which means 'the bitter pill'. A vestige of truth survived in their legends – they believed that the black hole was itself a demon who was tricked into devouring the planet, only to spit it out because it was poison.

Since the Beast was imprisoned, the planet has been in orbit around the black hole K-37 Gem 5. If the Beast escapes, the planet will be destroyed.

## SANCTUARY CREW

Since the death of their captain, the principal members of the Sanctuary Base 6 crew are: Zachary Cross Flane (Acting Captain), Ida Scott (Science Officer), John Jefferson (Head of Security), Danny Bartock (Ethics Committee), Tobias Zed (Archaeologist) and Scootori Manista (Trainee Maintenance). There is also a complement of 50 Ood.

The base was brought to the planet in sections that snap together, and established so that the crew can find the energy source that stops it from being pulled into the black hole.

## ANCIENT RUNES

The words of the Beast appear as runic symbols on ancient artefacts discovered by Toby – so ancient that the TARDIS cannot translate them. The Beast also speaks through those he has possessed.

An Ood serves Rose her meal and tells her: 'The Beast and his armies shall rise from the Pit to make war against God.' Toby hears a disembodied voice before he is possessed, and runes are burned into his face and hands. As the Beast takes control of him, he tells his colleagues he understands the runes: 'These are the words of the Beast…'

# THE SATAN CODE

The Beast was created entirely as a computer-generated image (CGI) by effects house The Mill – there was no model, no costume and no actor, as such. Even more amazingly, it was devised in just six weeks by two of the Mill's animators, working from designs drawn up by Nicholas Hernandez. He, in turn, was working from an idea provided by another Mill employee, who actually worked in the despatch department.

As with all computer-generated characters, the Beast was created from the final design drawings as a rough, wireframe model that could be animated. Then each frame of the Beast was given colour and texture until it looked just like a real – hellish – creature.

Though the Beast creature never actually speaks, its roars and movements had to be matched exactly with footage of David Tennant playing the Doctor. As happens so often in the making of *Doctor Who*, Tennant was acting against a plain green screen, which was replaced with The Mill's work.

The deep, terrifying voice of the Beast was provided by actor Gabriel Woolf, who played Sutekh in the 1975 adventure *Pyramids of Mars*.

# THE CARRIONITES

The ancient and awful Carrionites – from the Fourteen Stars of the Rexel Planetary Configuration – developed a science that was based on words instead of numbers. While humanity followed the mathematical route, creating formulae to explain the universe, the Carrionites pursued a form of science that exploits the power of language. To those who do not understand, it seems that the Carrionites are witches, who chant spells.

Long ago, the Eternals found the 'spell' – the right word – to banish the Carrionites into the Deep Darkness. It was thought they could never return, but the death of William Shakespeare's young son, Hamnet, released such grief in the great playwright that this brought back three of the Carrionites. In Elizabethan London, they set about using their 'magic' to have Shakespeare's words release all the Carrionites to feed on the world.

Hag-like appearance

Mother Bloodtide

Hooked nose

Lilith

Mother Doomfinger

Wrinkled, wizened skin

Evil eyes

# THE SHAKESPEARE CODE

The Doctor takes Martha to a play at the newly opened Globe theatre in Elizabethan London. They meet Shakespeare, who is completing his sequel to *Love's Labour's Lost* – called *Love's Labour's Won*. But he has fallen under the influence of three Carrionites, who are using his powerful words, coupled with the shape of the Globe theatre, to create a 'spell' that will release the other Carrionites from the Deep Darkness.

The Doctor encourages Shakespeare to rework the play's ending and the words of power are turned on the Carrionites, banishing them again. After some initial confusion, the audience expresses its appreciation of the one and only, effects-laden performance of *Love's Labour's Won*.

Written by
**Gareth Roberts**
Featuring
**the Tenth Doctor
and Martha**
First broadcast
**7 April 2007
1 episode**

### WILLIAM SHAKESPEARE

Widely regarded as the greatest poet and playwright in history, Shakespeare is in his mid-thirties and at the height of his success. He is a man so talented that his words can free the Carrionites; so grief-stricken by the death of his son that the Carrionites can twist his emotions to their need. He is perceptive enough to realise where – and when – the Doctor and Martha are from, but is not above 'borrowing' words that he overhears. One word of the Doctor's that appeals to him is 'Sycorax' – the name he will give to the witch-mother in *The Tempest*.

### DNA REPLICATION

One of the techniques the Carrionites use, which seems close to witchcraft, is DNA replication. From a small amount of a person's DNA they can bind a doll-like figurine to that person: whatever happens to the doll, happens to the person.

Using this technique, Lilith kills Lynley, Master of the Revels, when he threatens to stop the performance of *Love's Labour's Won*. She plunges the doll into a bucket of water, and so Lynley drowns. Later she uses the doll to make Shakespeare write the final scene of the play, and to try to kill the Doctor.

### THE GLOBE

The Carrionites have manipulated Peter Streete, who designed the Globe, to create a building to their specifications. The resulting fourteen-sided construction will amplify the words of power spoken at the end of *Love's Labour's Won*. His job done, Streete is driven mad by the Carrionites and consigned to Bedlam.

The Globe opened in 1599. It burned down in 1613, but was rebuilt. Puritans (who opposed the existence of theatres) demolished it in 1644. The Globe was recreated at London's Bear Garden and officially opened again in 1997.

## A MUSE OF FIRE

*The Shakespeare Code* was written by Gareth Roberts – an established and talented television writer who has worked on series from *Randall and Hopkirk (Deceased)* to *Coronation Street*, and and has written several episodes of *The Sarah Jane Adventures*.

Gareth Roberts is well known to *Doctor Who* fans for his novels: *Only Human* featuring the Ninth Doctor, Rose and Captain Jack, and the Quick Reads Tenth Doctor title *I Am a Dalek*. He also wrote a number of very popular classic *Doctor Who* novels. Here, he explains something of the Carrionites' background and history:

'The Fourteen Stars of the Rexel Planetary Configuration have been a mystery since the dawn of understanding in the universe. Legend has it that the Rexel stars are a prison door, sealed billions of years in the past, keeping the Carrionites in Deep Darkness. The Carrionites, legendarily, ate their own husbands and children. They are said to have developed a malevolent science of their own – using shapes, words, numbers and names to effect their attacks on hundreds of their neighbouring planets back at the dawn of time. They used the grief and suffering of others to enhance this science – which to us is indistinguishable from magic.

'The Eternals are said to have banished the Carrionites into Deep Darkness. It took the grief of a genius – Shakespeare, driven nearly insane by the death of one of his children – to allow a small group of them, led by Lilith, back into our universe, to plot the return of the others.'

From out night's parted veil vaunt wretched hags,

Whose former empery of blood and bone

Consigned to Deep Darkness, complot to steal

Th' impressions of our fantasies in words

Thereby to blot out realm, the world, and all.

Vile bounded power awak'd by boundless grief

Made form by poet's trumpeted renown

Takes shape from shapes poured subtly in the ear

Of lunatics, to wreck the globe from 'Globe'.

Yet providence provides two saviours near

The Doctor and his incomparable maid

      (Their voyages not hemmed in

      by space nor time)

      They know a curse to curse

      this damned spite

      With its foul title, baleful

      Carrionite.

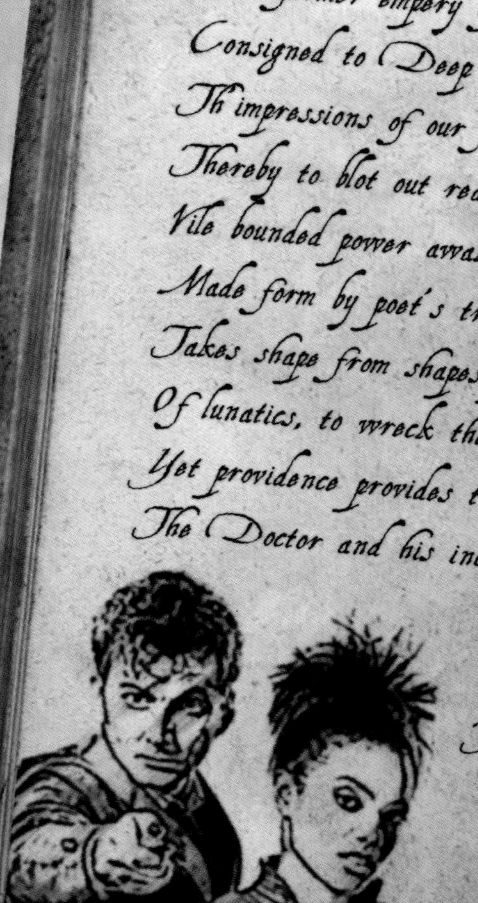

William Shakespeare

(channelled by Gareth Roberts)

# ALL THE WORLD'S A STAGE

Although all the action of *The Shakespeare Code* takes place in London, the *Doctor Who* production team used a variety of locations and techniques to recreate the Tudor city. Extensive use was made of the recreated Globe theatre, but the Elephant Inn, where Shakespeare stays, and the Carrionites' dwelling on Allhallows Street were found elsewhere.

One very useful location was the Lord Leycester Hospital on the main street in Warwick. Despite being on a busy modern road, the building has been used before for Elizabethan dramas, and provided an authentic backdrop. The final effect of placing the building in the heart of a medieval cityscape of London was achieved by The Mill, who supplied the digital painting of the background and city.

The Mill also created the impressive finale, as the Carrionites arrive in force at the Globe and fly round the audience like ethereal spirits. The wizened, hag-like figures of Mothers Doomfinger and Bloodtide (below), and their 'daughter' Lilith when in witch-form, were achieved using prosthetic make-up supplied by Neill Gorton and Millennium FX.

# CASSANDRA

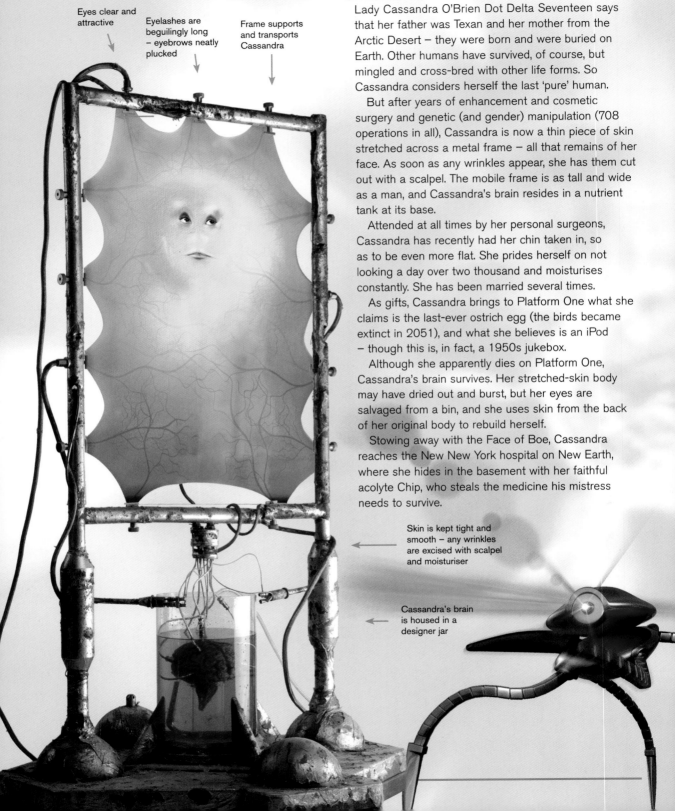

Eyes clear and attractive

Eyelashes are beguilingly long – eyebrows neatly plucked

Frame supports and transports Cassandra

Skin is kept tight and smooth – any wrinkles are excised with scalpel and moisturiser

Cassandra's brain is housed in a designer jar

Lady Cassandra O'Brien Dot Delta Seventeen says that her father was Texan and her mother from the Arctic Desert – they were born and were buried on Earth. Other humans have survived, of course, but mingled and cross-bred with other life forms. So Cassandra considers herself the last 'pure' human.

But after years of enhancement and cosmetic surgery and genetic (and gender) manipulation (708 operations in all), Cassandra is now a thin piece of skin stretched across a metal frame – all that remains of her face. As soon as any wrinkles appear, she has them cut out with a scalpel. The mobile frame is as tall and wide as a man, and Cassandra's brain resides in a nutrient tank at its base.

Attended at all times by her personal surgeons, Cassandra has recently had her chin taken in, so as to be even more flat. She prides herself on not looking a day over two thousand and moisturises constantly. She has been married several times.

As gifts, Cassandra brings to Platform One what she claims is the last-ever ostrich egg (the birds became extinct in 2051), and what she believes is an iPod – though this is, in fact, a 1950s jukebox.

Although she apparently dies on Platform One, Cassandra's brain survives. Her stretched-skin body may have dried out and burst, but her eyes are salvaged from a bin, and she uses skin from the back of her original body to rebuild herself.

Stowing away with the Face of Boe, Cassandra reaches the New New York hospital on New Earth, where she hides in the basement with her faithful acolyte Chip, who steals the medicine his mistress needs to survive.

But when Rose and the Doctor arrive, Cassandra devises a new plan – to steal Rose's body and implant her own consciousness inside it. She then tries to blackmail the Sisters of Plenitude, threatening to tell the people of New Earth the truth about how their treatments are derived.

After the Doctor has sorted out the trouble on New Earth, he takes Cassandra back – in Chip's dying body – to her own past, to the last time she was truly happy: a drinks party for the Ambassador of Thrace, which was the last occasion when someone told her she was beautiful.

## CHIP

Cassandra's loyal servant Chip is actually a force-grown clone. Cassandra has modelled him on the last person who ever told her she was beautiful.

In fact, this encounter was a self-fulfilling prophecy and a time paradox. It is Cassandra herself, inside Chip's body, that the Doctor takes back to tell her earlier self she is beautiful. So Cassandra later models the cloned Chip on himself, as she saw him at the party.

#  LIVES OF THE RICH AND THIN

An extract from Vox B MacMallican's bestseller, translated by Russell T Davies

Many have tried to write a biography of the Lady Cassandra O'Brien Dot Delta Seventeen, and many have died mysteriously in the process. She has guarded the secrets of her past with lawyers, bile and the occasional dagger. This much we know: she was born as Brian Edward Cobbs, in the ruins of the Walsall Apology, in the Old Calendar Year of 4.99/4763/A/15.

Cassandra often made outlandish claims about her parentage. Stories of lords and ladies and Eskimos would seem to be blatant lies; certainly, her title was a complete invention – the Dot Delta Seventeens appear nowhere in Burke's Extrapolated, and there is evidence that the 'Lady' was purchased for 50 klim at the Instant Royalty Bazaar.

Not much is known about her early years. There is evidence of a Mr B. E. Cobbs, registered as a security guard at Klime Enterprises in the OC Year A/32. Two years later, a Miss B. E. Cobbs marries Harry Klime, the billionaire owner of the company. Six months later, Harry Klime is found dead, having fallen on his own garden rake, five times. Mrs Cobb-Klime inherited the empire, but when police called in a rake expert, she cashed in her shares and promptly vanished.

In the OC Year A/60, a thumbprint matching that of Mrs Cobbs-Klime was found on the body of a murdered punter at the Linkladen Bordello, on the lawless border world of Rit. The bordello's madam, a lady by the name of Kitty Gillespie, vanished that night and was last seen boarding the shuttle to Sant's World.

And it's here, on Sant's World, twenty years later, that we find the first record of a woman operating under the name Cassandra. First, an actress by the name of Cassandra Hoots appears in B-movie gems such as *Mind My Legs* and *Run, Betty, Run*. This woman marries the studio boss, Ivor Cannabone, and after Ivor's death beneath a falling piano, Mrs Cannabone becomes head of the company. In this year, the original Brian Cobbs suddenly resurfaces, as the star of the musical biopic *Look At Me Laughing!* The reviews are terrible, fifteen critics and two surgeons mysteriously die, and Brian is never heard of again.

In the OC Year B/01, Cannabone Pictures collapses, but Cassandra flees the planet, travelling in steerage (perhaps this is what prompted her later collection of poems, *Forlorn and Lonely, Sitting On A Box of Chickens*). But soon she's seen on the arm of royalty, consorting with the one-thousand-year-old Prince Regent Lucius at the Fifteenth Pylomic Games. Marriage swiftly follows. Of course, a terrible gliding accident soon befalls the entire Lucius Family, leaving Princess Cassandra as the only living heir, but now, for the first time, I can exclusively reveal, that this was no –

(These were the last words written by MacMallican, before her sudden and mysterious death by fountain pen.)

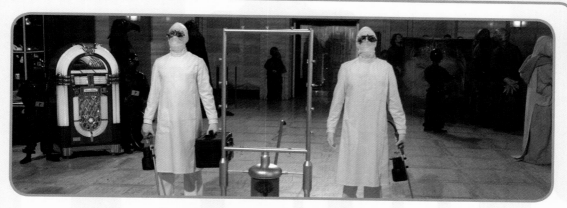

 # MAKING UP CASSANDRA

From the start of production on *The End of the World*, it was apparent that Cassandra's face would have to be a computer-generated image, and her voice would need to be added in post-production. However, a prop was needed for the actors to relate to, and she had to respond and speak in real time during filming. So a 'stunt' Cassandra was built – a static face that the other actors could react to and 'play off'. This was removed for some sequences, and the empty frame prop used, so that the computer-generated face could be added cleanly later.

As well as a 'stunt' face, Cassandra had a voice double. Actress Clare Cage spoke Cassandra's lines off-stage during recording. Clare's voice was then removed when Cassandra's 'real' voice – that of noted actress Zoë Wanamaker – was added.

## SCRIPT EXTRACT

CASSANDRA glides in.
A metal frame, six feet tall, three feet wide. Only an inch deep.
And stretched across the frame, a piece of canvas – bolted into
the frame, pulled tight. Except this isn't canvas. It's skin.
Right in the middle, there are two eyes and a mouth. No nose, no
chin, nothing but eyes and mouth. The eyes are bulging, but the
mouth has no depth; it's just lips and teeth, no actual mouth
behind it. When the lips are open you can see right through.
The whole frame is supported on a sleek metal truck. At the
base, in a glass jar, a brain bubbles and glows from
within, wires connecting it to the frame.

CASSANDRA
Moisturise me.

# THE CELESTIAL TOYMAKER

Although he dresses like an imposing, medieval Chinese nobleman, the Toymaker is an incredibly powerful being who has lived for thousands of years. He spends his time playing games. If he loses, the price he pays is the destruction of his world, but he is powerful enough to rebuild it. (His winning opponent is destroyed with the world.) If his opponents lose, they are added to the domain as his toys. The Doctor calls him 'a power for evil. He manipulates people and makes them into his playthings.'

Traditional Chinese clothes

The Toymaker is probably immortal

Toymaker turns people into toys

### THE TRILOGIC GAME

The Trilogic Game consists of a pyramid made of numbered layers that form the playing pieces. There are three points, A, B and C, on the board arranged in a triangle. Similar to the game 'Towers of Hanoi' (played with circular pieces), the player has to move the pyramid from point A to point C, moving one layer at a time, and never placing a larger piece on top of a smaller piece.

An added complication is that the new pyramid has to be completed at position C in exactly 1023 moves.

Other games the Toymaker forces his opponents to play include:
· Blind Man's Buff – with cheating dolls
· Musical Chairs – with chairs that kill whoever sits down on them
· Hopscotch – across a lethal, electrified floor

# THE CELESTIAL TOYMAKER

The TARDIS materialises in the domain of the Toymaker, who turns people into his playthings. The Toymaker makes the Doctor invisible and forces him to play the fiendishly difficult Trilogic Game. In order to escape, the Doctor and his companions must defeat the Toymaker and his toys in a variety of games of the Toymaker's choosing. If they lose, they will be added to the Toymaker's toy collection, but if they win, the Toymaker's domain will be destroyed – along with the winning players.

The Doctor imitates the Toymaker's voice to make the winning move in the Trilogic Game from the safety of the TARDIS – and so he and his companions survive the cataclysmic destruction.

Written by
**Brian Hayles**
Featuring
**the First Doctor,
Steven and Dodo**
First broadcast
**2–23 April 1966
4 episodes**

## PLAYTHINGS

All the Toymaker's subjects are, in actual fact, toys. He takes two dolls from their dolls' house and they become Joey and Clara. After they lose their game against Dodo and Steven, Joey and Clara become dolls again.

The Toymaker threatens to break Sergeant Rugg and Mrs Wiggs the cook like a stack of plates. Other playthings include a robot, naughty schoolboy Cyril, and the Hearts family – the King, Queen and Knave – who are really playing cards.

## RETURN VISIT

The Toymaker says that the Doctor has visited his domain before, but did not stay long enough to play any of the games. This may be because the Doctor has heard of the Toymaker, too.

'You and your games are quite notorious,' the Doctor tells him. 'You draw people here like a spider does to flies … and should they lose the games they play, you condemn them to become your toys for ever.'

# THE CLOCKWORK ROBOTS

Mask and wig cover main clockwork mechanism

Repair Droid 7

Clockwork body of robot covered by ball gown or other contemporary clothing

Gloves cover clockwork 'hands' with replaceable tool attachments

The Clockwork Robots are responsible for the maintenance and repair of the spaceship the SS *Madame de Pompadour*. The Clockwork Woman shown here is actually Repair Droid 7. The robots are operated by clockwork so that they will work even in the event of a total power failure.

When the ship breaks down catastrophically and suffers 82 per cent systems failure in an ion storm, the robots attempt to repair it. They are programmed to do this in any way they can – even if it means using the crew and passengers as spare parts.

Searching for Reinette – the real Madame de Pompadour – in 18th-century France, the robots disguise themselves in contemporary clothing and wigs, and wear ornate masks as if for a masked ball.

# THE GIRL IN THE FIREPLACE

The Doctor, Rose and Mickey find themselves on a damaged spaceship in the 51st century, which is linked through 'time windows' to 18th-century France. Using the windows, the Doctor meets Reinette and finds she is being menaced by Clockwork Robots. These are repair robots from the ship, who have been trying to get it working again using any spare components they can find – including the crew.

The Doctor visits Reinette several times and they form a close friendship. But can he prevent the robots from using her head to repair the ship? With Rose and Mickey about to be used for spare parts, it is up to the Doctor and his new friend Arthur – a horse – to save the day.

Written by
**Steven Moffat**
Featuring
**the Tenth Doctor,
Rose and Mickey**
First broadcast
**6 May 2006
1 episode**

### REINETTE

Jeanne-Antionette Poisson was born on 29 December 1721. As a child, she was taken by her mother to a fortune teller, who told the girl that one day she would become the mistress of a king. After this she became known by the nickname Reinette – which means 'little queen'.

In 1741, she married and became Madame d'Etoiles. Reinette met Louis XV at the masked Yew Tree Ball, and indeed soon became the king's mistress. She legally separated from her husband, and Louis XV made her Marquise de Pompadour. She died in April 1764.

### TIME WINDOWS

Using the tremendous reserves of power on the damaged spaceship, the Clockwork Robots have opened windows to 18th-century France. They are trying to locate Reinette at the age of 37 (the age of the ship), but the windows are not accurate enough, so they open many of them, all along her lifeline.

The relative time between the ship and France is not fixed: a few minutes may pass on the ship, but many months or even years have gone by in Reinette's world. So the Doctor appears not to age, but he sees Reinette at various points in her life.

### COMPATIBILITY

Programmed to repair the ship in any way that they can, the robots use 'components' from the bodies of the crew and passengers as spare parts. A human eye replaces a damaged camera lens; a heart (*above*) operates as an efficient fluid pump…

With the ship's main memory circuits destroyed, the robots need to replace the computer command circuit. They assume that the brain of the real Madame de Pompadour, at the same age as the ship, can form a suitable alternative to the damaged systems.

## SS MADAME DE POMPADOUR

Shown here are some of the original designs for the ship. While the interior was created as a studio set, the exterior of the ship was a computer-generated image (CGI).

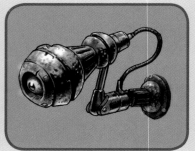

# SCRIPTING THE CLOCKWORK ROBOTS

The script for this episode was by acclaimed writer Steven Moffat. He describes the central character of this story – the girl in the fireplace:

'Reinette Poisson is a girl with one dream: to be the consort of a king. She has been trained, educated and refined into one of the most beautiful and learned women of her age. A dancer, an artist, an actress, a friend to philosophers and writers, and – one day, she hopes – the lover of Louis XV of France.

'But Reinette has nightmares, too. Some nights, she will hear the deep, slow tick of a clock – and, turning, see that the clock on the mantel is broken. She will feel

that something is close to her in the shadows of her room. Under her bed. Outside her window. Just out of sight in the corridor behind her. Something that ticks, something more machine than human. Something that wants her.

'In her dream, sometimes she sees a strange metal world of clanging corridors and clicking chambers, where strange Tick Tock men in grinning masks mass in the shadows – and somehow she knows these clockwork creatures dream of her too.

'But, in the confusion of her nightmares, there is also hope. A man is coming. A man who saved her once in the past and will one day return to save her future…

'At a magical fireside that is the gateway between one world and another, the girl with one dream will meet a man with two hearts. And she might just break them both.'

## STAGING THE BALL

Recreating the spectacular majesty of Versailles for television was a huge challenge for the *Doctor Who* production team – even without having to add alien Clockwork Robots. But it was a challenge that they rose to magnificently, as the pictures in this section show.

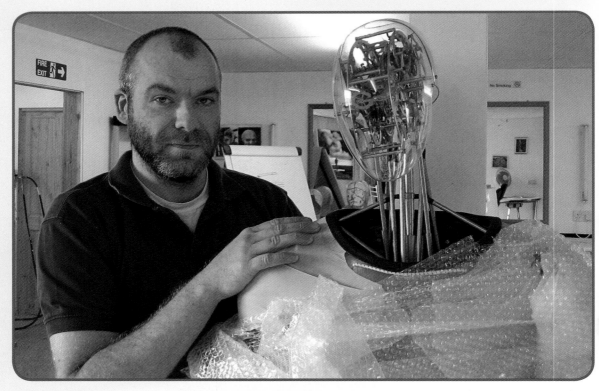

## MAKING THE CLOCKWORK ROBOTS

Although only seen briefly in the finished episode, the Clockwork Robot was every bit as beautiful as the Doctor says. There was a single head and shoulders for the Clockwork Robot, which was dressed in a costume, wig and mask. Neill Gorton and his team at Millennium FX worked from a design 'mood sheet' showing pictures of carriage clocks and close-ups of clockwork constructions. From this they designed and then built the Clockwork Robot's head and shoulders, and also the arm.

Constructed by Millennium FX, the head was tilted and swivelled by means of levers inside the chest and operated from behind. The clockwork inside the head actually worked – the various wheels and cogs form an intricate, working mechanism. The arm was also fully functional. With its various attachment tools, it was operated using a system of flywheels and wires. The result was a beautifully intricate and totally convincing clockwork robot.

Rods connect
directly into brain

Electronically
synthesised
voice

Enhanced vision
circuits

Cybus
Industries
symbol
covers vital
components

Hydraulic
cables, control
wires and pipes
carrying fluid

Gauntlet-like
hands are
highly dextrous
as well as
strong

In our universe, the Cybermen were created
on the planet Mondas, later migrating to
another world – Telos. Mondas was the twin
planet of Earth, so there has always been an
affinity between the origins of the Cybermen
and our own planet. In the parallel universe
the Doctor, Mickey and Rose visit, the
Cybermen are created on Earth itself. The
location may have changed, their design
might be subtly different, but the Cybermen
are the same – terrifying – creatures.

The globally powerful Cybus Industries
creates the Cybermen in huge factories
from living humans, replacing their bodily
organs and limbs with mechanical versions.
They also 'enhance' the brains, removing the
weakness of emotion and the sense of pain.
The resulting Cybermen are incredibly strong
and ruthlessly efficient, but without fear or
emotion or humanity.

Vision circuits are more powerful than a standard Cyberman's

Adapted brain is visible through protective casing

Sockets for pipes that can constantly feed nutrients and vital fluids to Cyber Controller

Exo-skeleton acts as a tough, protective shell for the Cyberman

Cyber Controller is even more powerful than other Cybermen

The leader of the Cybermen is the Cyber Controller. On the parallel Earth where the Doctor and his friends witness the birth of the Cybermen, the Controller is the Cybermen's creator, John Lumic, converted into a Cyberman. The Cyber Controller has the same basic design as the Cybermen, but differs in several ways.

# CREATING THE CYBERMEN

The Cybermen were the creation of Doctor Kit Pedler, who was a medical researcher when he was recommended to script editor, Gerry Davis, as someone who might be useful as an adviser to *Doctor Who*.

As a doctor, one of Pedler's greatest fears was 'dehumanising medicine'. He foresaw a time when spare-part surgery reached the stage where it was commonplace, even cosmetic. There would come a point where it was impossible to tell how much of the original human being remained. The resulting Cybermen, he thought, would be motivated by pure logic coupled with the overriding desire to survive. They would sacrifice their entire bodies and their minds in the quest for immortality.

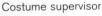

Costume supervisor Sandra Reid had the job of creating the first Cybermen. Although the look of the Cybermen would change and evolve with almost every story in which they appeared, the initial design included the main elements that make the Cybermen recognisable: the blank mask-like face, 'jug handles' connected to a light in the head, cables and rods to enhance the limbs, and the large chest unit.

## SCRIPT EXTRACT

The sleeve on the arm of one of them slips back. Instead of flesh there is a transparent 'arm-shaped' forearm containing shining rods and lights. There is a normal hand at the end of it. A close-up of one of their heads reveals a metal plate running between centre hair line front and occiput...

They are tall, slim with one-piece close-fitting silver mesh uniform. Their faces and hands are normal but under the hair on the head is a long shining metal plate stretching from centre hair line front to occiput. (This could be disguised by a hat.) Their faces are all rather alike, angular and normally good looking. On the front of their trunks is a mechanical (computer-like) unit, consisting of switches, two rows of lights, and a short moveable proboscis. They carry (exotic) side-arms. At elbow joints and shoulders there are small ram-like cylinders acting over the joints.

# THE TENTH PLANET

The Doctor, Polly and Ben arrive at Snowcap Base in the Antarctic, in 1986, as it monitors a space probe. A new planet enters the solar system, drawing power first from the space probe – resulting in its destruction – then from Earth itself. Cybermen arrive at Snowcap, intent on using a Z-Bomb installed there to destroy the Earth before their own planet, Earth's twin, Mondas, absorbs too much energy.

With Cybermen arriving on Earth in force, the Doctor close to collapse and Polly a prisoner, it is up to Ben to fight back. He discovers the Cybermen are susceptible to radiation and manages to hold them off for long enough for Mondas to explode.

Written by
**Kit Pedler & Gerry Davis**
Featuring
**the First Doctor,
Ben and Polly**
First broadcast
**8–29 October 1966
4 episodes**

### CYBER DATA

These first Cybermen have human hands, and perhaps the remains of their faces survive beneath the material that covers them. They plan to take humans back to Mondas and convert them into Cybermen like themselves. When the Cybermen speak, the mouth opens and an electronic, altered, voice comes out.

But the Cybermen are susceptible to radiation, and they also draw the power that keeps them alive from their home planet. When Mondas explodes, the human material of the Cybermen 'dissolves', leaving a shrivelled husk…

### CYBER NAMES

The scripts for *The Tenth Planet* attributed individual names to each of the Cybermen. These were never used in the televised story, but they were retained in the cast listings. The names of the Cybermen were: Krail, Talon, Shav, Krang, Jarl, and Gern.

The practice of naming the Cybermen was never repeated, although the final scripts for the second Cyber story – *The Moonbase* – do retain the name of Cyberman 'Tarn' from a previous draft. In his later novelisation of the story, writer Gerry Davis specifies that Tarn is the Cyberleader.

### MONDAS

Mondas was an ancient name for Earth. The Cybermen describe their home as Earth's 'twin', and explain that aeons ago Mondas drifted away from Earth on a journey to the edge of space. Now it has returned…

The energy of Mondas is nearly exhausted and the Cybermen have brought Mondas back to drain energy from Earth. The Doctor, however, realises that Mondas will absorb too much of Earth's energy, so all they need to do is wait. He is right – and Earth's twin is ultimately destroyed.

 # THE MOONBASE

Written by
**Kit Pedler**
Featuring
**the Second Doctor,
Ben, Polly and Jamie**
First broadcast
**11 February–4 March
1967
4 episodes**

The Doctor and his friends arrive on the moon in 2070 to discover that the crew of a moonbase is battling against a strange plague. The base uses a Gravitron to control Earth's weather, and the Cybermen have infected the sugar supply in order to disable the crew. They kidnap and 'convert' victims of the plague before taking over the base.

Ben, Polly and Jamie fight back, destroying the Cybermen with a mixture of solvents that attacks and dissolves their chest units. But many more Cybermen are on the way. The Doctor finally defeats the Cybermen by using the Gravitron to influence the moon's gravity so that the Cybermen and their ships are hurled off into deep space.

## CYBER DATA

The Cybermen that attack the Moonbase are of a different design to those of *The Tenth Planet*. The human hands have been replaced with three-fingered metal claws, the chest unit is more streamlined, and the body is a silver suit with tubular exo-skeleton and cabling. The face has changed from a cloth-covered mask to a blank, metal, skull-like helmet. The 'light' is now integrated into the headpiece rather than being separate. A small aerial extends from the chest unit when a Cyberman communicates by radio.

## AUGMENTATION

The 'altered' humans that the Cybermen control wear probes attached to their forehead held together in a 'mesh'. When this 'cap' is removed the men become immobile.

They are controlled from a box with aerials using a sonic beam, which the Doctor is able to disrupt by altering a tone control on a console.

The Cybermen use a cylindrical capsule to transfer humans between their ship and the Moonbase without the need for spacesuits.

## CYBERMATS

The Cybermats are small, metallic creatures, not unlike rodents. They have eyes, antennae and a segmented tail. Underneath they move on rows of filaments, and they have what seem to be rows of teeth. They can home in on human brainwaves to attack.

Similar Cybermats, but with spines down their back, no antennae, and solid, unfaceted eyes, are used to attack Station 3 in *The Wheel in Space* and destroy stocks of bernalium there (see page 56).

In *Revenge of the Cybermen* (see page 58), the Cybermats disseminate the plague that kills most of the crew of Nerva Beacon. These Cybermats are longer, with segmented bodies and a small red sensor at the front. The Doctor adapts one to attack the Cybermen with gold dust.

# TOMB OF THE CYBERMEN

Arriving on the planet Telos, the Doctor, Jamie and Victoria meet an archaeological expedition led by Professor Parry. His team is planning to excavate the last remains of the Cybermen. They find the Cybermen's city, where the last Cybermen are frozen in huge honeycomb-like tombs below ground. But logicians Kaftan and Klieg plan to revive the Cybermen and form an alliance with them.

Attacked by Cybermats, and with Kaftan's servant Toberman part-converted into a Cyberman, the Doctor manages to refreeze the tombs. The Cyber Controller is destroyed as the Doctor booby-traps and closes the doors to the City. He does not see that a single Cybermat has escaped…

Written by
**Kit Pedler & Gerry Davis**
Featuring
**the Second Doctor, Jamie and Victoria**
First broadcast
**2–20 September 1967**
**4 episodes**

## CYBER DATA

The Cybermen died out five centuries ago, but nobody knows why. In fact they realised they were in danger of becoming extinct and retreated into their city – which is actually a giant trap designed to lure future converts to the Cyber race.

The control systems form a logic and intelligence test: anyone who passes will revive the Cybermen. These intelligent humans will then be captured and used as raw materials – eventually becoming the first of a new race of Cybermen.

## THE CONTROLLER

The Cyber Controller is a taller Cyberman with no chest unit and less piping. The Controller's head has an enlarged cranium, lit from within, with visible veins, and lacks the usual 'handles' of the other Cybermen. Like other Cybermen, the Controller needs to revitalise himself when his power levels run down. The Doctor tries to trap him inside a recharging cabinet, but he smashes his way out.

In *Attack of the Cybermen* (see page 61), the Controller is seen not to have been destroyed.

id="2" /> # THE WHEEL IN SPACE

**Written by**
**David Whitaker**
**from a story by Kit Pedler**
Featuring
**the Second Doctor, Jamie and Zoe**
First broadcast
**27 April–1 June 1968**
**6 episodes**

The Doctor and Jamie arrive on a spaceship – the *Silver Carrier* – which has apparently drifted off course. They are taken to the nearby Station 3 – the Wheel. In fact, the Cybermen have sent the *Silver Carrier* and are concealed on board. They send Cybermats over to the Wheel to destroy the bernalium they need to power their X-ray laser.

With a meteorite storm approaching (again, engineered by the Cybermen), the crew of the Wheel find there is bernalium on board the *Silver Carrier* and bring it back to the Wheel. But the Cybermen are concealed inside the crates. The Doctor manages to neutralise the Cybermats and destroy the Cybermen on the Wheel before their main force arrives. The recharged X-ray laser destroys the Cybership.

## CYBER DATA

The Cybermen's bodies and external tubing and hydraulics are more streamlined, and the eyes have 'teardrop' holes at the outside lower corner. There is a similar hole below the mouth.

The Cybermen on the *Silver Carrier* are concealed and preserved inside large egg-like membranes. The Cybermen break out through the shells to operate the Cybermats and put their plans into operation. The Cybermats are carried to the Wheel in smaller egg-like protective bubbles, which sink through the hull.

## CYBER PLANNER

The Cybermen attacking the Wheel are given orders by a Cyber Planner. The Planner is a large bulbous metal object with thin filament attachments within a cradle, not unlike a large stylised Cyberman head mounted on a tiny body.

In *The Invasion* (see page 57), Tobias Vaughn contacts the Cybermen via a Cyber Director concealed behind a wall in his office. The Cyber Director seems to have an organic component at the core of a circular electronic structure that turns and pulses with sound and light.

## CONTROLLED HUMANS

The Cybermen are able to take control of humans they come into contact with. The Doctor devises a way of resisting Cyber control using a metal plate and resistor taped to the back of the neck.

The Cybermen are able to project mental images from Vallance's brain. He stares into a control box and thinks of each individual human being at present on the Wheel, forming the image in his eyes. The images are then relayed to the Cyber Planner, which advises that 'The Doctor is known and recorded.'

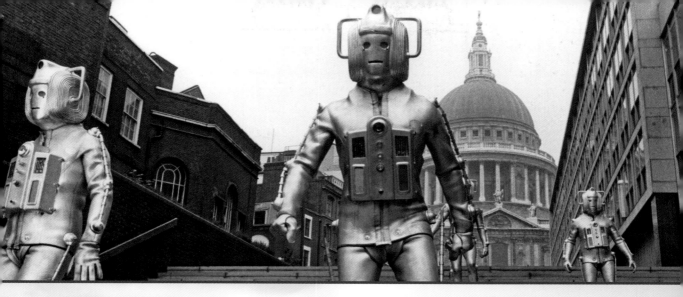

# THE INVASION

The Doctor, Jamie and Zoe meet up again with Lethbridge-Stewart – now a Brigadier, in charge of the newly formed UNIT organisation. UNIT is investigating the world's biggest electronics manufacturer – International Electromatics – and its managing director, Tobias Vaughn.

Vaughn is in league with the Cybermen, who are being shipped to Earth and reanimated at IE's warehouses. They are then distributed through the London sewers, ready to take over when a hypnotic signal is transmitted through IE's products. With Earth paralysed, the Doctor persuades Vaughn to help defeat the Cybermen. Zoe helps the RAF destroy the Cyber fleet in orbit.

Written by
**Derrick Sherwin,
from a story by Kit Pedler**
Featuring
**the Second Doctor,
Jamie, Zoe and UNIT**
First broadcast
**2 November–21
December 1968
8 episodes**

### CYBER DATA

The Cybermen are again 'streamlined', this time with enlarged helmets. They refer to a previous encounter with the Doctor on 'Planet Fourteen' (possibly Telos).

Attacked by UNIT forces, the Cybermen are apparently immune to bullets, but can be destroyed with well-aimed bazookas and grenades.

As in previous stories, the Cybermen can control human minds. Major General Rutlidge is under Vaughn's control and warns Vaughn of the Brigadier's attempts to deal with IE.

### TOBIAS VAUGHN

Tobias Vaughn, managing director of International Electromatics, has a cybernetic body, though he refuses to allow his brain to be altered. When he is shot in the chest by Professor Watkins, he simply looks down at the smoking holes in his shirt front, and laughs.

Vaughn eventually agrees to help the Doctor after realising that the Cybermen have betrayed him. They have promised him he will rule Earth, but then they decide to destroy all life with a Cyber-megatron Bomb.

### CEREBRATRON MENTOR

Professor Watkins has developed the Cerebratron Mentor to produce excessively powerful emotional pulses as an aid to learning. But Vaughn intends to mass-produce the machines as a weapon to control the Cybermen after they invade – emotions being alien to the Cybermen. Vaughn tests the machine on one Cyberman, which is driven mad and rampages through the London sewers.

But Vaughn's plans to mass-produce the Cerebratron Machines are thwarted when UNIT rescues Watkins.

# REVENGE OF THE CYBERMEN

Written by
**Gerry Davis**
Featuring
**the Fourth Doctor,
Sarah Jane and Harry**
First broadcast
**19 April–10 May 1975
4 episodes**

All but a handful of the crew of Nerva Beacon have been wiped out by a plague disseminated by Cybermats. The Doctor realises that the Cybermen are close by – hoping to annihilate the nearby Voga, planet of gold. Gold is lethal to Cybermen, and they must destroy Voga to ensure their survival.

The Doctor is captured and sent down to Voga with two other humans, all three with bombs strapped to them. The Cybemen plan to detonate the bombs to destroy Voga. But when the Doctor escapes and defuses the bombs, the Cybermen decide instead to fill Nerva with bombs and crash it into the planet. The Doctor returns to Nerva and prevents the collision, while the Vogans obliterate the Cybermen's ship with a missile of their own.

### CYBER DATA

The Cybermen who attack Voga have teardrop eyes and enlarged helmets. They are led by a Cyberleader who is distinguished – for the first time in the series – with a black helmet. He can send a signal to other Cybermen from his chest unit. Their weapons are mounted into the top of the head. This new multi-barrelled weapon can stun or kill.

The Cybermen and their equipment are affected by the gold dust on Voga, but seem impervious to the Vogans' bullets – which are presumably therefore not made of gold.

### VOGA

Voga is the legendary Planet of Gold, all but destroyed by the Cybermen in the Cyberwar. The remains have drifted through space until caught by Jupiter's gravity. The Vogans have survived the journey in a survival chamber built into the caves of Voga.

The leader of the City is Tyrum, while the routes to the surface of Voga are controlled by Vorus and his Guardians. Vorus has secretly worked with a human, Kellman, to lure the Cybermen to Nerva Beacon. Here he plans to destroy them using a Skystriker missile.

### GOLD

Gold is lethal to Cybermen. It is non-corrodible and coats their breathing apparatus – suffocating them. During the Cyberwar, the humans discovered this weakness and developed the 'glitter gun' using the gold that Voga could provide. Now the Cybermen plan to destroy Voga – the planet of gold – before assembling a new Cyber army for a new campaign.

The Doctor uses gold dust and pellets from Voga to destroy several Cybermen – even loading a Cybermat with gold to attack them in the same way as it injected humans with the plague.

# EARTHSHOCK

An archaeological team is all but wiped out by strange androids, and the Doctor and his friends are drawn in when they discover the bomb the androids were guarding. The Doctor manages to defuse the bomb, and traces the control signal back to a space freighter en route for Earth.

An army of Cybermen, concealed on the freighter, emerges to take control. With their bomb defused, they now plan to crash the freighter into Earth, destroying a vital conference forming an alliance against them.

The Cybermen evacuate, and the Doctor escapes. But Adric, still on board, disrupts the controls, and the freighter travels back in time. It crashes into prehistoric Earth, wiping out the dinosaurs and killing Adric.

Written by
**Eric Saward**
Featuring
**the Fifth Doctor,
Adric, Nyssa and Tegan**
First broadcast
**8–16 March 1982
4 episodes**

### CYBER DATA

These Cybermen are slimmer, with tubing largely built into their bodies rather than fitted externally. Though they maintain their usual blank-faced appearance, a vestigial chin can be seen moving behind the transparent mouth guard.

The Cybermen are still vulnerable to gold – such as Adric's badge, which the Doctor grinds into the Cyberleader's chest unit.

These Cybermen are again led by a Cyberleader, distinguished by the black tubing at the side of his head. He is assisted by a Cyber Lieutenant.

### SILHOUETTES

Two androids guard the Cyber bomb in the cave system on Earth. Simple, humanoid forms with featureless oval heads, one seems female and one male. They are remotely controlled by the Cybermen, who are able to observe events via the androids' visual circuits. Presumably, as they are referred to as androids, there is no organic material inside them. They are not detected by the scanning equipment used by Captain Scott's troopers.

The androids fire deadly rays from their hands, but can be destroyed by concentrated blaster fire.

### DEACTIVATION

On several occasions, Cybermen are deactivated, either for preservation or while in transit.

In *The Tomb of the Cybermen* and *Attack of the Cybermen*, we see the ice tombs on Telos, where the Cybermen wait in cryogenic suspension. In *The Wheel in Space*, Cybermen are stored in large egg-like membranes, while in *The Invasion* they are transported to Earth in cotton-wool-like cocoons. In *Earthshock*, the Cybermen stored on the freighter are encased in plastic and revived by a signal from Cyber control.

# THE FIVE DOCTORS

Written by
**Terrance Dicks**
Featuring
**the first five Doctors**
First UK broadcast
**25 November 1983**
**1 feature-length episode**

The first five incarnations of the Doctor and their various companions find themselves brought to the Death Zone on Gallifrey. Here, in ancient times, the Time Lords staged battles between different life forms.

With the Fourth Doctor trapped in a time eddy, the other Doctors make their way to the Dark Tower – battling various creatures including a Dalek and an army of Cybermen along the way. The Tower is the tomb of Rassilon – founder of Time Lord society. But corrupt Time Lord President Borusa has been using the Doctors to get him access to the tower so he can claim Rassilon's gift of immortality. However, the gift when he gets it is not all he expected, and he is incarcerated for ever.

### CYBER DATA

The Cybermen in this feature-length twentieth-anniversary special are almost identical to those in *Earthshock*.

They come up against another creature brought to the Death Zone – a Raston Warrior Robot, one of the most perfect killing machines ever devised. Its armaments are built in and sensors detect the slightest movement. It produces arrows and blades from its hands, and can teleport itself over short distances. It destroys a team of Cybermen with ruthless efficiency.

### THE DEATH ZONE

The Death Zone on Gallifrey is outside time and space. Here the ancient Time Lords gathered alien creatures and forced them to fight as entertainment.

Borusa has drawn several old enemies of the Doctor to the Death Zone to make the Doctor's quest to get to the Dark Tower more interesting and urgent. These enemies include the Master, a Yeti and a lone Dalek.

The Dalek is destroyed when it fires in a reflective corridor – its energy bolt reflects back and destroys the Dalek, revealing the thrashing creature inside.

# ATTACK OF THE CYBERMEN

The Doctor and Peri trace a distress call to Earth, 1985. It is from Lytton, who previously worked for the Daleks (*Resurrection of the Daleks*, see page 92), but is now seemingly in league with the Cybermen, who have a base in the London sewers. The Cybermen want to crash Halley's Comet into Earth so that Mondas will not be destroyed in 1986 (*The Tenth Planet*, see page 53). They also want to destroy the surface of their own planet Telos (in the future), which will destroy the native Cryons – who are actually employing Lytton to help steal the Cybermen's time vessel.

The Doctor manages to ignite a store of explosives within the Cyber city, destroying it, along with the Cybermen and their Controller.

Written by
**Paula Moore**
Featuring
**the Sixth Doctor and Peri**
First broadcast
**5–12 January 1985**
**2 episodes**

### CYBER DATA

The Cyber guards patrolling the dark London sewers are painted black as a form of camouflage. Cybermen have an inbuilt distress call, and will react to the distress of their own kind.

The tombs on Telos are of a different design to *The Tomb of the Cybermen* (see page 55), with larger cubicles arranged along corridors. The Cyber Controller is a standard Cyberman complete with chest unit, but again with an enlarged helmet devoid of 'handles'. The Cyberleader explains that the Controller was merely damaged in *The Tomb of the Cybermen*.

### CRYONS

The Cryons, the original inhabitants of Telos, used to live in refrigerated cities beneath the planet's surface before the Cybermen arrived. Cryons cannot survive in above-freezing conditions – at warmer temperatures they boil and die.

The Cryons have picked up Lytton's distress signal and asked him to help them destroy the Cybermen. They want Lytton to steal the Cybermen's only (captured) time vessel. Without it, the Cybermen will not be able to avert the destruction of Mondas, so will be forced to stay on Telos and not destroy it.

### BATES AND STRATTON

The Cybermen have captured a time ship, which is piloted by a crew of three. Two of the original crew, Bates and Stratton, are part of a working party mining the surface of Telos with an explosive called vastial.

Both Bates and Stratton have been partially converted into Cybermen. Their arms and legs have been replaced with cybernetic ones. Their bodies may be Cybernetic or they may be wearing protective suits on the surface of Telos. However, their brains have been unaffected by Cyber conditioning.

 # SILVER NEMESIS

Written by
**Kevin Clark**
Featuring
**the Seventh Doctor
and Ace**
First broadcast
**23 November–7
December 1988
3 episodes**

The Nemesis is a statue of Lady Peinforte made from a living metal, validium. It was launched into space by the Doctor from Windsor in 1638. Now it is returning to the point where it was launched, and when reunited with its bow and arrow will reach a critical mass. Lady Peinforte wants the power the statue holds, and travels to 1988 with the arrow. A group of neo-Nazis want the power, and travel from South America with the bow. The Cybermen also want the Nemesis, and arrive in force to claim it.

The Doctor activates the statue and seemingly gives it to the Cybermen. But when it reaches their hidden Cyber fleet, the statue explodes and destroys the Cybermen.

### CYBER DATA

Immune to machine-gun fire, the Cybermen are terrified of gold. They are killed by Lady Peinforte's gold-tipped arrows and by gold coins that Ace fires at them with a catapult.

One Cyberman has a device that detects the gold on Lady Peinforte's arrows. But the Cyberleader detects Ace has only one coin left without it.

With a fleet of thousands of shielded Cyber warships waiting invisibly in space, they plan to use the power of the Nemesis to transform the Earth into their base planet – the new Mondas.

### VALIDIUM

Validium is a living metal created as the ultimate defence for Gallifrey by Omega and Rassilon.

The Nemesis statue was made by Lady Peinforte in her own likeness from validium that fell into the meadow behind her house in the 17th century. The Doctor launched the statue into space in 1638 so the metal could never attain critical mass. For this, the statue needs to be reunited with its bow and arrow.

The Nemesis 'comet' circles the Earth once every 25 years (and generates destruction whenever it comes near).

### WALKMEN

The Cybermen have taken over two humans, fitting them with special Cyber-technology headsets that look like headphones, through which instructions are relayed. These controlled humans attempt to assassinate the Doctor and Ace, shooting at them as they leave an open-air jazz session.

When Ace destroys the Cybership with her Nitro-9 explosive, the Cybermen kill their programmed servants, assuming they are to blame and have betrayed their masters. The Doctor says the transformed men were effectively dead already.

# JOHN LUMIC

Lumic is the man who created Cybus Industries on the parallel Earth and invented the technology the company is based on. He is a dying man – frail and only kept alive by a life-support system built into his wheelchair. But Lumic has a vision, a dream of perpetual life. He wants to take humanity to the next stage of its development. He believes that, like one of his company's products, the human race is ready for an upgrade – an upgrade that is Lumic's only hope of survival. With the Cybermen a reality, Lumic will himself become their controller. But only when he has exhausted the final breath in his human body.

Oxygen mask easily accessible

Despite his condition, Lumic dresses immaculately

Life-support equipment

Motorised wheelchair

# RISE OF THE CYBERMEN and THE AGE OF STEEL

Written by
**Tom MacRae**
Featuring
**the Tenth Doctor,
Rose and Mickey**
First broadcast
**13–20 May 2006
2 episodes**

The Doctor, Rose and Mickey arrive on Earth. Or do they? There are differences that tell them they have arrived in a parallel universe. Huge Zeppelins hang in the sky over London. Rose's father is alive – a rich and powerful man – but Rose herself has never been born. And information is controlled and disseminated by the powerful Cybus Industries.

John Lumic, the owner and director of Cybus, has plans to take his corporation's control even further – beyond information and technology. As people disappear off the streets and Mickey meets an alternative version of himself, can the Doctor and his friends stop the creation of one of the Doctor's most deadly and fearsome foes?

## CYBUS INDUSTRIES

Cybus Industries has advanced the development of the whole planet with its inventions and products. Owned and run by the charismatic John Lumic, Cybus disseminates all news and current affairs information via a daily download sent directly to the earpods of every subscriber. But now Lumic wants to go further. Crippled and confined to a wheelchair, he believes his only hope of survival is another upgrade – this time for humanity itself. He sees the human brain as the most complex piece of software in existence, and plans to take it forward to the next stage. Cybus can improve the brain – removing painful and inefficient emotions. Cybus can upgrade the body – replacing inefficient organs and limbs with durable, strong plastic and steel.

## RE-SCRIPTING THE CYBERMEN

The job of reviving the Cybermen and updating them for the new series was given to writer Tom MacRae. MacRae has written for various television series and has also scripted several one-off plays. He remembered the Cybermen from the original series as 'big silver robot people', and wanted the new version to be much more than mere monsters – he felt they not only had to look impressive but should also recapture the credible motivation and purpose of their earliest appearances. He explains:

'The new versions look wonderful too, of course. But I wanted more than just spectacle. I wanted to give the Cybermen a proper place in the scheme of things – a motivation and a plan. I think, given their back-story, the Cybermen are very interesting and I wanted to draw that out. I wanted to get away from the straightforward monstrous villains of the end of the original series and make them more *human*, and therefore more scary. My starting point, and it's true to the original idea behind the Cybermen when they first appeared, is what if science went wrong? What if medical augmentation went too far? I wanted to approach that in a more modern way.

'The story itself is actually a very simple and very sad human story. It's a downfall story that's become almost supernatural, though there's no magic, it's all science. Lumic is not an evil genius, he's a man who is very ill and desperate to save himself, and in the process he's gone a bit mad. But everything he does and everything that happens stems from that.

'A good script needs a mix of both story and set pieces. I don't like horror stories that are all set piece with no narrative to bind them. The set pieces have to be there for a reason, and a reason which we understand. So when the Cybermen crash through the windows it's an impressive and exciting sequence, but we know *why* they're doing it.'

### SCRIPT EXTRACT

ROSE
But what are they?

THE DOCTOR
Cybermen

SMASH! – the French windows shatter –

SMASH! – another set –

SMASH! – another set – glass flying

THE CYBERMEN enter the room. Tall, steel giants. Impassive metal faces. Hints of Art Deco in their design. Cyberman after Cyberman after Cyberman.

## RECREATING THE CYBERMEN

The design of the new Cybermen was a month-long process, involving every part of the *Doctor Who* design team. Eventually, with a rough design agreed and the Art Deco style of the story settled on, the job of finalising that design and creating the Cybermen themselves fell to Millennium FX.

First they designed the head, which had to move independently of the body, rather than being a 'helmet' with restricted movement, as had been the case with previous Cyber costumes.

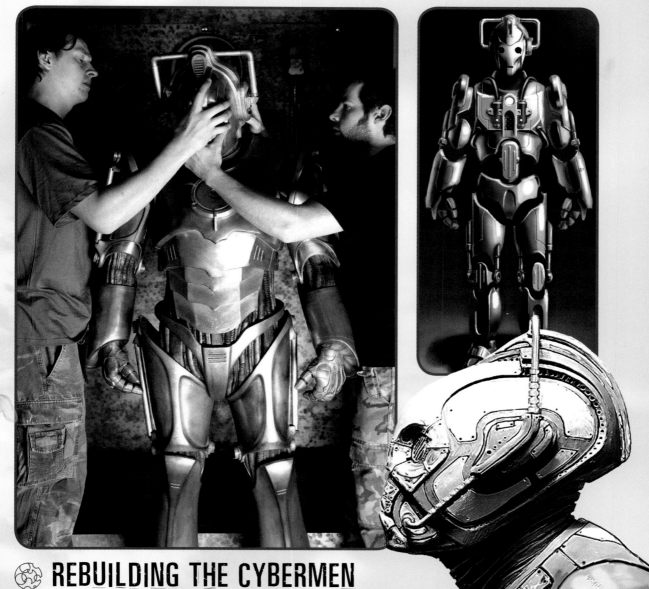

## REBUILDING THE CYBERMEN

Millennium FX created various drawings and clay models of possible Cyber heads before making a maquette – a small model – of the final design from clay. Next they made a full-sized clay sculpture of the entire Cyberman and took moulds from it to create the various parts of the costume from fibreglass.

Ten Cyberman costumes were made. The head was in nine sections, while the rest of the body had over forty component pieces. They achieved the metallic effect by adding aluminium powder to the final layer of fibreglass, and hand-polishing each separate piece until it gleamed. The exception to this was the hands – which were gloves made from soft, silver-tinted silicon. The result was the most terrifying Cyberman design yet.

## THE CYBER CONTROLLER

The Cybermen have been led by their Cyber Controller in two previous *Doctor Who* stories – *The Tomb of the Cybermen* and *Attack of the Cybermen*.

In *The Tomb of the Cybermen*, first broadcast in September 1967, the second incarnation of the Doctor managed to seal the Cybermen back into their ice tombs on the planet Telos. In *Attack of the Cybermen*, first broadcast in January 1985, the Sixth Doctor battled against a revived and redesigned Cyber Controller.

The Cyber Controller for the 2006 series of *Doctor Who* was again a Cyberman of a slightly different design. This Controller was also, for a while, wired into a Cyber throne.

# THE CYBERMEN

When ghostly, grey, translucent figures began to appear all round the world, there was panic. But after a while it became apparent that these figures were doing no harm, and people started to assume they must be ghosts. The figures were thought to be the spirits of loved ones who had died, returning to the real world to visit their former friends and families. But the truth was far more sinister…

In a sense, these figures *were* from another world – but not any afterlife. They were coming through the Void between universes, slipping through cracks created by a Void Ship. Their origin was a parallel Earth: similar to, yet in some ways very different from, our own. Once they arrived fully in our world, the millions of ghostly figures could be seen clearly for what they really were: Cybermen.

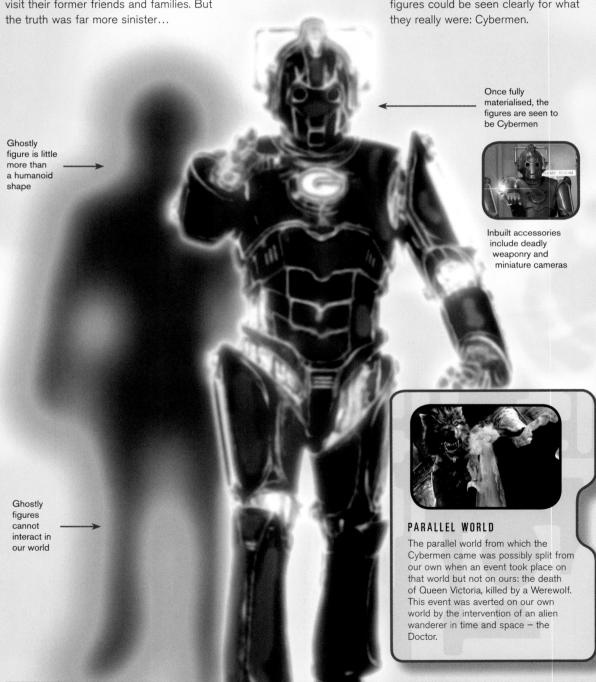

Ghostly figure is little more than a humanoid shape

Once fully materialised, the figures are seen to be Cybermen

Inbuilt accessories include deadly weaponry and miniature cameras

Ghostly figures cannot interact in our world

## PARALLEL WORLD

The parallel world from which the Cybermen came was possibly split from our own when an event took place on that world but not on ours: the death of Queen Victoria, killed by a Werewolf. This event was averted on our own world by the intervention of an alien wanderer in time and space – the Doctor.

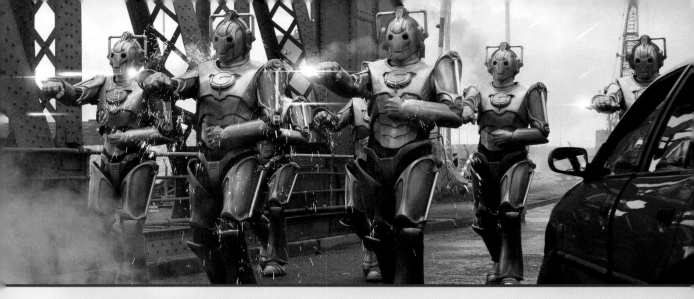

##  ARMY OF GHOSTS

Jackie is convinced that she is being visited by the ghost of her father. Sure enough, the Doctor and Rose see a grey, translucent figure appear in her kitchen – and other 'ghosts' appear around the world. But they are being brought into existence by scientists at the Torchwood Institute. The Doctor goes to Torchwood Tower, where he tries to persuade Yvonne Hartman that the experiments are damaging the very fabric of reality.

Meanwhile, Rose finds Mickey, who has returned from the parallel world where she last saw him. They investigate a mysterious Sphere that came through the Void. The ghosts materialise fully – as Cybermen – and then the Sphere opens and its occupants emerge: Daleks!

Written by
**Russell T Davies**
Featuring
**the Tenth Doctor, Rose and Mickey**
First broadcast
**1 July 2006**
**First of 2 episodes**
**(see page 107)**

### TORCHWOOD

The Torchwood Institute was established by Queen Victoria after she was nearly killed by a Werewolf, and was named after Torchwood House, where the incident happened. Torchwood's headquarters are in Canary Wharf Tower. The Institute collects and investigates alien technology. Refusing to go metric, Torchwood upholds the tenets of the British Empire.

In charge is Yvonne Hartman, a woman so single-minded that she is able to resist her conversion into a Cyberman and fight back – doing her duty, for Queen and country.

### THE GHOST SHIFT

Torchwood's experiments on the Sphere have opened the cracks between worlds, and the Cybermen can come through. The Sphere is a Void Ship, which has no real existence until the breach between reality and the Void is opened.

The Ghost Shift is the term Torchwood use to describe the times when they energise the cracks between reality and the Void, to bring the 'ghosts' through. They do not realise how fragile reality has become, and continue their experiments, allowing the army of millions of Cybermen to materialise fully on Earth.

### CYBER CONVERSION

The Cybermen have hidden conversion equipment inside Torchwood Tower, to 'upgrade' humans. They are ready to begin full conversions, and turn many Torchwood personnel into Cybermen, including Yvonne Hartman. They also partially convert some personnel before they reveal their presence. These people, conditioned with a brain implant attached to their earpods, are remote-controlled by the Cybermen. One of the partial converts is a young woman called Adeola – a cousin of the Doctor's future companion Martha Jones.

 ## SCRIPTING ARMY OF GHOSTS

Russell T Davies, lead writer and executive producer of *Doctor Who*, found the idea of pitching the Daleks and the Cybermen against each other irresistible. Despite the classic series running for so long, the two most popular of *Doctor Who*'s monstrous enemies had never met in battle. They sometimes featured together in 'guest' appearances in the same episode: in the Doctor's hallucinations in *The Mind of Evil*; and when the Doctor shows the Time Lords the evils he has fought, in *The War Games*. The closest they came to an encounter was in *The Five Doctors*, where a lone Dalek chases the First Doctor in the Death Zone on his home planet Gallifrey, while an army of Cybermen pursues his other incarnations.

It must have been daunting to bring the two super-monsters together, but Russell T Davies explains, in behind-the-scenes book *Doctor Who: The Inside Story*, why he did it:

'It's irresistible to put them together; it's begging to be done... Bronze and steel – they're just meant to clash. You've got to keep raising the stakes ... I wanted to create battleground Earth, where the human race is trapped in the middle of two giants scrapping. I always think that, in the mythology of the series, they're like gods ... These are two great big creatures from hell and they're sent into hell at the end ... For there to be hell on Earth, it means Daleks versus Cybermen, and the stakes have got to be that high for the Doctor to lose Rose at the end ... for the ending to be truly cataclysmic.'

## CYBER INVASION

Although the invading Cybermen seem frighteningly real, many were computer-generated. It is typical of the quality of the effects provided by The Mill that it's impossible to tell which are which.

   The ghosts were also created by The Mill, based on shots of actors in black suits against green screens. The scenes were shot without the ghosts and they were added afterwards. When they materialised fully, these figures were blended with the outlines of the Cybermen.

### INVASION SCRIPT

In the original script, Adeola's frightening encounter with the Cybermen did not reveal who had actually infiltrated Torchwood Tower:

```
The shadow is silent, unmoving. Just
 one more curtain of thick polythene
  between them; maybe, this close,
   the shape around its head visible;
   a handle-type structure ...
   She reaches out, she parts the
   polythene ...

  HIGH ANGLE POV looking down at
Adeola. And she just stares up. Rigid.
In shock. Hold.
```

It was not until the Doctor found the cordoned-off area that they were revealed:

```
A shadow's hand reaches up. The edge
of the hand slices through the tight polythene, top to bottom, like a knife
through butter, the metal hand protruding through –

THE DOCTOR
Cybermen.

And the CYBERMEN step through!
```

# THE CYBERMEN

On Christmas Eve in 1851, the Doctor encounters a new type of Cyberman – the Cybershades. Created by a group of Cybermen that have found themselves in Victorian times, the Cybershades are made out of local, contemporary materials using the techniques and technology available to the Cybermen. The Cybershades are more agile and less noticeable in London than standard Cybermen. They can run, climb and jump, but they are not equipped to administer lethal electric shocks, like normal Cybermen.

Crouched and constantly moving like hags or witches, the Cybershades seem to retain some emotional features. They are constantly hissing, as if angry at humanity as they carry out the orders of their masters. They are used primarily for reconnaissance and to instil fear in the Victorian Londoners.

Rags and skin less out of place than Cyber-armour

Cybershade can leap and climb

Hands and helmet created from available materials

Far more agile than standard Cyberman

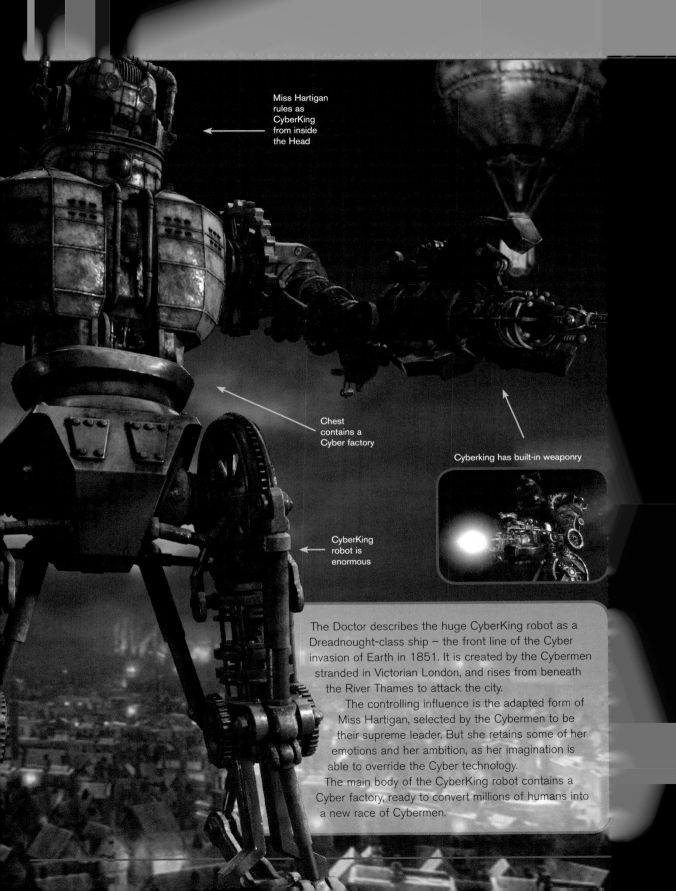

Miss Hartigan rules as CyberKing from inside the Head

Chest contains a Cyber factory

CyberKing robot is enormous

Cyberking has built-in weaponry

The Doctor describes the huge CyberKing robot as a Dreadnought-class ship – the front line of the Cyber invasion of Earth in 1851. It is created by the Cybermen stranded in Victorian London, and rises from beneath the River Thames to attack the city.

The controlling influence is the adapted form of Miss Hartigan, selected by the Cybermen to be their supreme leader. But she retains some of her emotions and her ambition, as her imagination is able to override the Cyber technology.

The main body of the CyberKing robot contains a Cyber factory, ready to convert millions of humans into a new race of Cybermen.

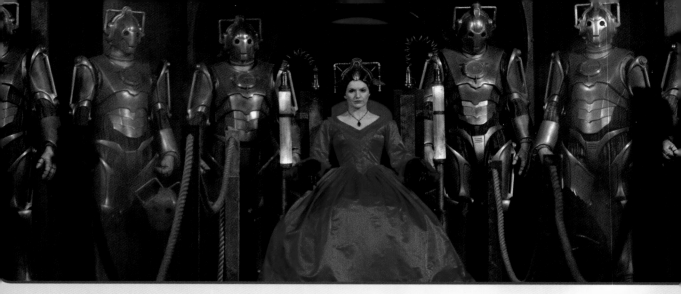

 # THE NEXT DOCTOR

Written by
**Russell T Davies**
Featuring
**the Tenth Doctor**
First broadcast
**25 December 2008**
**1 feature-length episode**

The Doctor arrives in London on Christmas Eve 1851 – and finds that another Doctor is battling against the Cybermen. At first he thinks this other Doctor is a future incarnation of himself. But gradually he realises this is not the case. And when the Other Doctor shows him his TARDIS, it turns out to be a hot-air balloon.

The two men join forces to fight the Cybermen and their deadly new Cybershades. They discover a huge work area where the Cybermen and their ally, the ambitious Miss Hartigan, are using children as slave labourers to construct a massive CyberKing. The Doctor helps Miss Hartigan to see the error of her ways, and the CyberKing is destroyed.

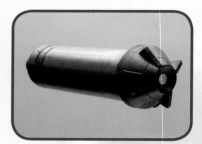

### THE OTHER DOCTOR

The man who thinks he is the Doctor is actually Jackson Lake. He has been traumatised by a chance encounter with the Cybermen – in which his wife was killed and his son abducted. Absorbing information from Cyber records, Lake learns of the Doctor and his mind is so shocked he believes himself to be the Doctor.

With the help of his friend Rosita, Jackson tries to live up to the Doctor's morals and bravery, and is able to help the real Doctor defeat the Cybermen and save his son, Frederic Lake.

### MISS HARTIGAN

Matron of St Joseph's Workhouse, Mercy Hartigan supplies child labour for the Cybermen, and helps them in their plan to take over London.

The Cybermen decide to convert Miss Hartigan into a CyberKing – their ultimate leader. But the power of her ambition and imagination causes the process to fail and she retains those human qualities. Despite her callous hatred for many of her fellow humans, the Doctor is able to show her the damage she is doing, and this causes the destruction of the CyberKing robot and the Cybermen.

### INFOSTAMPS

Infostamps contain compressed data. Each infostamp can hold masses of information – like the entire history of London from 1066 to 1851. Normally, the Cybermen exchange data using more sophisticated wireless technology. But when they are trapped in 19th-century London, they find themselves low on power and have to resort to cruder methods of information transfer.

When Jackson Lake absorbs information about the Doctor from one of these infostamps, his brain is tricked into believing that he really is the Doctor.

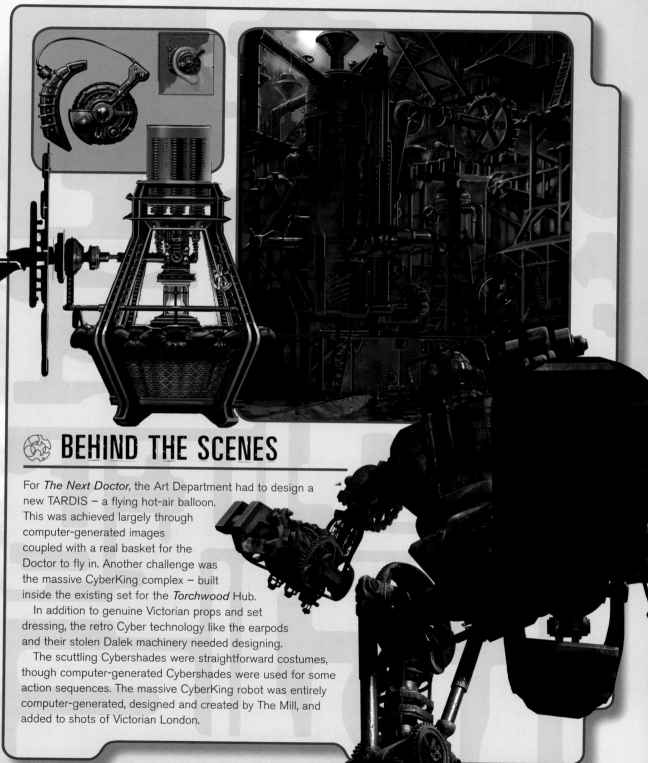

## 🌀 BEHIND THE SCENES

For *The Next Doctor*, the Art Department had to design a
new TARDIS – a flying hot-air balloon.
This was achieved largely through
computer-generated images
coupled with a real basket for the
Doctor to fly in. Another challenge was
the massive CyberKing complex – built
inside the existing set for the *Torchwood* Hub.

   In addition to genuine Victorian props and set
dressing, the retro Cyber technology like the earpods
and their stolen Dalek machinery needed designing.

   The scuttling Cybershades were straightforward costumes,
though computer-generated Cybershades were used for some
action sequences. The massive CyberKing robot was entirely
computer-generated, designed and created by The Mill, and
added to shots of Victorian London.

Horns have been a symbol of power since the dawn of Man

The classic image of the Devil is based on a race memory of the Dæmons

A Dæmon is able to grow to giant size or shrink so as to be practically invisible – releasing or absorbing heat energy in the process

The saturnine Dæmons are from the planet Damos – 60,000 light years away – and first came to Earth nearly 100,000 years ago. Glimpsed throughout history, they have secretly helped humanity to evolve, and have entered myth as the traditional image of the Devil. The effects of their psionic science have been part-remembered as magic and superstition. But to the Dæmons, human evolution and development is simply an experiment, and if humanity doesn't perform well enough, the Dæmon left on Earth will destroy the world.

Azal, the last of the Dæmons, will appear three times before deciding the fate of Earth: either he will destroy it, or he will pass on his great power – but with the Doctor around, things are rarely that simple.

## THE MASTER

Like the Doctor, the Master is a Time Lord – he is an old friend and colleague of the Doctor. But, unlike the Doctor, he craves power and longs to see the human race destroyed. The Master summons Azal using the villagers' violent emotions – their fear and hatred. He harnesses their psychic energy and hopes to persuade Azal to bequeath him his enormous power.

Cloven hooves for feet

# THE DÆMONS

The Doctor and Jo visit Devil's End, where Professor Horner is excavating an ancient burial mound. But inside is the crashed spaceship of Azal, last of the Dæmons, an ancient race who've been experimenting with human evolution. The Dæmon has been summoned by the Master, who is posing as the local vicar and manipulating the local villagers.

With the Brigadier and UNIT unable to reach them, the Doctor and Jo enlist the help of a local white witch to combat the revived Dæmon, an animated gargoyle, hostile villagers and some homicidal morris dancers.

Azal appears for a final time and prepares to kill the Doctor, but Jo's offer to die in the Doctor's place confounds Azal, who is destroyed.

Written by
**Guy Leopold**
Featuring
**the Third Doctor,
Jo and UNIT**
First broadcast
**22 May–19 June 1971
5 episodes**

## DEVIL'S END

The whole area is steeped in the Dæmons' mythology and black magic. Nearby villages include Witchwood and Satanhill, while the village pub is named the Cloven Hoof.

The burial mound containing Azal's ship is called the Devil's Hump, and local legends predict death and destruction if it is opened… Previous attempts to excavate Devil's Hump have ended in disaster.

In the notorious cavern beneath the church, the witches of the 17th century hid from the fires of witch-hunter Matthew Hopkins.

## THE HEAT BARRIER

Using the psionic science of the Dæmons and the power of the black magic coven he commands, the Master creates a heat barrier around Devil's End to keep UNIT out, trapping the Doctor and Jo in the village. The barrier is a huge dome, a mile high at the centre, above the village church. The barrier can be seen only as a 'heat haze' and a charred line across the ground.

The Doctor is able to help UNIT create an energy exchanger to make a hole in the barrier, so the Brigadier and his troops can enter.

## BOK

Bok is the pet name given by the Master to a stone gargoyle-like figure animated by the power of Azal. The gargoyle's eyes glow red and it can fire a destructive force from its finger. The Doctor escapes from Bok by warding it off with a trowel – iron has ancient magical properties – and chanting an incantation (part of a Venusian lullaby: 'Close your eyes, my darling – well, three of them, at least…').

Bok explodes when shot, but re-forms and attacks the UNIT troops again. When Azal is destroyed, Bok becomes inanimate stone.

# THE DALEKS

The Daleks are the most hated and feared life form in the universe. Originally from the planet Skaro, their empire eventually grew to cover much of known space. While they appear to be armoured robots, their casings are really survival chambers. The hideous creatures inside are the result of a thousand-year war between the Kaleds and the Thals. A Kaled scientist, Davros, experimented to discover the ultimate mutated form of his race, designing a travel machine to enable the creatures to survive. Now dependent on radiation, and powered by static electricity, the Daleks' only ambition is the conquest of all other life forms and the total extermination of their enemies.

Luminosity dischargers light up when the Dalek speaks

Data from the Dalek's eye is transferred directly into the brain of the Dalek creature

Power slats absorb energy to power Dalek's motive system

'The sucker cup on the Dalek's arm can manipulate and be used as a weapon. It produces a tremendously powerful vacuum.

The main chamber is where the Dalek creature is housed within the casing – floating in a nutrient-rich fluid, and attached directly by positronic linkages into the various on-board systems

The gyroscopic stabilisation system enables the Dalek to remain upright even in adverse circumstances

Some of these globes replace the external sense organs, while others contain additional capabilities including high explosive charges for offensive action or self-destruct

The casing of the Dalek is made from an incredibly tough and durable metal called Dalekenium

 # THE DALEKS

The TARDIS arrives on Skaro, a planet all but destroyed by a thousand-year war that ended with the detonation of an immensely powerful neutron bomb. In a huge metal city, left intact by the bomb, the Doctor and his companions discover the Daleks – hideously mutated survivors of the war, kept alive inside metal war machines powered by static electricity, and dependent upon the radioactivity in the atmosphere. The Daleks are determined to wipe out the Thals – their opponents in the war, now mutated into perfect blond-haired humanoids. The Doctor persuades the pacifist Thals to attack the Dalek City and defeat the creatures before they can release radioactive waste into the atmosphere.

Written by
**Terry Nation**
Featuring
**the First Doctor, Ian, Barbara and Susan**
First broadcast
**21 December 1963 –1 February 1964 7 episodes**

### DALEK DATA

The Daleks of this story are of a uniform, metallic silver appearance (with blue sense-globes). They are powered by static electricity, which they pick up from the metal floor of their city, and they cannot travel beyond its limits. They have a xenophobic hatred of the Thals and are determined to exterminate them.

The Daleks hope to use Thal anti-radiation drugs to enable them to leave their survival casings. But the drugs are deadly to them – the Daleks realise they have become dependent on the radiation and need it to survive.

### SKARO

The planet Skaro, the twelfth planet in its solar system, has been laid waste by the war between the Daleks and the Thals, which ended centuries ago. The only surviving structure seems to be the Dalek City, which stands in a desert close to the Petrified Jungle. Here the intense heat of the neutron bomb has turned the soil to ash and the trees and flowers to brittle stone.

Behind the city is a range of mountains, and then the Lake of Mutations – named after the hideous and deadly mutated monsters that survive in its glowing waters.

### THE THALS

Since the war, the Thals have mutated due to radioactive fallout and the residue of chemical and biological weapons. But, unlike that of the Daleks, their mutation has come full circle. Now they are a race of tall, Aryan humanoids.

Because of their history they are staunchly pacifist, refusing to fight the Daleks, even though they know this means they will die. They have become farmers, but the rains have not come and their crops have failed. They have no alternative but to turn to their old enemies – the Daleks – for help.

# THE DALEK INVASION OF EARTH

Written by
**Terry Nation**
Featuring
**the First Doctor, Ian, Barbara and Susan**
First broadcast
**21 November–26 December 1964**
**6 episodes**

In 2157, the Daleks invade Earth. Their plan is to drill through the Earth's crust and blow out the planet's core with a penetration explosive capsule. They will then install a guidance system and pilot the Earth like a giant spaceship.

The Doctor and his companions arrive in a devastated London and help the human resistance fighters. But after an attack on the main Dalek landing site goes disastrously wrong, they have to flee London. They make their separate ways to the Daleks' main mining operations in Bedfordshire, where the Doctor and his friends manage to divert the Dalek bomb intended to blow open the Earth. Instead it destroys the invaders.

### DALEK DATA

The Daleks in this story can now travel outside the confines of their city, invading other worlds. They have enlarged 'fenders', and pick up power through a receiver dish on the backs of their casings. The base of a Dalek is seen to be flat, when it is lifted by rebelling miners.

They are led by the Black Dalek – also called the 'Supreme Controller'. There is also mention of a separate 'Supreme Command'. The Saucer Commander is seen, a predominantly black Dalek, but with alternating black and silver flanges on its base section.

### ROBOMEN

Because there are relatively few Daleks on Earth, they operate on intelligent prisoners and turn them into living robots – Robomen. The so-called 'transfer' operation controls the human brain, at least for a time. But after a while, the processing breaks down and the Robomen go insane and kill themselves.

The Daleks relay instructions to the Robomen through a helmet grafted onto the skull that picks up high-frequency radio waves. The helmet flashes when in communication, and the Daleks always know when a Roboman is attacked.

### THE SLYTHER

The revolting Slyther is a 'pet' of the Black Dalek, used to enforce the curfew at the Dalek mine in Bedfordshire. Presumably brought to Earth from the planet Skaro, the Slyther roams the mine area at night in search of food – humans. The Slyther's horrific, screaming cries strike terror into the mine workers.

When Ian is confronted by the grotesque creature, he manages to evade it by jumping into a large bucket suspended over one of the mine shafts. The Slyther tries to follow, but falls to its death at the bottom of the shaft.

 # THE CHASE

The Dalek Supreme sends an execution squad to pursue the Doctor and his companions through time and space. They almost catch the Doctor on the desert planet of Aridius, but the TARDIS escapes first to the Empire State Building, then the *Mary Celeste*, where the Daleks terrify the crew into abandoning ship. After a narrow escape from an apparently haunted house, the Daleks corner the time travellers on Mechanus.

Here the Doctor and his friends are captured by the robot Mechonoids. When the Daleks arrive, there is a pitched battle between Mechonoids and Daleks. As it rages, the Doctor and his friends escape – Ian and Barbara taking the Daleks' time machine to get home to 1960s London.

Written by
**Terry Nation**
Featuring
**the First Doctor,
Ian, Barbara, Vicki
and Steven**
First broadcast
**22 May–26 June 1965
6 episodes**

### DALEK DATA

The Daleks in this story have vertical slats over the bands round their mid-sections, like armour-plating. This basic design would remain fundamentally unchanged over the coming years.

The Daleks create a robot duplicate of the Doctor to trick his companions. The double assumes (from previous encounters) that the young girl with the Doctor is Susan – she is in fact Vicki – enabling Ian to spot which Doctor is who!

The Daleks know of the Mechonoids, and the two sides seem evenly matched when they meet in battle.

### DALEK TIME TRAVEL

For the first time we see the Daleks travel through time. They also use a time machine, which is bigger inside than out, in *The Daleks' Master Plan*. In other stories they use either small, portable time machines – as in *Day of the Daleks* – or 'time corridors' that link specific times and places. In *The Evil of the Daleks*, they have a time corridor from Skaro to Maxtible's house in 1866, and from there to London in 1966. In *Resurrection of the Daleks*, a time corridor links the Dalek ship in the future with a warehouse in London in 1984.

### THE MECHONOIDS

The Mechonoids are robots sent from Earth to prepare the planet Mechanus for colonisation. They have built a city on huge stilts, 1500 feet (450 metres) above the jungle of Mechanus, and wait for the colonists, who, because of interplanetary wars, will never come.

But until human immigrants with the right control codes arrive, the Mechonoids treat all other life forms as specimens for study, or enemies to be destroyed with their flame-thrower weaponry. Weakened by fire, their city collapses when the Daleks attack.

# THE DALEKS' MASTER PLAN

Written by
**Terry Nation
and Dennis Spooner**
Featuring
**the First Doctor, Steven
and Katarina**
First broadcast
**13 November 1965
–29 January 1966
12 episodes**

Following on from *Mission to the Unknown* (see below), the Daleks' plan for conquest is nearing completion when the treacherous Guardian of the Solar System – Mavic Chen – delivers the taranium core of their Time Destructor to Kembel. But the Doctor manages to steal the taranium and escape in Chen's ship.

As the Doctor tries to keep the taranium core from them, the Daleks and Chen pursue him through space and time, from the prison planet Desperus to ancient Egypt. Finally, back on Kembel, he operates the Time Destructor and destroys them. Sadly, space agent Sara Kingdom who has been a loyal companion to the Doctor and Steven, is also killed by the device.

## MISSION TO THE UNKNOWN

In a single-episode story that does not feature the Doctor, Space Agent Marc Cory is investigating the sighting of a Dalek ship in the year 4000. He soon discovers they have a base on the planet Kembel. But his crew are infected by homicidal Varga plants, imported from Skaro, and they themselves start to mutate into deadly Vargas. Elsewhere on Kembel, the Daleks are negotiating with representatives of the six outer galaxies to destroy the solar system. Cory records a message of warning, but before he can send it he is found and exterminated.

## THE DALEK DELEGATES

The members of the Dalek Alliance (except Mavic Chen) are the rulers of the outer galaxies: Sentreal; Zephon, Master of the Fifth Galaxy; the Masters of Celation and Beaus; Trantis, the representative of the largest of the outer galaxies; Malpha and Gearon.

Mavic Chen is the Guardian of the Solar System. Not content merely to rule Earth's galaxy, Chen plans to betray the Daleks and take control with a fleet of Earth security vessels. But the Daleks are just as perfidious, and they exterminate Chen before he can betray them.

## SPECIAL SPACE SECURITY

The SSS is Earth's elite defence and security force. Its top agents include Marc Cory – exterminated by the Daleks on Kembel – and Bret Vyon who was sent to find Cory. When Vyon allies himself with the Doctor, he too is killed – branded a traitor by Mavic Chen and assassinated by his own sister, Agent Sara Kingdom.

After the Doctor proves to Sara that Vyon was innocent, she helps the Doctor and Steven to destroy the Daleks, even at the cost of her own life. She ages to death on Kembel when the Time Destructor is activated.

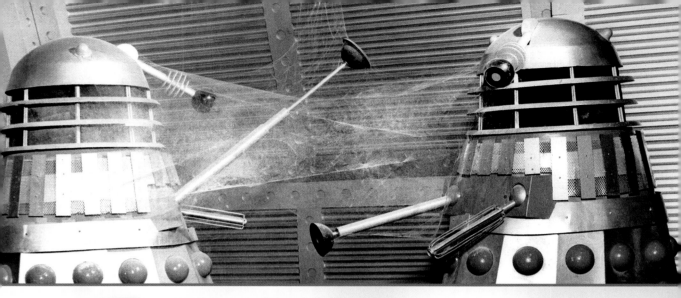

 # THE POWER OF THE DALEKS

On the Earth colony Vulcan, a space capsule is recovered after being buried for over 200 years in a mercury swamp. Inside, scientist Lesterson discovers three inert Daleks. Not knowing what they are, he reactivates one. The newly regenerated Doctor and his friends struggle to convince the colonists that the (disarmed) Daleks are not harmless, friendly or servile. But then a rebel group tries to use the Daleks to help them seize power. The Daleks have set up a secret facility to create a Dalek army and, as the humans fight each other, Daleks emerge from the capsule to exterminate all humans! But the Doctor manages to turn their power source against them and the Daleks are destroyed. Or are they?

Written by
**David Whitaker**
Featuring
**the Second Doctor, Ben and Polly**
First broadcast
**5 November–10 December 1966**
**6 episodes**

### DALEK DATA

While pretending to be servile and obedient to the human colonists, a Dalek seems to recognise the newly regenerated Doctor. Disarmed by the scientist Lesterson, the Daleks are forced to operate from a position of weakness. They scheme to secure the power supply that will place them in a dominant position from which they can destroy the colony.

When their weapons are returned, their firepower is as awesome as ever. One Dalek gun fires through two-inch thick tungsten steel by way of demonstration to the rebel leaders.

### DALEK PRODUCTION LINE

The three Daleks in the capsule set up a conveyor-belt production line to make empty casings into which the Dalek creatures are placed. The top section of the Dalek is then lowered into place before the complete Dalek emerges, ready to do battle with the human colonists.

The Dalek creatures may have been stored in the secret area of the capsule, or they may have been manufactured or bred specifically when needed. The Dalek creatures are placed inside the newly created Dalek casings as part of this production process.

### STATIC POWER

The Daleks can store power, but they require a static electrical circuit for permanent energy. The Doctor likens static power to their blood: 'a constant life-stream'.

In *The Daleks*, the metal floors were wired to provide the Daleks with power; they could not leave their city. In *The Dalek Invasion of Earth*, the Daleks picked up power through receiver dishes attached to their backs. It may be that the slats over the Daleks middle sections store and supply power. These slats have been evident in all Dalek design since *The Chase*.

# THE EVIL OF THE DALEKS

Written by
**David Whitaker**
Featuring
**the Second Doctor,
Jamie and Victoria**
First broadcast
**20 May–1 July 1967
7 episodes**

The Daleks steal the TARDIS and lure the Doctor and Jamie to scientist Theodore Maxtible's house near Canterbury in 1866. Here Jamie is tested by having to rescue Victoria (the daughter of another scientist) while his emotions are recorded. The Daleks want to distill 'the Human Factor', which will show why humans have always defeated them.

Back on Skaro, the Dalek Emperor reveals that the Doctor has refined the Dalek Factor – the impulse to exterminate – which they will spread through Earth history. But the Doctor 'infects' some Daleks with the Human Factor and they begin to question the orders of their leaders. With a Dalek civil war raging, the Doctor, Jamie and Victoria escape.

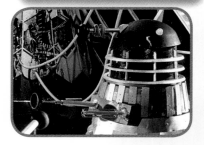

### DALEK DATA

The Daleks are commanded by black Dalek Leaders, with black domes and mid-sections. These are also the Emperor's guards, and they battle the humanised Daleks to protect their leader.

When the top is blown off a Dalek in the civil war, a glutinous gunge erupts from inside its casing, which may issue from the Dalek creature's protective environment.

The Doctor explains that the Dalek City is huge and mainly below ground. Within the city, we see the Emperor's throne room and various other facilities including the weapon shop.

### THE EMPEROR DALEK

The Daleks' supreme leader is the Emperor – a massive Dalek built into the very fabric of the Dalek City on Skaro. Despite the Doctor's assertion that this is the 'final end' of the Daleks, the Emperor is not totally destroyed in the civil war.

In *Remembrance of the Daleks*, the Dalek Emperor seems to be a 'normal' Dalek with an enlarged globe replacing its top section, and no eyestalk. When this globe opens, its occupant is revealed to be Davros. In *The Parting of the Ways*, the Emperor is once again an immobile colossus built into the Dalek flagship.

### ALPHA, BETA, OMEGA

Once revived, the three test Daleks in which the Doctor implants the Human Factor are just like children. The Doctor says they will grow up quickly, and names them Alpha, Beta and Omega.

In their child-like state, the test Daleks play 'trains' and spin the Doctor round as he rides on their fenders. 'Dizzy Doctor', they intone with glee, and sing their new names. The Doctor strikes up a bizarre friendship with the three Daleks.

Before long, Alpha, Beta and Omega begin to question orders, and the Dalek race soon descends into civil war.

# DAY OF THE DALEKS

The Doctor investigates a mysterious attack on diplomat Sir Reginald Styles, and discovers that guerrillas from the 22nd century are trying to assassinate him. They believe Styles sabotaged a peace conference in their past – our present – and the resulting wars gave the Daleks another chance to invade Earth.

In the Dalek-ruled future, the Doctor and Jo struggle to avoid capture and to learn what really happened. But as the Doctor returns to put history back on track, the Daleks – and their ape-like servants the Ogrons – prepare their own attack on the conference. The Daleks are finally destroyed when one of the guerrillas blows up Sir Reginald's house.

Written by
**Louis Marks**
Featuring
**the Third Doctor, UNIT and Jo**
First broadcast
**1–22 January 1972**
**4 episodes**

### DALEK DATA

From now on, the Dalek eye has a black 'pupil' rather than a solid white disc. The chief Dalek is gold, and the other Daleks are dark grey.

The Daleks use their Mind Analysis Machine to establish the Doctor's identity.

Bullets and mortars have no apparent effect on Daleks during their attack on Auderly House.

The Daleks have time-travel technology, but it is only rudimentary. But the equipment is not reliable and requires fixed points to be established between time zones.

### OGRONS

The ape-like Ogrons are a form of higher anthropoid that used to live in scattered communities on one of the outer planets. The Daleks use them to supplement human security forces.

Ogrons are very simple, very honest, very loyal and very strong. Apparently immune to the Doctor's Venusian karate, one Ogron is felled by a blow to the head with a carafe of wine.

In *Frontier in Space* (1973), the Ogrons are seen to be working for the Daleks again, under the direction of the Master, operating from a base on the Ogron planet.

### AN ALTERNATIVE INVASION

The Daleks have managed to invade because of a time paradox. The Doctor discovers that the peace conference was destroyed not by Styles, but by one of the future guerrilla fighters trying to assassinate Styles to prevent the very war this causes.

Under Dalek rule, Earth is run like a giant labour camp, its raw materials mined and taken to Skaro to supply the expanding Dalek empire. Rather than deploy a massive occupation force, the Daleks use traitorous humans to control the population, aided by Ogrons.

# PLANET OF THE DALEKS

Written by
**Terry Nation**
Featuring
**the Third Doctor
and Jo**
First broadcast
**7 April–12 May 1973
6 episodes**

The Doctor and Jo follow a group of Daleks to the planet Spiridon. Here they find a group of Thals (see page 81) on a suicide mission to prevent the Daleks learning how to be invisible. The Daleks are studying the native – invisible – Spiridons, who they have enslaved. The Thals believe there are only a dozen Daleks on the planet, but the Doctor discovers a massive Dalek army in an underground ice cavern – 10,000 Daleks, held in suspended animation.

As the Daleks prepare to unleash a deadly bacteria to destroy the Thals, the Doctor and his friends fight their way into the Dalek base. They manage to flood the Dalek army with liquid ice, freezing it for centuries.

## DALEK DATA

Most Daleks have an automatic distress transmitter, which may be activated if the casing is opened, even after the Dalek is deactivated. Spiridon has been totally subjugated with the usual Dalek technique, which the Doctor describes as, 'mass exterminations, followed by absolute suppression of the survivors.'

The Daleks' guidance system uses high-frequency radio impulses, which the Doctor manages to jam to confuse one Dalek. The cold of the Spiridon night slows the Daleks' mechanical reflexes – they hardly function at all at sub-zero temperatures.

## INVISIBLE DALEKS

From studying the Spiridons, the Daleks have discovered an anti-reflecting light wave that enables them to become invisible. Generating this light wave takes enormous power, however, so the Daleks can stay invisible for only short periods.

Some of the Daleks suffer from light-wave sickness as a side effect and deactivate. When the Doctor and his Thal friends find a deactivated invisible Dalek, they use spray paint to make it visible again. The Dalek has completely shut down, but may still be able to send an automated distress call.

## THE DALEK SUPREME

The Black Dalek in early Dalek stories was also referred to as the Dalek Supreme. In this story, it is seen to be black and gold with enlarged dome lights and is said to be 'one of the Supreme Council'. There is mention of a ruling council in *The Daleks*.

The Supreme Dalek is referred to in later stories – including *Destiny of the Daleks* and *Revelation of the Daleks* – as opposed to Davros. A Supreme Dalek also appears in *Resurrection of the Daleks* and as leader of the rebel Daleks in *Remembrance of the Daleks*.

# DEATH TO THE DALEKS

The TARDIS loses power and lands on Exxilon. The Doctor meets up with a stranded group of humans mining for parrinium, the antidote to a space plague. Sarah finds a huge city, but is captured by native Exxilons. A group of Daleks arrives, also apparently looking for parrinium. They too lose power and their guns fail, forcing them into an uneasy alliance with the humans. But the Daleks are planning to take all the parrinium.

Equipped with machine guns, the Daleks take over. Meanwhile, the Doctor and a rebel Exxilon, Bellal, enter the city, the source of the power drain. They destroy it, but the Dalek ship leaves as power is restored. It is destroyed by Galloway, one of the humans, using a Dalek bomb.

Written by
**Terry Nation**
Featuring
**the Third Doctor
and Sarah Jane**
First broadcast
**23 February–16 March
1974
4 episodes**

## DALEK VOICES

As recognisable as the Dalek's distinctive pepperpot shape is its grating metallic voice. This was created by treating the actor's voice with a 'ring modulator', which adds and subtracts an input signal's frequency (in this case the actor doing the Dalek voice) from an internal oscillator's frequency. Unfortunately, the frequency used was never noted, and so Dalek voices tended to alter between stories. The earliest Dalek voices were provided by Peter Hawkins, a well-known voice artist. He was joined by David Graham, a regular voice actor for Gerry Anderson. Later, Roy Skelton provided Dalek voices, as did Michael Wisher (*above*), who was also the original Davros. Other actors have also given voice to the Daleks – most notable in recent times being Nicholas Briggs (*left*), who also wrote and directed the audio CD series *Dalek Empire*. A talented writer, actor and voice artist (as well as a massive fan of the Daleks), Nick has provided voices for all the Daleks in *Doctor Who* since 2005, as well as for other creatures including the Nestene Consciousness, the Adherents of the Repeated Meme, the Cybermen and the Judoon.

## DALEK DATA

The Doctor says that the Daleks move by psycho-kinetic power, which is why only their armaments and spaceship are affected by the power loss. Inside each Dalek, the Doctor says, is a 'living, bubbling lump of hate'.

One Dalek survives an electric shock of 7,000 volts inside the Exxilon City, while another self-destructs when it 'fails' by letting a prisoner escape. While usually fitted with a standard gun, in *Death to the Daleks*, they replace their inactive blasters with machine guns, which they describe as 'moderately efficient'.

 # GENESIS OF THE DALEKS

Written by
**Terry Nation**
Featuring
**the Fourth Doctor,
Sarah Jane and Harry**
First broadcast
**8 March–12 April 1975
6 episodes**

The Time Lords despatch the Doctor to Skaro in the distant past to avert the creation of the Daleks. He arrives at the end of a thousand-year war between the Thals and the Kaleds. Anyone mutated by the chemical and biological weapons is banished outside their huge domed cities. Crippled Kaled scientist Davros has realised the mutation process is irreversible. So he has invented a 'travel machine' that will ensure the survival of the creature he knows his race will become – the Dalek.

But he makes the Daleks ambitious creatures of hate, without feeling or pity for inferior life forms. The Doctor manages to slow Dalek development, but leaves as the Daleks take over Skaro and exterminate Davros.

### DALEK DATA

Davros calls his prototype Dalek a Mark III Travel Machine. All the Daleks he creates are gunmetal grey in colour. The first Dalek is able to detect that the Doctor and Harry are aliens, and its immediate response is that they should be exterminated.

It is impossible to know at what point the Daleks decide they no longer need Davros. Once they have secured the Kaled Elite's bunker, they start up the automated Dalek production line Davros has set up – and when Davros's henchman Nyder tries to stop it, they exterminate him.

### DALEK ORIGINS

While *Genesis of the Daleks* is the definitive account of the creation of the Daleks, the *TV Century 21* Dalek comic strip of 1965 gave another account. The Daleks here were war machines developed by Yarvelling of the short, warlike, blue-skinned Dalek race. The Daleks plan to destroy the Thals with a neutron bomb, which is prematurely detonated by a meteorite storm and, two years later, Yarvelling's dying action is to adapt his war machine to carry the mutated remains of his people.

### DAVROS

Crippled and deformed, Davros has based his Dalek machines on his own life-support system. The Dalek base resembles his wheelchair, and its voice sounds like Davros's own electronically modified and enhanced speech.

Davros is the head of the Kaled Elite Scientific Corps – a group of the best scientists, headquartered in a bunker some miles from the main Kaled dome. He is a brilliant scientist and ruthless politician, who will stop at nothing to ensure the success of his Dalek project.

 # DESTINY OF THE DALEKS

The Doctor and Romana arrive on Skaro where they meet the Movellans, who are locked in a stalemate in a war against the Daleks. The Daleks are digging through the remains of their ancient city to find and revive Davros, in the hope he can give them an advantage in their unending war.

The Movellans are a robot race, and they hope the Doctor can give them a similar advantage. The Doctor captures Davros, but the Daleks exterminate their human slave-workers until the Doctor surrenders. As the Movellans prepare to depart and destroy the planet, the Doctor frees the slave-workers to take over their ship. He tricks Davros into destroying the approaching 'suicide' Daleks and Davros is taken to Earth for trial.

Written by
**Terry Nation**
Featuring
**the Fourth Doctor
and Romana**
First broadcast
**1–22 September 1979
4 episodes**

### DALEK DATA

Davros was not destroyed, it seems, but went into suspended animation after being shot by the Daleks in *Genesis of the Daleks*. In the intervening centuries, the Daleks have become dependent on their battle computers. They now believe their creator can help them defeat the Movellans, and they are willing to sacrifice themselves, if need be, to rescue him.

A group of Daleks strap explosives to their armour that will be detonated when they close on the Movellan ship – destroying themselves and their enemy.

### THE MOVELLANS

The Movellans appear to be beautiful humanoids. In fact they are ruthless robots, locked in a war with the Daleks. The battle computers of both fleets are so evenly matched they anticipate and neutralise the other's every move. Led by Commander Sharrel, the Movellans believe the Doctor can solve this stalemate – which he can: whichever side turns off its battle computers will become unpredictable and win the war. The Doctor is able to disrupt the Movellans' control systems with his K-9 dog whistle.

### TYSSAN

Starship Engineer Tyssan was serving with Earth's deep space fleet and has been a prisoner of the Daleks since he was captured two years ago. About 50 captives have been sent from a Dalek prison ship to work in the excavations on Skaro. If any prisoner escapes, five others are executed in retaliation.

Left for dead, Tyssan manages to escape and helps the Doctor. He leads the other prisoners against the Movellans and Daleks. When Davros is captured, Tyssan returns him to Earth to stand trial.

# RESURRECTION OF THE DALEKS

Written by
**Eric Saward**
Featuring
**the Fifth Doctor,
Tegan and Turlough**
First broadcast
**8–15 February 1984
2 episodes**

Ninety years after Davros was imprisoned in suspended animation, the Daleks come to free him. The Movellans have won the war, developing a deadly Dalek virus. The Daleks need Davros – to find an antidote.

The Doctor and his friends find samples of the virus in a warehouse in present-day London. The Daleks capture the Doctor by means of a time corridor linking London in 1984 to their ship. They intend to duplicate him and send him to assassinate the Time Lord High Council. But as Davros betrays the Dalek Supreme and turns his own Daleks against him, the virus is unleashed – which also affects Davros. The Dalek ship is destroyed by a Dalek 'duplicate' human who reverts to his true nature.

## DALEK DATA

The Daleks are able to duplicate humans – including a bomb-disposal squad sent to investigate the canisters of virus stored in a warehouse in London. The Dalek Supreme claims that Dalek duplicates now occupy key positions on 20th-century Earth.

Davros has a device concealed in his chair that enables him to take over humans and even Daleks. Planning to destroy the Daleks and start again with his Dalek project, Davros releases the virus – only to find it affects him too.

## DALEK CREATURES

Until *Dalek*, the creature inside the Dalek has rarely been revealed, but we have seen glimpses. In *The Daleks*, a four-fingered claw emerges from under a Thal cape where the Doctor and Ian have dumped the creature from inside one Dalek. Dalek embryos are clearly seen as green, sponge-like creatures in *Genesis of the Daleks*. 'Young' Dalek creatures, writhing with tentacles, are placed inside Daleks on the production line in *The Power of the Daleks*, and in *Resurrection of the Daleks* a Dalek creature escapes from its destroyed casing. It tries to strangle a soldier before being shot by the Doctor and his friends.

When a Dalek is destroyed in *The Evil of the Daleks*, the pulsing, writhing gunge inside is revealed. In *The Five Doctors* and *Resurrection of the Daleks* (right), the dead Daleks are seen. And in *Revelation of the Daleks*, Natasha finds her father, Stengos – or rather just his head – being mutated into a new Dalek creature by Davros.

# REVELATION OF THE DALEKS

At Tranquil Repose, wealthy and important people with incurable diseases can be cryogenically frozen to await a cure for their ailments. But the 'Great Healer' in charge is actually Davros. He is building a new army of Daleks from the most intelligent cryogenic sleepers, and using the rest to create concentrated food protein, which is saving the galaxy from starvation.

Davros lures the Doctor to Tranquil Repose to exact his revenge. But the double-crossing Kara has also sent an assassin, Orcini, to kill Davros. The Doctor and Peri escape as a group of Daleks loyal to the Dalek Supreme arrives to capture Davros and take him back to Skaro for trial. Orcini detonates a bomb, sacrificing himself to destroy Davros's army.

Written by
**Eric Saward**
Featuring
**the Sixth Doctor
and Peri**
First broadcast
**23–30 March 1985
2 episodes**

### DALEK DATA

Davros is mutating the humans at Tranquil Repose into Dalek creatures. The creatures' brains are cultivated in incubators, then transplanted into nascent, transparent Daleks that grow into 'adult' machine-creatures. Davros's Daleks are ivory coloured, with gold sense-spheres and 'trim'.

The Skaro Daleks easily defeat Davros's new Daleks in battle, and plan to put Davros on trial for crimes against the Daleks. They plan to recondition Davros's Daleks to obey the Dalek Supreme.

### TRANQUIL REPOSE

Tranquil Repose is a cemetery combined with a facility where the terminally ill, amongst others, can be cryogenically suspended until a later date – for example when a cure for their ailment is discovered. A local DJ provides a 'personalised entertainment system'.

However, the theory does not work, as in practice nobody wants the cryogenically suspended people back – in many cases they would be in conflict with those currently in power. Also, the galaxy can barely support the current population.

### ORCINI

Temporarily excommunicated from the Grand Order of Oberon, Orcini is a feared assassin. It is said he has only to breathe on a victim for him to die. He has an artificial leg with a faulty hydraulic valve (the leg is blown off by a blast from a Dalek gun). When Orcini is seated, the valve is inclined to jam – but he refuses to have it fixed as it is a constant reminder of his own mortality. He lost his leg the one time he did not listen to the instincts of his squire, Bostock. To cleanse his conscience he gives his fee to charity.

# REMEMBRANCE OF THE DALEKS

Written by
**Ben Aaronovitch**
Featuring
**the Seventh Doctor
and Ace**
First broadcast
**5–26 October 1988
4 episodes**

The Doctor and Ace arrive in London in 1963, where the Doctor left the so-called Hand of Omega for safety. But now two groups of Daleks are after this powerful device, which can be used for manipulating stars. Imperial Daleks, led by their Emperor, battle against 'Rebel' Daleks led by the Dalek Supreme. The Doctor teams up with a military unit led by Group Captain Gilmore to destroy both factions. The Imperial Daleks win the battle, using their Special Weapons Dalek. The Emperor is revealed to be Davros – who uses the Hand of Omega despite the Doctor's warnings. But the Doctor has tricked Davros, and the device destroys first Skaro, and then the Imperial Dalek mothership over Earth.

## DALEK DATA

The Imperial Daleks are an ivory colour with gold 'trim'. Their slats are moulded into the bodywork rather than attached, and the eye and sucker arm are of a different design. The Dalek creatures are different too – a claw emerges to attack the Doctor, and they have functional appendages and mechanical prostheses grafted on. They are led by the Emperor – a Dalek with a spherical head, which is revealed to contain Davros.

The Rebel Dalek faction is led by the black-and-silver Dalek Supreme. These Daleks are of a gunmetal-grey design.

## SPECIAL WEAPONS DALEK

The heavily battle-marked Special Weapons Dalek has no external eyestalk or sucker arm, just a single enlarged gun that can be tilted and rotated with the top half of its casing. The Imperial Daleks are losing to the Rebel faction until the Special Weapons Dalek is deployed from the Dalek shuttle that lands in the school playground.

The Rebel Daleks' projected-energy weapons leave no tissue damage but scramble the victim's insides, but they seem not to affect the Special Weapons Dalek – which can destroy several Rebels with a single blast of its own gun.

## DALEK BATTLE COMPUTER

The Dalek battle computer is a Dalek base with headset attached – a bio-mechanoid control device for a young human.

The Doctor explains that the Daleks' major drawback is their dependency on rationality and logic, and the solution is to get a human – preferably young and imaginative – plug them into the system and slave their ingenuity and creativity to the battle computer.

In this case, the human is a young schoolgirl. She recovers after the Dalek Supreme is destroyed.

# CREATING THE DALEKS

In 1963, *Doctor Who*'s story editor David Whitaker asked Terry Nation to write the second-ever *Doctor Who* story – the result was *The Daleks*, and the series would never be the same again.

The descriptions of the Daleks in Terry Nation's scripts gave little idea of the tremendous visual impact his monsters would achieve. The first appearance of a Dalek was at the end of the Episode 1 of *The Daleks*, where just the sucker arm is seen as it menaces Barbara:

```
SEEN ONLY BY THE AUDIENCE, A PANEL SLIDES OPEN AND
THERE EMERGES FROM IT A PAIR OF MECHANICAL ARMS.
BARBARA HEARS THE SOUND BEHIND HER AND TURNS IN
TIME TO SEE THE THING THAT IS ADVANCING ON HER.
ONLY ITS ARMS ARE SEEN BY THE AUDIENCE AS THEY
PIN BARBARA'S ARM TO HER SIDE AND SHE STARTS
TO SCREAM.
```

Later, in Episode 2, the Daleks were fully revealed:

```
STANDING IN A HALF CIRCLE IN FRONT OF THEM
ARE FOUR HIDEOUS MACHINE-LIKE CREATURES.
THEY ARE LEGLESS, MOVING ON A ROUND BASE.
THEY HAVE NO HUMAN FEATURES.
  A LENS ON A FLEXIBLE SHAFT ACTS AS AN EYE.
ARMS WITH MECHANICAL GRIPS FOR HANDS(WE
HAVE SEEN THESE ARMS BEFORE, MOVING UP BEHIND
BARBARA)
THE CREATURES HOLD STRANGE WEAPONS IN THEIR HANDS.
ONE OF THEM GLIDES FORWARD. IT SPEAKS WITH AN ECHOING METALLIC VOICE.
```

It was the job of BBC designer Raymond Cusick to bring these descriptions to life. Cusick based his design around the shape of a man sitting on a chair. To this basic shape he added the sucker arm and gun (originally at different levels) and an eye at the top of the creature. The job of building the four Dalek machines was subcontracted to a company called Shawcraft Models.

Despite slight modifications for later stories – most notably the addition of 'slats' over the middle-section bands round the Dalek – the basic design of the Dalek remained unchanged and is immediately recognised around the world.

# REINVENTING THE DALEKS

The task of re-imagining the Daleks for the 21st century was embraced by the series' design team, who welcomed the challenge. Led by production designer, Edward Thomas, the team set about reworking the look of the Daleks.

Right from the beginning, they were determined that the overall shape and instantly recognisable image of the Dalek should remain basically the same. This would be a revision and a refinement of the original, rather than a complete reinvention.

A measure both of the team's success and of the intense interest surrounding the revived series was that, within hours of its (supposedly secret) filming debut at the Millennium Stadium in Cardiff in 2004, the new Dalek had its own full-page spread in *The Sun*.

## BUILDING DALEKS

Two complete Daleks were actually built for the episode *Dalek* – one highly damaged Dalek, and one in pristine condition. Working from Matt Savage's original concept drawings and paintings, models and miniatures supervisor Mike Tucker and his team set about the task of recreating the iconic monster. Using elements from the original 1960s Daleks, they updated and improved the Dalek using state-of-the-art materials and technology.

The original Daleks were operated completely manually by the actors inside. But Mike Tucker and his team created a radio-controlled version of the head, complete with controllable eyestalk and lights. This allowed actor Barnaby Edwards to concentrate on the other aspects of Dalek movement, although a 'standard' head was also created as an emergency back-up.

As well as a change of colour scheme and extra detailing and design refinements, a 'dog-tag' symbol was added under the eye – in effect, a simple way for each Dalek to be identified.

 # DALEK

Written by
**Robert Shearman**
Featuring
**the Ninth Doctor
and Rose**
First broadcast
**30 April 2005
1 episode**

Answering a faint distress signal, the Doctor and Rose arrive at Henry Van Statten's private museum of alien artefacts, located deep beneath the deserts of Utah. Van Statten has one live specimen – a damaged and dying Dalek. Reactivated by a touch from Rose, the Dalek breaks free of its 'cage' and, in the absence of any other orders, sets out to exterminate all humans – starting with Van Statten's private army. Rose is trapped with the Dalek, while the Doctor struggles to find a weapon to use against it.

But the Dalek has been contaminated by the human DNA it absorbed from Rose, which is now affecting its reasoning and outlook. Rather than live with the shame of being 'impure', the Dalek destroys itself.

## VAN STATTEN

A ruthless businessman who secretly owns the internet, Henry Van Statten develops new technology from alien artefacts.

He has the largest private collection of alien objects in the world. This includes the milometer from the Roswell spaceship, a Slithen claw, an alien musical instrument, a variety of weaponry, a hairdryer, and the head of a Cyberman.

After the battle with the Dalek, Van Statten's new PA Diana Goddard orders his surviving security guards to wipe Van Statten's memory and abandon him. His bunker is sealed with concrete.

## ADAM

Adam is in charge of acquiring alien artefacts for Van Statten. He was recruited by Van Statten's head-hunters – who search the world for geniuses – and has no false modesty about his own abilities. With an eye on his own long-term survival, Adam has kept some uncatalogued weapons in his office in case he ever needs to escape from Van Statten.

After the destruction of the Dalek, Rose invites Adam to join them and travel in the TARDIS. But Adam quickly shows that he is not cut out to be a companion of the Doctor…

## POWER OF THE DALEK

Fifty years ago, the Dalek fell through the sky and landed on the Ascension Islands, where it burned in its crater for three days – constantly screaming, driven mad…

When Rose touches it, the Dalek is able to absorb her genetic material and extrapolate the biomass to re-energise and break free. It absorbs power – blacking out much of the USA – to regenerate itself, and downloads the entire internet. Bullets cannot penetrate the damaged Dalek's casing. When powered up, they are stopped by a force shield that surrounds the Dalek.

## SCARY STORIES

Award-winning theatre and television writer
Rob Shearman was given the enviable task of
bringing back the Daleks and reinventing them
for the 21st-century audience. He describes
what a daunting – and scary – task it was:
'When I was a kid, I was too scared to
watch *Doctor Who*. It was my sister's fault,
and the way she described the Daleks. They
sounded terrifying! For years I was afraid
even to put rubbish in the dustbins.

'Being asked to write for them was just as frightening. They're
truly iconic – the ultimate monster, vindictive and brutish and
spitting out laser bolts of hate. Their design is brilliant, losing
the human shape so they seem wholly alien. But their
characters are gleefully familiar – Daleks are everything
we want to be when we're children, if we didn't have
parents or teachers to get in our way!
'Bringing them back after over fifteen years off screen
was a collaborative effort, and everyone wanted to
emphasise that there's a real emotional creature inside that
pepperpot casing – far more frightening than a bland robot.
It was a great responsibility to take these monsters loved and
feared by my generation, and make them loved and feared
again. But it was tremendously satisfying.
'And, yes, I'm still scared of dustbins. My sister and the Daleks
– they've both got a lot to answer for.'

Black-domed Emperor's Personal Guard Dalek

The supreme leader of the Daleks – their Emperor – has taken several different forms in the past. After the Great Time War wiped out most of the Dalek race, the few survivors were ruled by an Emperor who, having led them from the wilderness and created new Dalek life, believes itself to be the god of all Daleks.

This enormous Dalek Emperor is wired into the Daleks' flagship. The surviving Daleks have waited, slowly infiltrating humanity and taking the refugees and dispossessed to create new Daleks, only one cell in a billion being 'pure' enough for them to use. Now, with an army of new Daleks, the Emperor is ready to purify the Earth – by fire.

## THE EMPEROR'S PERSONAL GUARD

Traditionally, the Dalek Emperor's personal guards are distinguished from other Daleks by their black dome sections. On the Dalek flagship they hover close to the Emperor, constantly observing and protecting their leader. These Daleks also have an additional, highly powerful weapon in place of the sucker arm that ordinary Daleks use.

On Skaro, before the Great Civil War, the Black Dalek Leaders formed the personal guard of the Dalek Emperor, which was built into the very fabric of the Dalek City. During the Civil War they fought to protect the Emperor from rogue Daleks that the Doctor had impregnated with the Human Factor and that questioned the authority of the Emperor. Despite the Emperor's attempts to prevent the battle spreading into the throne room, its personal guards were forced to retreat and the Emperor was severely damaged. The Doctor described the Civil War as 'The final end'.

The Dalek Supreme – one of the High Council of Daleks – has also been distinguished by its black livery. It was seen during the attempted Dalek invasion of Earth.

The Dalek Emperor creature itself is housed in a transparent life-support unit

Eyestalk uses enhanced Dalek visual technology

The enormous Dalek Emperor is plumbed into the very fabric of the Dalek flagship

Sense globes

Claw-like appendages for manipulation

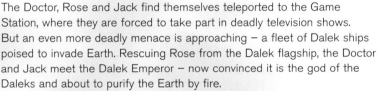

# BAD WOLF and THE PARTING OF THE WAYS

Written by
**Russell T Davies**
Featuring
**the Ninth Doctor,
Rose and Captain Jack**
First broadcast
**11–18 June 2005
2 episodes**

The Doctor, Rose and Jack find themselves teleported to the Game Station, where they are forced to take part in deadly television shows. But an even more deadly menace is approaching – a fleet of Dalek ships poised to invade Earth. Rescuing Rose from the Dalek flagship, the Doctor and Jack meet the Dalek Emperor – now convinced it is the god of the Daleks and about to purify the Earth by fire.

Captain Jack organises the defence of the station, while the Doctor returns Rose to Earth and works to create a Delta Wave that will destroy the Daleks. As the Daleks kill Jack and corner the Doctor, it is Rose who returns to save the day. But her solution will cost the Doctor his own life.

## THE GAME STATION

The Game Station is Satellite Five a century after the destruction of the Jagrafess (see page 172). Run by the Bad Wolf Corporation, it broadcasts game shows and reality TV to the population of Earth. The entire output goes through the brain of the Controller – a woman who was installed into the station's systems as a child. In fact, she is the conduit through which the Daleks are running the Game Station. She is able to bring the Doctor to the station and warn him about the Daleks. Realising her betrayal, the Daleks exterminate her.

## THE TIME WAR

Records of the Great Time War are scarce and unreliable, but after the Time Lords sought to eliminate the Daleks by sending the Doctor back in time to prevent their creation, the Daleks began to retaliate. As negotiations broke down, a full-scale war erupted within the Time Vortex and beyond that in the Ultimate Void. The Time Lords reached back into history for ever-more-terrible weapons, while the Daleks unleashed the Deathsmiths of Goth... For centuries the war raged, unseen by most of the universe. But the Higher Species watched and wept...

## THE BAD WOLF

During her time with the Ninth Doctor, Rose becomes aware of references to 'Bad Wolf', though she has no idea what they mean. Then she finds the Game Station is run by the Bad Wolf Corporation. Returned, unwillingly, to Earth, Rose realises the references are a message telling her she can save the Doctor and humanity. Spurred on by this, she opens the very heart of the TARDIS and becomes possessed by the power of the Vortex itself. She uses it to defeat the Daleks, and to send the Bad Wolf messages back into her past.

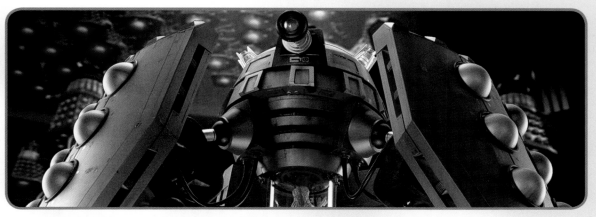

## EMPERORS OF THE DALEKS

The Dalek Emperor has taken several forms over the long history of the Daleks. According to some records, the first Dalek Emperor had a casing built from Flidor gold, quartz and the sap of the Arkellis flower that grew on Skaro before the Thousand Year War that led to the creation of the Daleks. It had an enlarged dome section.

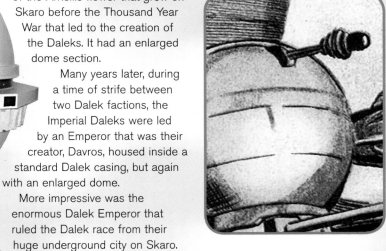

Many years later, during a time of strife between two Dalek factions, the Imperial Daleks were led by an Emperor that was their creator, Davros, housed inside a standard Dalek casing, but again with an enlarged dome.

More impressive was the enormous Dalek Emperor that ruled the Dalek race from their huge underground city on Skaro. Plumbed into the very structure of the Dalek City, the Emperor was badly damaged – possibly even destroyed – in the Great Civil War caused by the Doctor introducing the so-called Human Factor into the Dalek race. This caused infected Daleks to question the authority of the Emperor – and indeed the whole Dalek creed.

Order was eventually restored and the renegade Daleks destroyed. The Emperor led the Daleks into the Last Great Time War against the Time Lords that resulted in the apparent destruction of both races. The leader that survived and rebuilt the Dalek race, using genetic cellular material from kidnapped humans, saw itself as god of all Daleks.

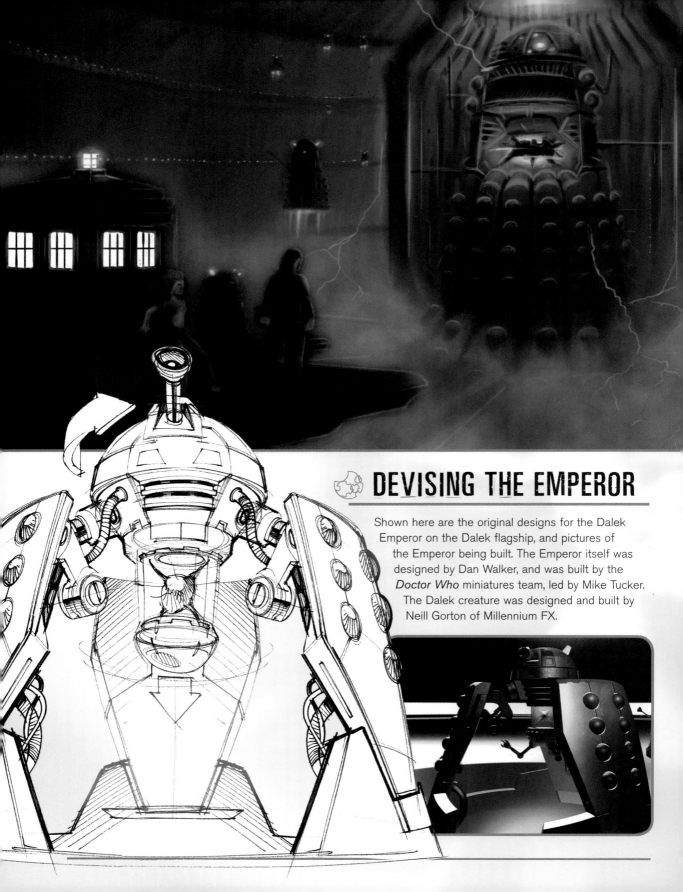

## DEVISING THE EMPEROR

Shown here are the original designs for the Dalek
Emperor on the Dalek flagship, and pictures of
the Emperor being built. The Emperor itself was
designed by Dan Walker, and was built by the
*Doctor Who* miniatures team, led by Mike Tucker.
The Dalek creature was designed and built by
Neill Gorton of Millennium FX.

# THE DALEKS

The Cult of Skaro was thought to be a myth – a legend, built up during the Great Time War between the Daleks and the Time Lords. It was rumoured that, at some point, the Dalek Emperor had established a secret order of Daleks, whose task was to think the unthinkable – to dare to *imagine*.

As the Doctor discovers, however, it was no myth. The Cult of Skaro is very real. More important even than the Emperor, the Cult of Skaro is made up of four Daleks who tried to think like the enemy, to get inside enemy minds and predict their strategies so as to give the Daleks an advantage in their wars. These Daleks have even given themselves names – as a part of becoming enough like the enemy to predict and counter their actions. They are called Sec, Thay, Jast and Caan.

Dalek
Thay

Dalek
Jast

Dalek
Caan

Dalek Sec
– leader of the
Cult of Skaro

# DOOMSDAY

Millions of Cybermen have materialised from an alternative Earth, and four Daleks emerge from their Void Ship. The Cybermen suggest an alliance, but the Daleks – the legendary Cult of Skaro – see them as pests and the two join battle. The Daleks win easily and open their Genesis Ark: hundreds of Daleks emerge in the skies over London, so the Doctor re-opens the Void. Contaminated with 'Void stuff', Daleks and Cybermen are sucked back into the empty space between universes.

But Rose, her mum and Mickey are trapped on the parallel Earth. To save both universes, the Doctor must close the holes into the Void. After a tearful farewell, he and Rose part, seemingly never to see each other again.

Written by
**Russell T Davies**
Featuring
**the Tenth Doctor, Rose and Mickey**
First broadcast
**8 July 2006**
**Second of 2 episodes (see page 71)**

### DALEKS VS CYBERMEN

In *Dalek* (see page 98), Van Statten has a Cyber head in his archives. When the Doctor was put on trial and exiled to Earth, he cited both the Daleks and Cybermen as menaces that had to be fought. In *The Five Doctors* (see page 60), a single Dalek was brought to the Death Zone on Gallifrey, along with many Cybermen.

But this is the first time that the Daleks and Cybermen have come into direct conflict. Even with just four Daleks taking on millions of Cybermen, the outcome is never in doubt. What the Cybermen view as a war, the Daleks see as 'pest control'.

### THE VOID

When the Daleks realised they couldn't defeat the Time Lords without being destroyed themselves, the Cult of Skaro devised a Void Ship to hide between the universes, waiting for the war to end.

The Void is nowhere, a place that doesn't exist. The TARDIS travelled through it when it took the Doctor, Rose and Mickey to an Earth where the Cybermen were being created. It fell through a crack that the Void Ship had left in the fabric of the universe. The Cybermen used similar cracks to come through to our own world.

### THE GENESIS ARK

During the Great Time War, the Time Lords took many Daleks prisoner and locked them in a huge prison. The Time Lords knew how to fit enormous spaces into tiny containers – just like the Doctor's TARDIS – so the prison was contained inside a large casket.

The Daleks captured the casket, and they hid it in the Void between universes, together with the Cult of Skaro. They called it the Genesis Ark because it was their future, their survival – a vast army of Daleks waiting to emerge once the war was over.

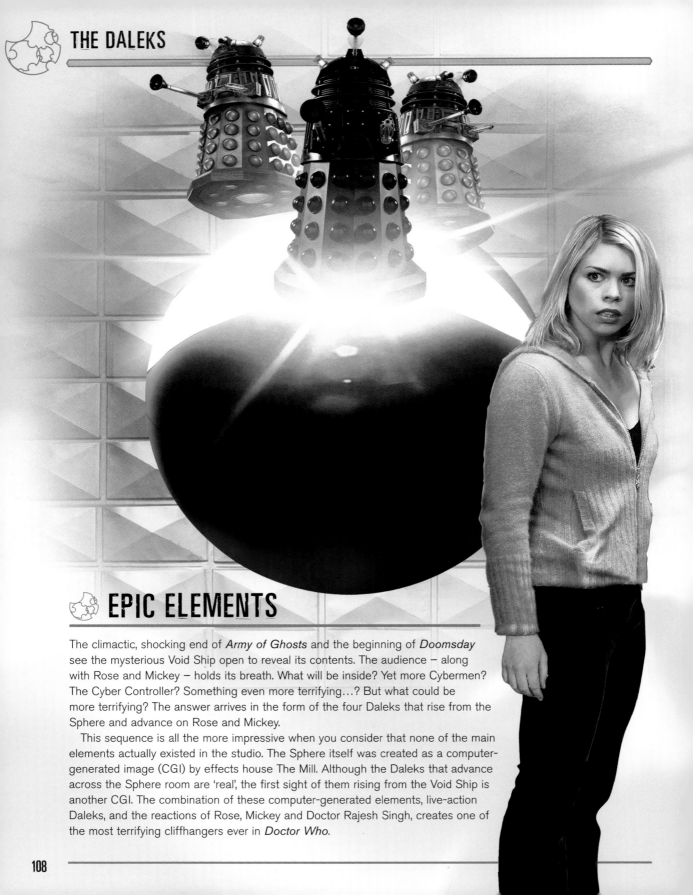

## EPIC ELEMENTS

The climactic, shocking end of *Army of Ghosts* and the beginning of *Doomsday*
see the mysterious Void Ship open to reveal its contents. The audience – along
with Rose and Mickey – holds its breath. What will be inside? Yet more Cybermen?
The Cyber Controller? Something even more terrifying…? But what could be
more terrifying? The answer arrives in the form of the four Daleks that rise from the
Sphere and advance on Rose and Mickey.

   This sequence is all the more impressive when you consider that none of the main
elements actually existed in the studio. The Sphere itself was created as a computer-
generated image (CGI) by effects house The Mill. Although the Daleks that advance
across the Sphere room are 'real', the first sight of them rising from the Void Ship is
another CGI. The combination of these computer-generated elements, live-action
Daleks, and the reactions of Rose, Mickey and Doctor Rajesh Singh, creates one of
the most terrifying cliffhangers ever in *Doctor Who*.

# THE FINAL END

More Dalek props were used for *Doomsday* than in any previous story. Even though *The Parting of the Ways* saw an army of thousands of Daleks, there were only three Dalek props used in that story. For *Doomsday*, four Daleks were used, with CGI again providing the thousands of Daleks seen swarming above London.

The original Dalek prop used in the episode *Dalek* was repainted black to become Dalek Sec. The design department had tried out different colour schemes on toy Daleks before deciding exactly how the black Dalek would look. The other Daleks in the Cult of Skaro – Thay, Jast and Caan – retained the bronze colour scheme of the previous stories.

Reproduced below are some of the storyboards used to plan the sequences showing the destruction of the Daleks as they are sucked back into the Void.

13.68.20   DALEKS PASS LEVERS AS THEY ARE SUCKED INTO VOID.

13.74.03

13.68.18   DALEKS GET SUCKED TO THE LEFT. PAN WITH THEM.

13.68.19   DALEKS GET SUCKED IN THROUGH WINDOW.

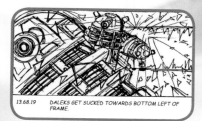

13.68.19   DALEKS GET SUCKED TOWARDS BOTTOM LEFT OF FRAME.

13.72.01   10 DALEKS HOVERING AND FIRING SUDDENLY

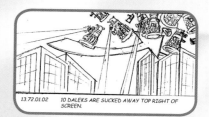

13.72.01.02   10 DALEKS ARE SUCKED AWAY TOP RIGHT OF SCREEN.

13.74.01.01   DALEK "EMERGENCY TEMPORAL SHIFT"

# THE DALEKS

Experimenting with the genetic structure of the human race, the Daleks created the Pig Men. They took ordinary human beings – such as the unfortunate Laszlo, a stagehand at the Laurenzi theatre – and turned them into creatures that were half-human, half-pig.

The Daleks also brainwashed the creatures they had created, so that the Pig Men became their unquestioning servants, ready to steal more humans for them: humans that were needed for another purpose – the Final Experiment.

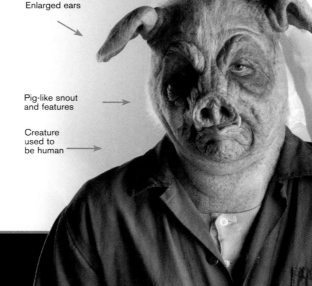

Enlarged ears

Pig-like snout and features

Creature used to be human

### DALEK-HUMANS

Unable to grow new Dalek embryos, the Cult of Skaro turn instead to the greatest resource that Earth has to offer them – its people.

In the secret caverns beneath Manhattan's new Empire State Building, the Daleks are storing over a thousand transgenically processed humans. Their minds have been wiped, and – held close to death – they have been conditioned to obey; to be like the Daleks. These humans are waiting to be reborn as new and deadly creatures. A massive blast of gamma radiation provided by a solar flare will splice human and Dalek genetic codes and waken the sleeping army – an army of Dalek-Humans ready to conquer the Earth.

Dalek and human fused together ←

Single blue eye ←

Features are reminiscent of original Dalek creature ←

Having tried – and failed – to create new Dalek embryos, the Cult of Skaro adopts another plan. As well as genetically adapting human beings to become Dalek-like, Dalek Sec is genetically bonded with a human being. The human chosen is Mr Diagoras, the man in charge of completing the Empire State Building. Diagoras has been working for the Daleks for a while, and they have noted his drive, and his determination to control New York.

Using a chromatin solution, Diagoras is pushed into the flesh of the Sec Dalek creature, and the two become one. To survive, the Dalek species must evolve and experience life outside their shells – the children of Skaro must walk again.

## DALEKENIUM CONDUCTOR

The Dalek plan to resurrect over a thousand processed people as Dalek-Humans depends on the channelling of a vast amount of power. To achieve this, the Daleks have created a conductor on the top of the new Empire State Building that will collect and provide gamma radiation from a massive solar flare. The conductor is made up of several panels taken from the casing of Dalek Thay.

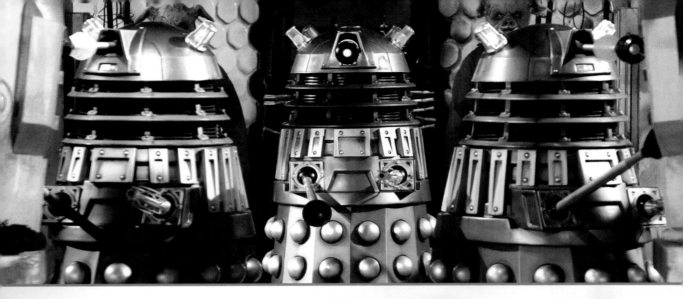

# DALEKS IN MANHATTAN and EVOLUTION OF THE DALEKS

Written by
**Helen Raynor**
Featuring
**the Tenth Doctor
and Martha**
First broadcast
**21–28 April 2007
2 episodes**

The Doctor and Martha arrive in 1930s New York and discover that the sinister Mr Diagoras is in league with the Daleks. The Cult of Skaro have escaped to New York and are using humans converted into pig-like creatures as slaves. Having failed to create an army of 'real' Daleks, they are planning to convert people into Dalek-Humans, and have a vast army hidden beneath the Empire State Building. When energy from a solar flare strikes a conductor installed in the building, the army will awaken.

But Dalek Sec genetically bonds with Diagoras and absorbs human DNA in an effort to evolve into a super-Dalek. Will Sec realise that the Dalek way is flawed? And can the Doctor stop the Daleks in time?

## HOOVERVILLE

The American boom of the 1920s came to an abrupt end with the Wall Street Crash in 1929: suddenly, shares were worthless. Millions of people lost their jobs. In New York many of those who were evicted from their homes ended up in Central Park, where a vast shantytown was set up. It was, rather sarcastically, named Hooverville, after US president Herbert Hoover. When the Doctor and Martha arrive they find Solomon keeping the people there in order, though Mr Diagoras is recruiting for Dalek slaves among the dispossessed.

## THE EMPIRE STATE BUILDING

Completed in 1931, New York's 102-floor Empire State Building was the highest building in the world until 1972. The distinctive mast where the Daleks place their Dalekenium conductor was originally designed as a mooring post for airships. But the architects were not to know that construction of the building would be taken over by the Cult of Skaro, working through the unprincipled Mr Diagoras.

The Daleks also constructed a secret base and laboratory beneath the structure where they stored their Dalek-Human army ready to be activated.

## THE FINAL EXPERIMENT

Believing themselves to be the last four Daleks in existence, the Cult of Skaro are determined to think unlike any other Daleks. But the audacity of Dalek Sec's plan to evolve the Dalek race by bonding human and Dalek flesh worries the other Daleks, and they warn Dalek Sec not to proceed with it. Ultimately, they are right: Sec is corrupted by his human side, and betrays them. But the Daleks are not defeated – not while one single Dalek survives. Dalek Caan escapes from New York, and his subsequent actions have implications for the entire universe…

# DALEK MILITARY COMPUTER

Installed in their transgenic laboratory, deep below the Empire State
Building, the Daleks' Military Computer is ready to coordinate their
war strategy as they unleash their army of converted Dalek-Humans.
The computer is operated by a Dalek that is plugged directly into the
systems and becomes one with the computer. Through the computer,
the Dalek can monitor the Dalek-Human army and issue orders
directly to it.

The system was originally designed for the leader of the Cult
of Skaro – Dalek Sec – to operate. But after Sec is genetically
bonded with Diagoras and begins to doubt underlying Dalek
philosophy, the other Daleks overrule his authority and Dalek Caan
assumes responsibility for all military strategy and operations.

When the other Daleks – Thay and Jast – are destroyed,
Caan is able to draw on enough power, possibly from the
Military Computer itself, to activate its emergency temporal
shift and escape from the Doctor and his allies.

## EPIC ELEMENTS

*Daleks in Manhattan* was written by one of *Doctor Who*'s script editors: Helen Raynor. Helen has written for both radio and for television, including an episode for each of the first two series of the *Doctor Who* adult spin-off series *Torchwood*.

Helen explained how she came up with the various elements of the story and brought them together into an epic struggle for survival:

'The Empire State Building was a gift, and it helped me settle on the 1930 date pretty early on. It's iconic, it was the tallest building in the world and there was enough mystery and controversy surrounding the "mooring mast" at the top to spark my curiosity. Being the highest building, the Empire State itself was in effect the tallest lightning conductor in Manhattan. Also, in 1931, the year it opened, Boris Karloff's creature in *Frankenstein* terrorised audiences by lurching into life after being animated by lightning… Irresistibly juicy ingredients. I always wanted the whole thing to feel like a family-show take on 1930s

horror films – everything from the shadowy sewers to the "mad scientist" transgenic lab could have come from a Universal Pictures Film. 'Russell T Davies had talked about using a theatre, and showgirls – which in itself is a bit *King Kong* – and the minute I thought of a theatre, I thought of *Phantom of the Opera* (Lon Chaney's Universal *Phantom* film was released only a few years earlier, in 1925). Which gave me poor faithful Laszlo – half-man, half-pig. He has Russell T Davies to thank for his survival – I originally killed him off, in a scene of indulgent, heartrending tragedy, which didn't ultimately sit well in our optimistic series. It would have been a right downer for kids at Saturday teatime. '1930 gave me a very specific time in the Depression as well. Just one year after the Wall Street Crash, while America was still in deep shock – before Roosevelt's "New Deal" was even a glimmer of light on the horizon. Ours is a family-show take on the Central Park "Hooverville" – the real thing would have been much more brutal. But it still has the feel of real desperation – the need to survive. A theme which fed right into the heart of the Dalek story....'

# BRINGING DALEKS TO LIFE

As well as New York in 1930, the Empire State Building, Pig Men and the theatre, there was something else that Helen Raynor had to include in her script. The executive producers of *Doctor Who*, Julie Gardner and Russell T Davies, shocked Helen by asking her to write a Dalek story:

'It was one of the hardest secrets I've ever had to keep (from March 2006 to Christmas, thank you very much).

'The story started like they all do: a big chat with Russell T Davies, where we talked about the Daleks and Nature, Destiny, Survival, Evolution, Imagination, Heresy – all key ingredients in the final mix. Daleks come with a big history, and an almost mythical status, which makes them amazing. So I went back to basics. What did I remember about them as a child? Why were they so scary? The grating voice, the remorseless onward glide – all the physical manifestations of

DOCTOR WHO III cryogu

| DOCTOR WHO III | | cryogu | |
|---|---|---|---|
| DRAWN BY | ian bunting | DATE 05/10/06 B> | PROP. |
| PRODUCER | | DIRECTOR | DOP: | CONSTRUCT. |
| PROD DESIGNER | | ASSOC DESIGNER | SFX | CGI: |
| SUP ART DIR/DES | | SUPV CLR ART DIR | | ELECTRICAL |
| S/B ART DIR | | SET DECORATION | COSTUME | GRAPHICS |

that will to power, that single-mindedness, that drive to exterminate everything else. Writing them really made me appreciate how perfect their design is. They look like what they are. And they certainly look at home in 1930 – military Art Deco, that's a Dalek for you.

'The "back to basics" approach took me back to all of the Dalek stories, but especially *Genesis of the Daleks*, which tells the story of their creation. It's a brilliant story about survival, and the need to become strong, removing human weaknesses; human emotion. What we were writing now was a companion piece to that, in a way – the need to survive, but now to contemplate reversing the process. Because the Dalek conundrum in these episodes is: If humans are weak, and we are strong – why are there millions of humans, and four of us?

'The origin of the Dalek race was genetic mutation, and it's the way to their future. So says Dalek Sec – a prophet and orator, and every inch a match for the Doctor. Together, they make a plan that could end the genocidal wars of the Daleks. If only…'

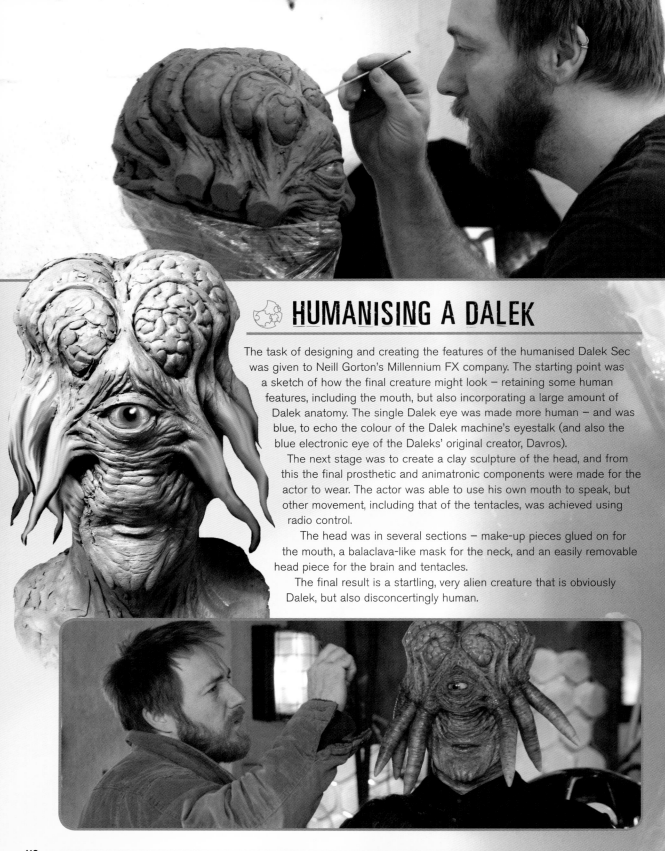

# HUMANISING A DALEK

The task of designing and creating the features of the humanised Dalek Sec was given to Neill Gorton's Millennium FX company. The starting point was a sketch of how the final creature might look – retaining some human features, including the mouth, but also incorporating a large amount of Dalek anatomy. The single Dalek eye was made more human – and was blue, to echo the colour of the Dalek machine's eyestalk (and also the blue electronic eye of the Daleks' original creator, Davros).

The next stage was to create a clay sculpture of the head, and from this the final prosthetic and animatronic components were made for the actor to wear. The actor was able to use his own mouth to speak, but other movement, including that of the tentacles, was achieved using radio control.

The head was in several sections – make-up pieces glued on for the mouth, a balaclava-like mask for the neck, and an easily removable head piece for the brain and tentacles.

The final result is a startling, very alien creature that is obviously Dalek, but also disconcertingly human.

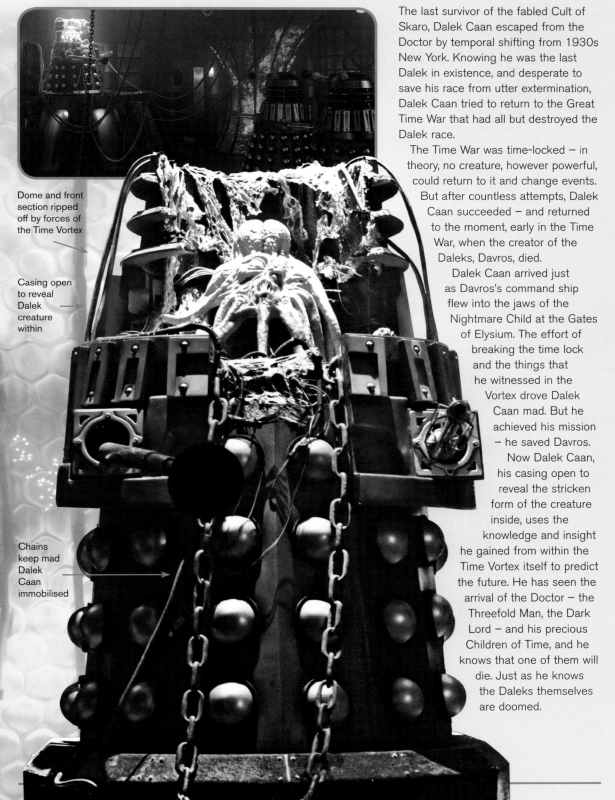

The last survivor of the fabled Cult of Skaro, Dalek Caan escaped from the Doctor by temporal shifting from 1930s New York. Knowing he was the last Dalek in existence, and desperate to save his race from utter extermination, Dalek Caan tried to return to the Great Time War that had all but destroyed the Dalek race.

The Time War was time-locked – in theory, no creature, however powerful, could return to it and change events. But after countless attempts, Dalek Caan succeeded – and returned to the moment, early in the Time War, when the creator of the Daleks, Davros, died.

Dalek Caan arrived just as Davros's command ship flew into the jaws of the Nightmare Child at the Gates of Elysium. The effort of breaking the time lock and the things that he witnessed in the Vortex drove Dalek Caan mad. But he achieved his mission – he saved Davros. Now Dalek Caan, his casing open to reveal the stricken form of the creature inside, uses the knowledge and insight he gained from within the Time Vortex itself to predict the future. He has seen the arrival of the Doctor – the Threefold Man, the Dark Lord – and his precious Children of Time, and he knows that one of them will die. Just as he knows the Daleks themselves are doomed.

Dome and front section ripped off by forces of the Time Vortex

Casing open to reveal Dalek creature within

Chains keep mad Dalek Caan immobilised

Electronic eye and other sensory organs

Long ago, on the war-ravaged planet of Skaro, a Kaled scientist called Davros found a way for his people to survive the thousand-year war against their enemies the Thals. Crippled and disfigured, Davros could live only with the help of a special wheelchair housing life support and sensory functions (see page 90).

Davros devised a travel machine and life-support system for the creature he knew his race would evolve into – mutated by the chemical, biological, and nuclear weapons of the war. He based it on is own life-support system – creating new life in his own image.

But Davros interfered with the mutation. He introduced genetic changes that he thought would equip the creatures for survival – he removed all emotions except for hatred of other life forms. He took away their capacity for love and pity and mercy. His creations – the Daleks – killed him for it.

But Davros did not die. Time and again, his Daleks returned for his help when they were in their direst need. Finally, Davros was destroyed during the Time War, when his command ship flew into the jaws of the Nightmare Child at the Gates of Elysium.

Or so it seemed.

But Davros was rescued by Dalek Caan, and immediately set about creating a new race of Daleks – using cells from his own emaciated body. He devised the Reality Bomb that would destroy all other life forms, and leave only the Daleks, reigning supreme…

Hand lost in previous encounter with the Doctor

Chair provides mobility and life support

Enhanced Dalekenium casing

Red and gold livery denotes rank

Additional luminosity discharger at rear of dome

The leader of the new race of Daleks created from Davros, the Supreme Dalek is a red Dalek with enhanced 'shoulder' sections and an additional luminosity discharger at the back of its dome. The Supreme Dalek commands the Dalek fleet from the control deck of the huge flagship known as the Crucible.

While the Supreme Dalek tolerates Davros, he does not defer to his creator – keeping Davros like a pet in the depths of the Crucible Vaults. With enhanced mental ability and defence systems, the Supreme Dalek is the only Dalek on board the Crucible to remain largely unaffected by Donna Noble's sabotage. But, weakened by its resistance to the effects, the Supreme Dalek is destroyed by Captain Jack Harkness.

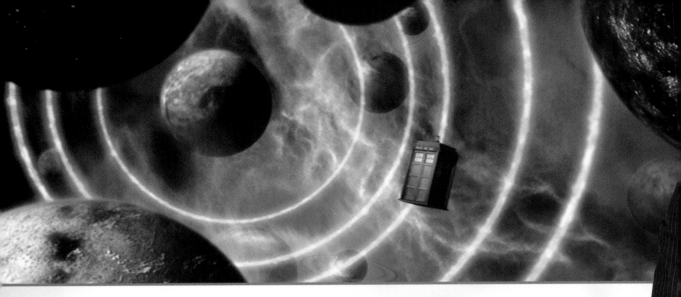

# THE STOLEN EARTH and JOURNEY'S END

Written by
**Russell T Davies**
Featuring
**the Tenth Doctor
and the Children of Time**
First broadcast
**28 June–5 July 2008
2 episodes**

The Earth is stolen – transported across space to the furthest reaches of the Medusa Cascade, along with 26 other planets. The Daleks have been recreated by Davros – saved from the Time War by Dalek Caan. They plan to use the powerful configuration of planets to power the ultimate weapon – the Reality Bomb.

The Doctor and his many friends are held captive by Davros. But a second Doctor has been created in a two-way biological metacrisis that also makes Donna part Time Lord, just as the new Doctor is part human. Donna defeats the Daleks, but at a terrible cost – the Doctor is forced to wipe Donna's memories of him so that she can survive…

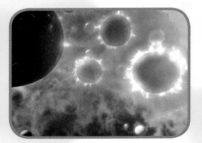

## THE OSTERHAGEN KEY

When the Daleks invade, Martha is sent on a mission by UNIT. She makes her way to a castle in Germany, which houses a secret underground control room. Here Martha can use the Osterhagen Key. Used in conjunction with two other keys in other secret stations, it will set off a chain of 25 nuclear warheads buried at strategic points beneath the Earth's crust.

This is the final option for the human race, when faced with such terrible suffering. The whole world will explode – stopping the Daleks from using their Reality Bomb, but at a terrible cost…

## THE CHILDREN OF TIME

Many of the Doctor's friends and companions are brought together by the events of the Dalek invasion of Earth. Davros refers to the Doctor's companions as 'the Children of Time' and gloats that the Doctor changes people for the worse – turning them into soldiers and killers.

But, while this strikes an unpleasant chord with the Doctor, he knows the truth. He inspires people and brings out the best in them. Now, more than ever before, the Doctor relies on his friends and companions not just to help him but to save the world. To save the universe.

## THE REALITY BOMB

Within their flagship Crucible, the Daleks have prepared their most powerful weapon ever: the Reality Bomb. This is powered by the exact configuration of the 27 stolen planets, linked together in a huge web generating tremendous energy.

This energy can then be directed across the entire universe and, through the rift at the Medusa Cascade, out into every alternative reality. It will cancel out the electrical field that binds all matter together. Structure falls apart – everything turns to dust, which becomes atoms, which become… nothing.

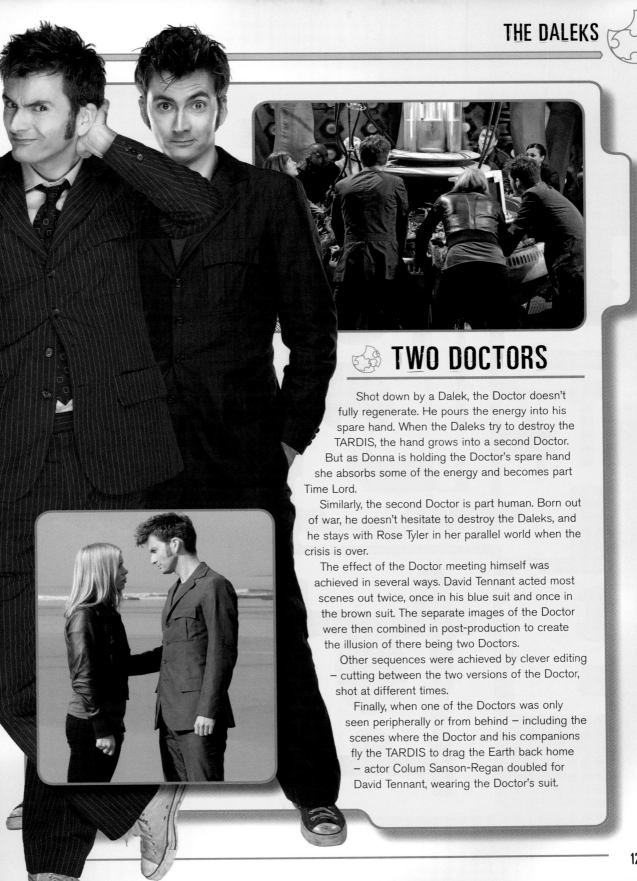

## TWO DOCTORS

Shot down by a Dalek, the Doctor doesn't fully regenerate. He pours the energy into his spare hand. When the Daleks try to destroy the TARDIS, the hand grows into a second Doctor. But as Donna is holding the Doctor's spare hand she absorbs some of the energy and becomes part Time Lord.

Similarly, the second Doctor is part human. Born out of war, he doesn't hesitate to destroy the Daleks, and he stays with Rose Tyler in her parallel world when the crisis is over.

The effect of the Doctor meeting himself was achieved in several ways. David Tennant acted most scenes out twice, once in his blue suit and once in the brown suit. The separate images of the Doctor were then combined in post-production to create the illusion of there being two Doctors.

Other sequences were achieved by clever editing – cutting between the two versions of the Doctor, shot at different times.

Finally, when one of the Doctors was only seen peripherally or from behind – including the scenes where the Doctor and his companions fly the TARDIS to drag the Earth back home – actor Colum Sanson-Regan doubled for David Tennant, wearing the Doctor's suit.

## SUPREME DESIGN

For *The Stolen Earth* and *Journey's End*, the Daleks would be led by the Supreme Dalek. An established part of 'Dalek lore', the Supreme Dalek – sometimes called the Dalek Supreme – had appeared in several previous stories, and been referred to in others. Usually depicted as a 'standard' Dalek with a black colour scheme, the Dalek Supreme that appeared in – and survived – *Planet of the Daleks* was a larger black and gold version.

In this story too, a new type of Dalek was designed. The script specified it should be 'deep metallic red' and the Art Department created several designs – shown above – before the final look of the Supreme Dalek was agreed. The final version had an extra dome light and bulky side panels that perhaps allowed it to plug into flagship systems.

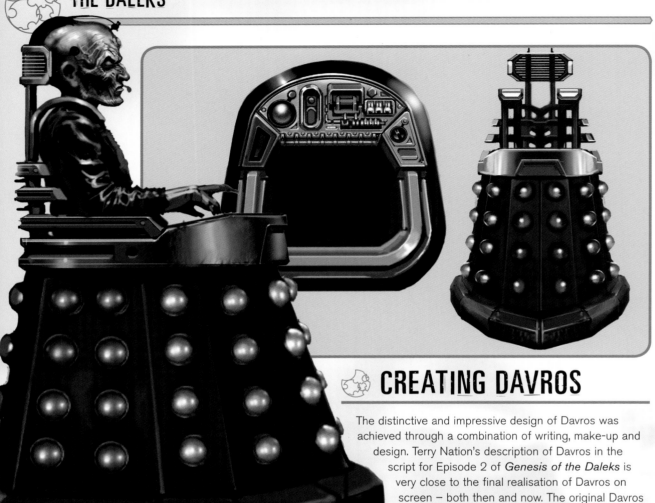

## CREATING DAVROS

The distinctive and impressive design of Davros was achieved through a combination of writing, make-up and design. Terry Nation's description of Davros in the script for Episode 2 of *Genesis of the Daleks* is very close to the final realisation of Davros on screen – both then and now. The original Davros chair was created by Visual Effects Designer Peter Day and his team, while the mask was sculpted by John Friedlander. The role was originally played by actor Michael Wisher – who rehearsed with a paper bag over his head to get used to the restricted vision the mask would provide.

For his reappearance in *The Stolen Earth*, Davros's chair was rebuilt to a similar but updated design by the *Doctor Who* Art Department. The mask was created by Neill Gorton of Millennium FX. The design was based on the original Davros mask, but updated to make the best use of new materials. The final mask actually consisted of several separate sections, and a glove was made for Davros's prosthetic metal hand. This time it was actor Julian Bleach who brought Davros to such eerie life.

### SCRIPT EXTRACT

The SHADOWED FIGURE gliding forward on its Dalek base... Into the LIGHT. REVEALING... DAVROS.
Half-man, half-Dalek, his face withered, an artificial blue eye blazing in his forehead. His torso swathed in a tunic like a black leather straitjacket. The metal hand always suspended above the Dalek-base's switches.

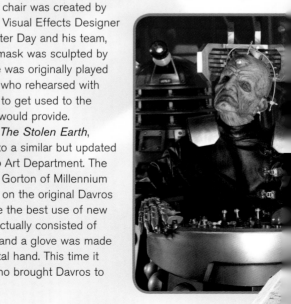

# DAVROS LIVES!

The origins of Davros are lost in mystery and myth. In his first televised appearance in *Genesis of the Daleks* by Terry Nation, Davros already looked very much as he appears in *The Stolen Earth* and *Journey's End*. In early drafts of these scripts, writer Russell T Davies included a flashback to Davros before he was disfigured:

### SCRIPT EXTRACT

EXT. SKARO - DAY

FX: CU DAVROS,
the MAN.
Gaunt,
strong, in
a dirty-
white
medic's
coat. FX
for the
BOILING RED
SKY behind
him...

FX:
REVERSE.
DAVROS a small figure
on a VAST PLAIN. DMP
of a RUINED WORLD.
A shattered domed
city; weird, warped
cliffs in the
distance. NUCLEAR
CLOUDS in the sky.

CUT TO:
INT. CRUCIBLE
VAULTS - NIGHT

DAVROS
And I swore, then.
To end it. I pledged
my life, to help
my people, to
ensure their
survival.

# THE DESTROYER

Curled horns ⟶

Demonic features ⟶

Clawed hands

Lord of Darkness and Eater of Worlds, the Destroyer is a demon-like creature summoned by the sorceress Morgaine when she thinks she is in danger of losing her battle against the Doctor and his friends. She calls the Destroyer into existence in our world.

Morgaine has the Destroyer chained with silver, which burns the creature and keeps it powerless. But Morgaine calls the Doctor's bluff and frees the Destroyer so it can claim the world to devour. As the Destroyer begins to consume the planet, the Doctor's old friend the Brigadier kills it with silver bullets.

Chainmail armour

Can be chained with silver ⟶

## MORGAINE

Morgaine is from a parallel world where a medieval culture has developed technology alongside magic, and the legends of King Arthur are actual fact. Although he's unsure how, the Doctor – in another incarnation – is Merlin, and Morgaine has sworn to destroy him.

Morgaine of the Faye, the Sunkiller – Dominator of the Thirteen Worlds and Battle Queen of the S'rax – also wants revenge on Arthur, unaware that he is already dead. She demands to face Arthur in single combat – but he was killed over a thousand years ago in the final battle. His 'body' is actually an empty suit of armour, with a note the future Doctor has written to himself in the helmet.

 # BATTLEFIELD

Knights in armour arrive from a parallel reality where technology and magic exist together and the legends of King Arthur are fact. Mordred battles against his enemy Ancelyn, and summons his mother, Morgaine, to help him. The Doctor and Ace find a UNIT convoy stranded beside Lake Vortigern. Under the lake is Arthur's spaceship, linked to the shore by an ancient tunnel that opens in response to the Doctor's voice. On board the ship is Arthur's body; he has been dead for centuries.

Morgaine tries to gain the upper hand by unleashing the powerful Destroyer to devour the world. But Brigadier Lethbridge-Stewart kills the creature with silver bullets, and Morgaine surrenders to the UNIT forces.

Written by
**Ben Aaronovitch**
Featuring
**the Seventh Doctor,
Ace and UNIT**
First broadcast
**9–27 September 1989
4 episodes**

## UNIT

A secret international organisation which the Doctor worked for in his third incarnation, UNIT is responsible for investigating unusual phenomena and alien threats to Earth.

UNIT's headquarters is in Geneva, with each member country providing military and technical personnel and local military facilities.

The UK section of UNIT is now commanded by Brigadier Winifred Bambera, following the retirement of UNIT's first UK commanding officer, Brigadier Lethbridge-Stewart.

## BRIGADIER LETHBRIDGE-STEWART

Brigadier Alistair Lethbridge-Stewart was a colonel in the British Army when he first met the Second Doctor. Having fought against deadly Yeti in the London Underground, Lethbridge-Stewart was promoted to Brigadier and put in command of UNIT's UK section.

The Second Doctor worked with him again to defeat the Cybermen. Throughout his third incarnation, the Doctor assisted the Brigadier, battling against Autons, Axons, misguided scientists, Daleks, and the Master. Now the Brigadier has retired and lives with his wife Doris.

## BESSIE

One of the conditions on which the Doctor originally agreed to work for UNIT was that he should have a car. He chose a yellow vintage car, which he called Bessie and modified extensively. Bessie has an anti-theft device that 'glues' the potential thief to the car, inertia-absorbing brakes, a 'Super-Drive' option for high-speed travel, and can even be operated by remote control.

Bessie's number plate was WHO1 throughout the Doctor's UNIT years, but for her reappearance in *Battlefield* this has been changed to WHO7.

# THE EMPTY CHILD

Gas mask appears fused to the face – and is actually flesh and bone

Massive head trauma on left side

Partial collapse of the chest cavity

Distinctive scar on back of hand

In the war-torn Britain of 1941, a young girl, Nancy, is living on London's blitzed streets. To survive, she and other street children steal food from the houses of people sheltering from German air raids. The children regard Nancy as their leader. But they are haunted by another child – a small boy wearing a gas mask, constantly searching for his mother.

The child can project his voice – incessantly asking 'Are you my mummy?' – through any communications equipment: the (unconnected) TARDIS telephone, a radio, even a music box and a typewriter. The 'empty' child is actually Nancy's 'brother' Jamie. He was killed in an air raid, and has been brought to life by alien technology.

## GAS-MASK PEOPLE

In the nearby Albion Hospital, patients and staff have been 'infected' by the boy. Their faces turned into gas masks, they too are searching for their mummy… In fact, the infection is caused by nanogenes that have escaped from a crashed Chula medical ship. Taking the dead Jamie's body as a template, the nanogenes 'repair' any humans they come into contact with – transforming their faces into gas masks, and recreating exactly the same injuries.

# THE EMPTY CHILD and THE DOCTOR DANCES

Looking for a crashed spaceship in London, the Doctor and Rose arrive during the Blitz of 1941 and discover that people have been infected by a strange, 'empty' child. The crashed ship was a Chula medical ship, and the interior was filled with nanogenes, which were released in the crash. These microscopic devices are programmed to repair Chula warriors on the battlefield. Now the nanogenes are set to remodel the entire human race on a terrified child augmented with fearsome military powers.

With the help of Captain Jack Harkness, and armed only with a sonic screwdriver and a banana, the Doctor and Rose reunite Jamie with his mother, and the nanogenes recognise – and reverse – the damage.

Written by
**Steven Moffatt**
Featuring
**the Ninth Doctor,
Rose and Captain Jack**
First broadcast
**21–28 May 2005
2 episodes**

## NANOGENES

The nanogenes do not understand the human physiology. They use the first human they find – Jamie – as a template and 'repair' all the others they come into contact with through him.

First the doctors and nurses who treat the child are affected, then the patients those doctors and nurses treat, and so on until the infection seems to become airborne. Infected people have no life signs – but they do not die. They have also been augmented and are ready to defend the crashed ship, and the Empty Child, with tremendous alien power at their disposal.

## THE CHULA SHIP

The Chula Ship – a large mauve cylinder – fell on Limehouse Green Station and is now cordoned off and under guard.

Captain Jack claims it is the last surviving fully equipped Chula warship. He is in fact lying, and is planning to sell the ship to the Time Agency – it is actually an ambulance, which he steered close to the TARDIS as bait for the Doctor and Rose (whom he believes to be Time Agents). Jack has parked the ship where he knows a German bomb will destroy it – after he gets his money, but before the Agents realise he has lied.

## NANCY AND THE CHILDREN

Nancy looks after the children who live rough on the streets of London during the Blitz. She organises the theft of food from houses during air raids. She enjoys mothering the children, making sure they behave in each house like guests rather than thieves.

The Doctor realises that Nancy has lost someone close to her – Jamie – and is looking after the children as a way of making up for it. He also works out that she is not Jamie's sister. She is actually the boy's mother – the mummy the Empty Child is desperately trying to find.

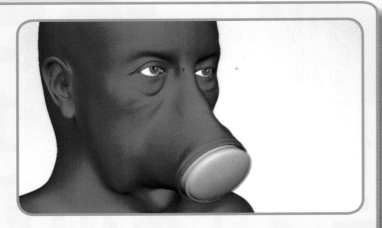

## BEHIND THE MASKS

While they looked completely authentic, the gas masks used in making *The Empty Child* and *The Doctor Dances* were actually created specially for the episodes by Millennium FX. The eye pieces were indeed taken from real gas masks – but modern, Russian ones. The designers sculpted the rest of the mask in clay and then took a mould of this model, from which the actual masks were made. Next they fitted the eyepieces and backed them with dark material to obscure the actors' eyes. The protruding filter was also specially moulded, with a section of it actually made from a baked bean tin!

The sequence in which Doctor Constantine turns into one of the gas-mask people was created by The Mill using computer-generated images (CGI). It was one of the most unsettling effects produced for the series. In fact, the story was packed with memorable images, with one sequence winning a viewers' award.

## RECREATING THE BLITZ

One of the greatest challenges in making *The Empty Child* and *The Doctor Dances* was to recreate the London of 1941 – and, in particular, a German air raid. But not only did the production team, led by director James Hawes, need to create that air raid, they also had to put Rose right in the middle of it.

This was achieved by combining live-action footage of Billie Piper playing Rose with CGI of the attacking planes and the London landscape, and a miniature barrage balloon created and filmed by the model unit.

# THE FACE OF BOE

Face of Boe is
housed within a
glass-fronted tank

Life support is
maintained within the
sealed environment

From the Silver Devastation,
the Face of Boe is incredibly
old, his origins shrouded
in mystery. He is held in a
fluid-filled life-support tank,
powered by antiquated,
steam-driven technology.

In *New Earth*, the Face of
Boe summons the Doctor.
But the important message
he has to impart waits until
they meet again in *Gridlock*,
when the Face of Boe finally
dies. The message is: 'You
Are Not Alone.'

The Doctor's friend and
companion Captain Jack
Harkness later tells the
Doctor that he was known
as the 'face of Boe'. Jack
is fated to live for ever, and
helps the Doctor defeat
the Master. Could he really
become the Face of Boe –
warning the Doctor of events
he has already witnessed
himself?

Motive power is
provided by steam-
enhanced systems

The Face of Boe
is incredibly old

## LEGENDS OF THE UNIVERSE

By J B Dane – an extract from the Stellar Edition, translated from the original hieromanx by Russell T Davies

It is said that the Face of Boe has lived for ever. Certainly, there is evidence that he was present when the stars of Andromeda were still nothing but dust. And his presence, billions of years later, at the End of the Earth, is on public record.

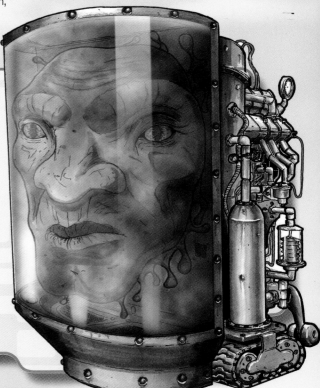

No one knows if the Face of Boe can die; perhaps not even the Face himself. His longevity is a mystery; it is not due to the gases of his tank, nor the coils of his DNA. It is as if he lives by will alone. Or by mistake. On the integrated planets of Cep Cassalon, the Face is known as 'the Creature that God Forgot'.

He has borne children; he was particularly fertile during the Fourth Great and Bountiful Human Empire, carrying three sons and three daughters. But all six Boemina lived a natural lifespan of forty years and no more. The Face of Boe watched his children die, and stayed watching while the world forgot they had even existed.

Legend has it that if the Face of Boe should die one day, then the sky will crack asunder. And it is said that he holds one, final secret; that he will speak this secret, with his final breath, to one person and one person alone. A homeless, wandering traveller…

### BOE DESIGN

The Face of Boe was originally just a minor character in *The End of the World*. For his return in *New Earth*, Neill Gorton and the Millennium FX team rebuilt the Face of Boe. Although he communicates telepathically, the prop's mouth could be moved. So for his final appearance in *Gridlock*, with great care, the Face of Boe was able to 'say' the final devastating message he gives to the Doctor – 'You are not alone.'

This completed the prophecy that the Face of Boe's final words would be a secret told to a homeless wandering traveller. It was only after *Gidlock* had been completed that writer Russell T Davies was reminded that his other prediction – as printed above – was that when Boe died the sky would crack asunder. Which is what happens for the trapped motorists when the Doctor and the Face of Boe open the roof of the motorway.

Son of Mine has stolen the body of schoolboy Jeremy Baines

Mother of Mine has stolen the body of school maid Jenny

Father of Mine has stolen the body of farmer Clark

The Family of Blood follow the Doctor to Earth in 1913. A short-lived species, they want to absorb the Doctor's Time Lord essence so that they can live for ever. They hunt by a strong sense of smell, and keep in contact with each other telepathically.

Having tracked the Doctor to Earth, they land their spaceship near the village of Farringham and steal bodies from local people. They must hunt for the Doctor, as they have no idea what he looks like. Their spaceship is invisible so that it will not attract attention. They use molecular fringe animation to create an army of deadly scarecrows that they use to attack the school where they believe the Doctor is hiding.

Daughter of Mine has stolen the body of Lucy Cartwright ⟶

## FAMILY FATE

As the Family discover, the Doctor is hiding from them not because he is scared, but to protect them. The Doctor knows that, if he is found by the Family of Blood, he will have to take drastic action – and this is what ultimately happens.

The Doctor traps them all for ever. Father of Mine is imprisoned underground, bound with unbreakable dwarf-star chains. Mother of Mine is thrown into the event horizon of a collapsing black hole. Son of Mine is trapped in the form of a scarecrow, and Daughter of Mine is hidden inside every mirror for all eternity…

Scarecrows brought to life by molecular fringe animation

Clothes made from sacking

Bodies made of straw

Brought to eerie life by molecular fringe animation, an army of scarecrows is used by the Family of Blood as its troops in the battle to find and capture the Doctor. They abduct humans so that the Family can steal their bodies to use as disguises.

The scarecrows are also used to attack Farringham School when the Family of Blood trace the Doctor there – though the Doctor has taken on a disguise of his own as history teacher John Smith.

When the Family is defeated by the recovered Doctor, the scarecrows cease to have any life of their own.

# HUMAN NATURE and THE FAMILY OF BLOOD

Written by
**Paul Cornell**
Featuring
**the Tenth Doctor
and Martha**
First broadcast
**26 May–2 June 2007
2 episodes**

The Family of Blood come to Earth in 1913, hunting for the Doctor. They want the Doctor's Time Lord essence and to live for ever. But the Doctor has gone into hiding. He has used a Chameleon arch to alter his physical form and his own memories so that he actually becomes John Smith – a history teacher at Farringham School in Herefordshire. Martha, her own memories intact, is also working at the school, as a maid. The Doctor intends to stay in hiding until the Family of Blood dies, rather than have to deal with them.

The Family finds the Doctor and creates an army of scarecrows to serve as their troops in the battle against the Doctor and his colleagues and pupils at Farringham School.

## JOHN SMITH

Realising he is being chased by the Family of Blood, the Doctor uses a Chameleon arch in the TARDIS to 'hide' his real personality inside a pocket watch. He becomes John Smith, a schoolteacher, and hides on Earth in 1913.

Smith believes himself human, though he keeps a diary of his strange dreams of a time and space traveller – 'A Journal of Impossible Things'. He falls in love with the school matron, Joan Redfern. John Smith gives up his love and his new life to become the Doctor again and defeat the Family of Blood.

## JOAN REDFERN

Joan is the Matron at Farringham School for Boys. To Martha's horror, Joan and John fall in love. But when the Family find 'Smith', Martha explains that he must become the Doctor again. At first, neither Joan nor John believes that the Doctor exists. But, with the Family of Blood on the rampage, the couple are forced to accept the truth of Martha's story. Though they both desperately want the Doctor to stay as John Smith – and live the long, fulfilling lives they would have together – Smith sacrifices himself to defeat the Family of Blood by once more becoming the Doctor.

## TIM LATIMER

A pupil at Farringham School, Tim is mildly psychic and realises that John Smith's fobwatch is vitally important. He takes the watch and hides it from the Family of Blood. Later he returns the watch to John Smith so he can again become the Doctor.

While he has the watch, Tim finds he can see visions of events that are yet to happen. One vision the watch helps him 'see' enables Tim to avoid dying in the Great War. His last sight of the Doctor – and Martha – is at a Remembrance Day service. Tim is an old man, but the Doctor and Martha have not changed at all…

## BRINGING THE FAMILY TO LIFE

Unusually for a *Doctor Who* television story, *Human Nature* started life not as a script but as a novel. After *Doctor Who* finished its original run on BBC Television in 1989, Virgin Publishing – which had taken over the Target books imprint of *Doctor Who* television novelisations – began publishing 'New Adventures' for the Seventh Doctor from 1991 to 1997. One of these was Paul Cornell's *Human Nature*, published in 1995.

Paul Cornell had written several previous *Doctor Who* novels for Virgin, and for *Human Nature* he devised a story about the Doctor making himself human and teaching at an English public school in the spring of 1914.

While the general themes and premise of the story – the Doctor becoming human and falling in love – remained the same when Paul Cornell adapted his book for the small screen, there were notable changes. In the book, the alien family – the Aubertides – hunt the Doctor after he has become human – he isn't actually hiding from them.

Martha took the place of the Doctor's companion in the book – Bernice Summerfield – and there were numerous other changes. Most notable was that in the book, the Doctor's 'essence' was contained in a biodata module disguised as a cricket ball, whereas for the television version this was changed to a pocket watch – foreshadowing Professor's Yana's fobwatch in the later episode *Utopia* (see page 205).

Russell T Davies suggested adding the scarecrows, and Paul Cornell soon realised that animated scarecrows would provide a spooky, Gothic and quintessentially English menace to enhance the original story.

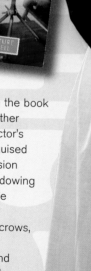

Dead body acts as host to the Gelth

Deep-rooted emotions and thoughts may still surface

Gelth appears as ectoplasmic mist from mouth

Gelth 'spirit' visible in the gas

The Gelth are ectoplasmic, ethereal, wraithlike creatures, which possess the dead at the Cardiff undertakers' Sneed and Company, in the late 19th century. They are trans-dimensional aliens that can travel through the junction point between two worlds, using beings with psychic ability as a bridge between dimensions.

Essentially gaseous creatures, in this world the Gelth 'live' in the gas pipes – the environment most suited to them. They claim there are very few Gelth left; they are the last of their kind and are facing extinction. But in fact they plan to invade the planet in their billions, killing humans and then possessing the bodies of the dead.

 # THE UNQUIET DEAD

The Doctor and Rose arrive in Cardiff on Christmas Eve in 1869. The Doctor meets Charles Dickens, while Rose finds herself at Gabriel Sneed's funeral parlour, where the dead are getting far too lively.

Enlisting the help of Dickens, Sneed and Gwyneth, the Doctor and Rose discover that the dead are being possessed by an alien race, the Gelth. Gwyneth is psychic and is able to contact them through a séance. They claim they are looking for new bodies so their race can survive.

Gwyneth creates a gateway for the Gelth to enter the real world. But they reveal that their true intentions are to kill everyone and live in their bodies. Gwyneth sacrifices herself to close the gateway and leave the Gelth stranded.

Written by
**Mark Gatiss**
Featuring
**the Ninth Doctor and Rose**
First broadcast
**9 April 2005
1 episode**

### GWYNETH

Sneed's servant girl, Gwyneth, came to work for him after her parents died of influenza when she was 12 years old. She is gifted with second sight and is able to track down Mrs Peace when the Gelth possess the old woman's dead body.

Gwyneth considers the Gelth to be angels sent by her dead mother. But after they arrive and reveal their true nature, the Doctor is able to convince her of the Gelth's intentions. Although her body is already dead, enough of Gwyneth lives on to destroy the Gelth by igniting the gas in Sneed's morgue.

### CHARLES DICKENS

Charles Dickens is in the last year of his life when he meets the Doctor and Rose. He is a tired, sceptical old man and is at first wary of the Doctor, accusing him of staging a phantasmagoric intrusion at the theatre. But the Doctor soon wins Dickens over by telling him he is the writer's number one fan.

At first Dickens does not believe in the existence of the Gelth, but their manifestation during Gwyneth's séance soon convinces him. He is shocked and disappointed to think that all his life he has misunderstood the true nature of the world. But by the end of the story, he is ready to open his mind to new ideas and to broaden his outlook.

## WHERE THE DICKENS?!

To create Victorian Cardiff, the *Doctor Who* team actually went to Swansea, which offered a more authentic-looking Victorian setting. The transformation of present-day Swansea into Cardiff on Christmas Eve, 1869 was a huge undertaking. Cars had to be excluded from the area, street signs replaced, extras dressed in appropriate clothing and made up with Victorian hairstyles, and snow had to be created. This attention to the smallest detail helped create a totally convincing Victorian winter scene.

# 🌀 BRINGING BACK THE DEAD

Many of the bodies brought to Sneed's funeral parlour just won't stay dead – in fact they're up and about, and off to the theatre. Sneed claims that one deceased sexton almost walked in on his own memorial service, and the late Mrs Peace kills her grandson, Redpath, and goes on to attend Charles Dickens' reading, as she had planned before her death.

In truth, the bodies are possessed by the Gelth, which emerge from the gas pipes as screeching blue ectoplasm, and enter the corpses, bringing them back to unnatural life.

But the 'union' of Gelth and body is weak and after a short while the zombie collapses, once more a lifeless corpse, as the Gelth leaves it.

While the walking dead at Sneed and Company were actors made up to look like cadavers, the Gelth themselves were computer-generated images (CGI), created using the face of actress Zoe Thorne as a starting point for the design of the creatures.

# GIANT MAGGOTS

The Giant Maggots are created when Global Chemicals dispose of waste from a revolutionary oil-refining process by pumping it down a disused coal mine. The green chemical slime causes maggots in the mine to mutate and grow to an enormous size. And not only is the glowing, green waste deadly to anyone who touches it – so are the maggots.

The Doctor and his friends from UNIT try to destroy the creatures with armour-piercing bullets, flame-throwers and fire bombs before they discover the real solution – the maggots can be poisoned with a type of fungus.

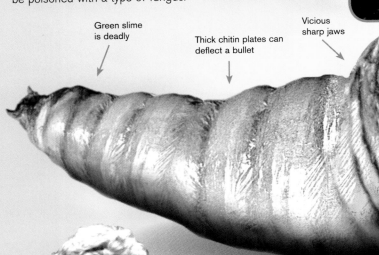

Green slime is deadly

Thick chitin plates can deflect a bullet

Vicious sharp jaws

## GLOBAL CHEMICALS AND BOSS

Global Chemicals is run by Jocelyn Stevens, and its mission is to control the world through technological advancement. The company is actually controlled by a giant super-computer – BOSS – which is linked directly to Stevens' brain. It plans to take over humanity to ensure huge profits for Global Chemicals, but the Doctor manages to convince Stevens that BOSS must be destroyed.

 # THE GREEN DEATH

A mysterious death at a disused coal mine leads to a UNIT investigation. Teaming up with a local group of ecologists, the Doctor discovers that Global Chemicals has been dumping deadly chemical waste down the mine, and the waste has caused maggots to mutate and grow in size.

While the Brigadier and his men try to contain the maggots, the Doctor confronts the real head of Global Chemicals – a megalomaniac computer called BOSS that has the ability to take over people's minds and is planning world domination.

With BOSS ready to act, the race is on to stop the maggots before they metamorphose into something even more deadly.

Written by
**Robert Sloman**
Featuring
**the Third Doctor,
Jo and UNIT**
First broadcast
**19 May–23 June 1973
6 episodes**

### PROFESSOR CLIFF JONES

Nobel prizewinner Professor Cliff Jones is in charge of an ecological group based in the Welsh village of Llanfairfach. He is a champion of the use of solar power, the tides, wind and other renewable energy sources, rather than using up the Earth's resources.

A new edible fungus his group is developing turns out to be deadly to the giant maggots and kills them. Cliff Jones asks the Doctor's assistant, Jo, if she will go with him on an expedition up the Amazon – as his wife. The Doctor's sadness is apparent when Jo agrees.

### METEBELIS THREE

For a long time, the Doctor has wanted to visit Metebelis Three, a famous blue planet in the Acteon Galaxy. But when he gets there, it is not what he's been expecting: as soon as he leaves the TARDIS, the Doctor is attacked by flying monsters.

He brings back one of the planet's blue crystals, though, and uses its mind-opening properties to break the control of BOSS. He gives the crystal to Jo as a wedding present, little knowing that it is the last great perfect crystal of power and that the giant spiders of Metebelis Three will soon want it back.

### GIANT FLY

As Professor Jones and his colleagues prepare to poison the giant maggots with their fungus, UNIT's Sergeant Benton finds a maggot that has entered a pupa stage. The maggots are about to change into something else.

Luckily only one of the maggots gets a chance to undergo this change before they are destroyed. It becomes a giant fly, attacking the Doctor and Benton from the air and squirting poisonous green fluid at them. The Doctor manages to swat it with his cape, and the beautiful but deadly creature is killed.

Head houses positronic brain imbued with a 'prime directive'

Massive and powerful

The last project Professor JP Kettlewell worked on at ThinkTank was a robot designed to replace human beings in a variety of difficult and dangerous tasks. Officially, the project was abandoned. But in fact, Kettlewell built his robot – codenamed K-1.

Although Robot K-1's Prime Directive is that it must serve humanity and never harm it, Kettlewell has helped ThinkTank Director Miss Winters and her colleague Arnold Jellicoe bypass this so they can use the Robot for their own purposes.

But the Robot reacts against the programming. It forms a sort of friendship with Sarah Jane – the only human ever to show it compassion and sympathy. When it sets out to destroy the world, she is the only person it is willing to spare…

### LIVING METAL – LIVING ROBOT?

Professor Kettlewell made his Robot from a 'living' metal. Attacked by UNIT, the Robot uses the energy from the Disintegrator Gun to grow to giant size.

But as well as its metal body, the Robot may also be able to develop its brain – to become more than merely an unfeeling automaton. When it accidentally kills Kettlewell, its creator, the Robot is driven mad. The Doctor describes the effect as 'suppressed Oedipus Complex'. The Robot determines to see that its creator's plan is carried out. Ultimately, the Robot's status as a 'living' thing leads to its destruction. The Doctor uses Kettlewell's research to create a 'virus' that corrodes the Robot's living metal.

Clamp-like 'hands'

Robot K-1 is made of 'living' metal

 # ROBOT

The Brigadier investigates a series of mysterious thefts of scientific components, which the Doctor realises can be used to build a Disintegrator Gun. A massive robot uses the gun to steal nuclear destructor codes.

Miss Winters, Director of ThinkTank, is using the Robot to get the codes so she and her colleagues can blackmail world governments. They seal themselves inside a nuclear bunker and prepare to launch the missiles.

With the Doctor's help, UNIT breaks into the bunker. But when the Brigadier uses the Disintegrator Gun to destroy the Robot, it grows to gigantic size and goes on the rampage. The Doctor is finally able to destroy the Robot using a metal virus.

Written by
**Terrance Dicks**
Featuring
**the Fourth Doctor,
Sarah Jane, Harry
and UNIT**
First broadcast
**28 December 1974
–18 January 1975
4 episodes**

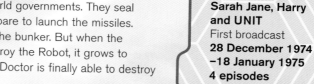

### THINKTANK

The National Institute for Advanced Scientific Research is colloquially known as ThinkTank. The Brigadier describes it as 'the frontiers of science research place'. As soon as ThinkTank work reaches the practical stage, it is handed over to someone with more resources and a bigger budget – usually the government.

The research for the Disintegrator Gun was pioneered at ThinkTank. The Director, Hilda Winters, is also in charge of the Scientific Reform Society. She sees the Disintegrator Gun as ideal for stealing the nuclear destructor codes.

### THE SRS PLAN

The superpowers, Russia, America and China, have handed details of their hidden atomic missile sites together with full operation instructions to Britain – apparently the only country that can be trusted with them. In the event of trouble, Britain would publish everyone's secrets and defuse the situation.

The Scientific Reform Society use the Robot (the SRS logo is based on the robot's head) to steal nuclear destructor codes from a cabinet minister. The SRS threaten to launch the world's atomic missiles if their demands are not met.

### DISINTEGRATOR GUN

Powerful enough to drill a hole in the moon or destroy a tank in a single blast, the Disintegrator Gun was designed by scientists at ThinkTank before being handed over to the British government. The first task Miss Winters and her colleague Arnold Jellicoe give Robot K-1 is stealing the components to make their own version of the gun.

Although the Brigadier manages to capture the gun, it doesn't help him destroy the Robot. Instead, the living metal it is made from absorbs the energy and it grows to giant size.

# GIANT SPIDERS

Some time in the future, an Earth spacecraft crashed on the planet Metebelis Three. Unable to repair their ship or signal for help, the survivors were forced to settle on the planet. But an ordinary spider from the ship found its way into the mountains of blue crystal that could enhance the power of the mind. The spiders became cleverer and larger, and eventually used their power over the human mind to take control of the settlers.

Many years later, a psychic link from present-day Earth to Metebelis Three enables the spiders to track down the last perfect crystal of power that was taken by the Third Doctor on his previous visit to Metebelis Three (see page 145). Ruled by Queen Huath, the spiders now seek the crystal on the instructions of the Great One – an enormous spider that lives in a crystal cave in the mountains. She needs the crystal to complete a crystalline matrix that will amplify her own brain waves and make her the most powerful creature in existence…

Spiders communicate telepathically with humans and other spiders

Spiders can strike people down with blue 'electronic web blasts'

Just like an ordinary spider, but huge

Spiders call themselves 'Eight-Legs' and refer to humans as 'Two-Legs'

# PLANET OF THE SPIDERS

The blue crystal the Doctor found on Metabelis Three (in *The Green Death*) is important to the giant spiders that live there in the far future – they want it back, and so open a route to contemporary Earth. While Sarah Jane Smith and Mike Yates investigate the Meditation Centre where the spiders are appearing, the Doctor's crystal is stolen.

   The Doctor and Sarah Jane travel to Metebelis Three, where they discover the giant spiders need the crystal to deliver to the Great One. The Doctor confronts the Great One, who is destroyed by the power of the crystal. But the Doctor's body is also devastated by the crystal radiation. The TARDIS takes him back to Earth, where he regenerates…

Written by
**Robert Sloman**
Featuring
**the Third Doctor,
Sarah Jane and UNIT**
First broadcast
**4 May–8 June 1974
6 episodes**

### THE SPIDER ON THE BACK

The Metebelis spiders can control humans telepathically. The controlling spider jumps onto the back of a human 'host', becoming invisible to other people, while exerting a telepathic influence and inflicting mental pain to subdue the host. Strong-minded people can fight back and regain control.
   Sarah Jane manages to throw off a spider when helped to fight it by the Doctor and the monk K'anpo – who is actually a retired Time Lord.

### THE GREAT ONE

The Great One, feared and worshipped by the spiders, is an enormous spider within a crystal cave. She needs the Doctor's crystal to complete a web of crystal she has woven to reproduce the pattern of her brain. She just needs one perfect crystal to complete it, and the Doctor's is the last such crystal.
   Once the web is completed, the Great One's every thought resonates within it and grows in power. She thinks this will maker her ruler of the entire universe, but she has built a positive feedback loop and its power destroys her.

### REGENERATION

K'anpo reveals that the Doctor's change of form is known as 'regeneration'. K'anpo helps the Doctor regenerate: 'All the cells of his body have been devastated by the Metebelis crystals. But you forget – he is a Time Lord. I will give the process a little push, and the cells will regenerate. He will become a new man…'
   K'anpo explains that he regenerated before coming to Earth from Gallifrey, and settling in Tibet. Now living in England, he has projected Cho-Je, an image of his future self, and he regenerates into this new, younger version.

# MAGNUS GREEL

After World War Five in the 51st century, the infamous minister of justice Magnus Greel was nicknamed the Butcher of Brisbane. He sent 100,000 people to their deaths and was branded a war criminal after the fall of the Icelandic Alliance. He escaped in his experimental time cabinet, arriving in 19th-century China, where he assumed the identity of the Chinese god Weng-Chiang and recruited members of the Tong of the Black Scorpion.

Powered by dangerous zygma energy, Greel's time cabinet has distorted his appearance. Greel tries to augment his life force by draining energy from young women, with a distillation device. Defeated by the Doctor, and desperate for nutrition, Greel dies from cellular collapse when the Doctor pushes him into the distillation chamber.

Leather mask hides distorted face →

← Talon-like clawed hands

### MR SIN - THE PEKING HOMUNCULUS

Greel has brought the Peking Homunculus back through time, disguising it as Li H'Sen Chang's ventriloquist's dummy – Mr Sin. The Homunculus was made as a toy for the children of the Commissioner of the Icelandic Alliance in the year 5000. It contained a series of magnetic fields operating on a printed circuit and a small computer as well as one organic component – the cerebral cortex of a pig. But the pig's brain took over the Homunculus, and the swinish instinct became dominant – it hated humanity and revelled in carnage. Eventually it is this instinctive nature that drives it to rebel against Greel.

# THE TALONS OF WENG-CHIANG

The Doctor takes Leela to Victorian London to visit the music hall, but they witness a murder and are attacked by Chinese thugs from the Tong of the Black Scorpion. Faced with a giant rat hiding in the sewers and a sinister stage-magician with an animated and homicidal ventriloquist's dummy, the Doctor loses all hope of a quiet evening out – he is up against Magnus Greel, a war criminal from the far future.

Greel has lost his time cabinet, and traced it to London. When he recovers it, the Doctor obtains the key, leading to a stand-off. Greel threatens the Doctor with a dragon statue that fires laser beams from its eyes. But the Doctor and his friends triumph, and Greel is killed.

Written by
**Robert Holmes**
Featuring
**the Fourth Doctor
and Leela**
First broadcast
**26 February–2 April
1977
6 episodes**

### LI H'SEN CHANG

The son of a peasant, Li H'Sen Chang's status has improved since he witnessed the arrival of Greel in his 'cabinet of light' and greeted him as the god Weng-Chiang. Now Chang tours the world helping Greel look for his missing time cabinet, which was taken by the emperor's soldiers and given to an Englishman.

Chang is now a magician, helped by the hypnotic powers that Greel has given him, and by his ventriloquist's dummy, Mr Sin. Betrayed by Greel, Chang is killed after his leg is bitten off by one of Greel's giant rats.

### GIANT RATS

Greel's testing of the zygma beam has created enlarged animals as a side effect. The Doctor finds a huge money spider in the basement of the Palace Theatre and an outsized rat hair on a corpse in the local mortuary. Greel is using the giant rats to guard the entrance through the sewers to his hidden base below the theatre.

The Doctor manages to rescue Leela from one of the rats by shooting it (with a Chinese firing piece that was – luckily – made in Birmingham). Another of the rats carries off Li H'Sen Chang, who later dies of his wounds.

### LITEFOOT AND JAGO

The Doctor and Leela are helped by Henry Gordon Jago (owner-manager of the Palace Theatre) and pathologist Professor George Litefoot. Jago's bluster and bluff manner cover a soft-hearted nature, and he admits to Litefoot that he's 'not so bally brave when it comes to it'.

Litefoot's father was palace attaché in China, and here he acquired Greel's time cabinet. He meets the Doctor and Leela while performing a post mortem for the police. When the Doctor and Leela go missing, Litefoot and Jago join forces to track Greel to his lair.

# THE HAEMOVORES

If Fenric, the quintessence of evil, has his way then thousands of years in the future, Homo sapiens will evolve into Haemovores: creatures with an insatiable appetite for blood. Fenric's manipulation of time has enabled the Ancient One (see below) to travel back from a future Earth dying in the pollution of the post-industrial age, to infect people and turn them into Haemovores since Viking times.

Once infected, the victim becomes a pale vampire-like figure. But over time they mutate into hideous, grey-green creatures that can live in the sea. Their destiny is bound to the will of Fenric – they are his 'wolves' – and predicted by the legends of Norse mythology. The 'infection' has followed the journey of the flask in which Fenric is imprisoned and which was stolen by Viking raiders.

Discoloured skin with pustules and suckers, possibly developed underwater

Faith can hold back a Haemovore – Russian Captain Sorin's faith in the Revolution; Ace's faith in the Doctor…

Clothing may be the best indication of the era when the victim was originally infected

Clawed, talon-like fingers

## THE ANCIENT ONE

The Ancient One, possibly called Ingiger, is the last living creature on a future Earth. Having watched the world die in the chemical waste, Ingiger was carried back by Fenric in a time storm to 9th-century Transylvania. Since only Fenric could return the creature to its own time, Ingiger sought the flask in which Fenric was trapped. A merchant bought the flask in Constantinople and Ingiger followed him through Europe, then pursued the Viking pirates who stole the flask.

Those it has killed and infected over the years have become Haemovores. But as it goes to spread the poison in the sea, the Ancient One kills the other Haemovores by thought. The Doctor manages to persuade Ingiger not to release the poison, but to kill Fenric instead.

# THE CURSE OF FENRIC

The Doctor and Ace arrive at a secret military base during the Second World War. Here, Doctor Judson's 'Ultima Machine' decodes German ciphers, while Naval Commander Millington has discovered a source of poison beneath a local church, and plans to use it to attack Germany. Also buried there is an ancient flask, which contains the essence of Fenric – an elemental evil from the dawn of time, trapped by the Doctor centuries ago.

Fenric is released, and his Haemovores attack the base. The Doctor again challenges Fenric, who succeeds and prepares to send the Ancient One to poison the seas so that mankind will be replaced by Haemovores. But the Doctor persuades the Ancient One to destroy Fenric.

Written by
**Ian Briggs**
Featuring
**the Seventh Doctor and Ace**
First broadcast
**25 October–15 November 1989**
**4 episodes**

## VAMPIRES

Jean and Phyllis have been evacuated from London during the Blitz, and are now billeted with Miss Hardaker in the Northumberland village near the naval base. They become friends with Ace.

Infected by a Haemovore while swimming in the sea, they mutate into vampire-like creatures. Returning to Miss Hardaker's cottage, they attack her – leaving her body drained of blood. The vampire-girls are destroyed by the Ancient One once Fenric has no further use for them, dissolving and rotting to dust.

## FENRIC

Fenric is an elemental force of evil, born out of the creation of the universe itself. Seventeen hundred years ago, the Doctor carved bones from the desert sands into chesspieces, and challenged Fenric to solve his puzzle. Fenric failed and as a result was trapped in the Shadow Dimensions, within an ancient flask.

Fenric's 'wolves' have unwittingly worked to bring about Fenric's escape, and are descendants of Joseph Sundvik, a Viking who buried the flask. Once freed, Fenric first takes over the crippled body of Doctor Judson (right), and later that of the Russian Captain Sorin. The Doctor again sets Fenric a chess problem, which he cannot resist. The solution involves the white pawns turning on their own king – just as the Ancient One turns on Fenric.

Aquatic face visible behind breathing mask

Oxygenated liquid (pale green)

Gills are supplemented by liquid rebreather

As the human race ventured deeper into space, they made enemies and formed alliances. One race that went with the humans, helping to claim the new frontier and establish colonies and settlements across the galaxy, was the Hath.

On the colony planet of Messaline, a mixed team of humans and Hath was sent to clear out the old mining towns and adapt the eco-system with a standard PT306. But the two races fell out and a conflict started – then escalated. Each side made use of recalibrated Progenation Machines to 'breed' new troops. Soon a war that had in fact lasted only days had claimed the lives of generations of Hath and humans.

Essentially amphibious, the Hath depend on oxygenated liquid to breathe. They can only survive out of water with specially constructed breathing apparatus, and communication with other species is difficult as their 'voices' are filtered through the liquid and emerge as bubbles and gurbles.

# THE DOCTOR'S DAUGHTER

The TARDIS is drawn to the planet Messaline, where humans and Hath are engaged in an unending war. Each side is using adapted Progenation Machines to create new soldiers. A girl, Jenny, is created from a genetic sample of the Doctor – his daughter. Both sides want to find the mythical 'Source', which turns out to be a terraforming device.

This discovery brings the war to an end – it has actually lasted for just seven days, but during that time generations of soldiers on both sides have been created and killed. But Jenny is shot, and dies in the Doctor's arms. Only after he has left with Donna and Martha, does Jenny awaken – and sets off into space in search of adventures, just like her 'father'.

Written by
**Stephen Greenhorn**
Featuring
**the Tenth Doctor,
Donna and Martha**
First broadcast
**10 May 2008
1 episode**

### JENNY

Created from a genetic sample taken from the Doctor's hand, Jenny is literally born to fight – a soldier. At first, the Doctor finds it hard to come to terms with the fact that his own flesh and blood, as it were, can be so dedicated to the art of war. But he comes to appreciate his 'daughter' and to respect her talent and ability.

Jenny takes a while to understand the Doctor's viewpoint. But she too comes to respect him and to envy the life he leads fighting injustice and advocating peace. She is shot but recovers – and sets off into space to emulate her father...

### THE SOURCE

Humans and Hath alike seek the Source – a mystical artefact housed in a temple and containing the last sigh of the goddess who created their world. In fact they brought the Source in their colonisation ship. It is a terraforming device designed to make the inhospitable mining planet of Messaline suitable for habitation.

The Source is a glass sphere containing a gaseous compound of ammonia, methane, hydrogen, amino and nucleic acids, and proteins. The terraforming process is triggered when the Doctor breaks the sphere and releases the gas.

### COBB

The leader of the humans in their war against the Hath, Cobb appears to be a middle-aged man. But in fact, created by a Progenation Machine, he is less than one week old.

Fiercely determined to defeat the Hath and claim the Source, Cobb is devastated when he discovers the truth. He blames the Doctor for bringing the conflict to an unsatisfactory – as he sees it – end, and shoots him.

But Cobb's shot doesn't find its target. Jenny intervenes, throwing herself in front of the bullet intended for her father...

##  SCRIPTING THE HATH

The writer of *The Doctor's Daughter* was Stephen Greenhorn, who had written *The Lazarus Experiment* for Series Three the previous year. One comment that Stephen made to lead writer Russell T Davies after working on his first script was that *Doctor Who* is unlike other television drama in that the lead character does not change and become different because of the events in that drama. The Doctor remains pretty much a constant, without undergoing significant shifts in character.

Taking this as something of a challenge, Russell T Davies decided to give Stephen Greenhorn a brief for his next script that would indeed necessitate a change for the Doctor. Russell T Davies briefed the writer to include a subterranean war on another planet, a traumatic experience for Martha so she is keen to return home at the end, a race of aliens that breathe and communicate through liquid… And the Doctor's daughter.

The Hath speeches were kept simple, and the Hath communication was printed in italic in the scripts. This meant that the actors could convey as much of the dialogue as possible – including swearing – through body language and the gurgling.

### SCRIPT EXTRACT

MARTHA
So what's it like out there?

PECK
*I don't know.*

MARTHA
You don't know? You mean you've never been?

PECK
*No.*

MARTHA
But aren't you curious? Don't you want to find out?

PECK
*No.*

MARTHA
Where's your sense of adventure?

# MAX CAPRICORN

The 'public face' of Max Capricorn is actually a hologram

Head maintained by nutrient feeds and electro-stimulation

Max confined to box-like mobile life support

Control maintained by direct brain-link

Founder of Max Capricorn Cruiseliners, there is little left of the original Max Capricorn, apart from his head. He is now built into a wheeled cyborg trolley that provides mobility and life support.

Voted off his own company board, Capricorn planned to get revenge by crashing the huge starship *Titanic* into an obscure planet called Earth. The new board would be blamed, and the company would be bankrupted by the claims for compensation.

Max Capricorn has blackmailed Hardaker, the Captain of the *Titanic*, into sabotaging his own vessel. Capricorn has no thought for the thousands of innocent people who will die on board – or for the millions who may be killed on Earth.

Halo becomes a deadly weapon

Blank metal mask for face, with hinged jaw

Like any electronic system, they are vulnerable to an electro-magnetic pulse

The robot assistants and information centres on board *Titanic* are designed to look like angels – fitting in with the Christmas theme of the voyage. The Host are incredibly strong, and have the ability to fly.

Although they are programmed to assist organic life forms and never harm them, Max Capricorn has reprogrammed the Host to kill any survivors. The Host pursue the Doctor and his friends through the ship, using their halos as deadly weapons.

### THE MAX BOX

Coming from a society that regards cyborgs as second-class citizens, Max has kept his condition a secret. For years he has been running Max Capricorn Cruiseliners by hologram. In fact, his head is the only humanoid component that remains, and he is confined to a mobile life-support system. Max Capricorn plans to survive the crash of the *Titanic* in a concealed Omnistate Impact Chamber on Deck 31. He will be rescued from the crash site by well-paid employees, and will then retire to the beaches of Penhaxico Two – where the ladies are apparently very fond of metal.

 ## VOYAGE OF THE DAMNED

Written by
**Russell T Davies**
Featuring
**the Tenth Doctor
and Astrid**
First broadcast
**25 December 2007
1 feature-length episode**

After a collision with what seems to be an ocean liner, the Doctor finds himself on board the starship *Titanic* – a replica of the original doomed ship – orbiting Earth on Christmas Eve. When a meteoroid strike disables the *Titanic*, the Doctor helps other survivors to get to safety.

But they are attacked by the reprogrammed Heavenly Host robots which are supposed to help the passengers. The Doctor discovers that the crash has been engineered by Max Capricorn – former owner of the cruise company. The waitress Astrid sacrifices her life to destroy Max Capricorn. With the help of Midshipman Frame and other survivors, the Doctor is able to prevent the *Titanic* from crashing into Buckingham Palace.

### TITANIC

Owned and operated by Max Capricorn Cruiseliners, the *Titanic* is a space cruiser from the planet Sto in the Cassavalian Belt. The passengers are there to get experience of various primitive cultures along the way. And to enjoy Christmas.

The Heavenly Host provide information and assistance, while the ship's historian, Mr Copper, is on hand to explain local customs. But the Doctor realises that former salesman Bayldon Copper is relying on the dubious information he learned studying Earthonomics at Mrs Golightly's Happy Travelling University.

### ASTRID

Astrid Peth has always wanted to travel and see the universe – so she became a waitress on the luxury star cruiser *Titanic*. She befriends the Doctor and, with his help, joins a party from the starship making a shore leave visit to Earth on Christmas Eve. She is one of the survivors of the meteoroid strike that cripples the *Titanic*.

Astrid sacrifices her own life to save the Doctor – and Earth – from Max Capricorn. The Doctor tries to save her, using a teleport bracelet, but he is too late. Astrid becomes stardust, travelling the universe for ever.

### THE SURVIVORS

The few who survive the meteoroid strike are hunted down by the Heavenly Host. But the Doctor and Astrid are helped by the self-centred businessman Rickston Slade, Midshipman Frame from the crew, and Mr Copper the tour guide.

Others are tragically killed after the meteoroid strike. These include Morvin and Foon Van Hoff, who won their tickets in a competition. A diminutive, spiky-headed Zocci named Bannakaffalatta dies after using his cyborg body to emit an electromagnetic pulse that temporarily disables the Heavenly Host.

### RAISING THE TITANIC

The beautiful *Titanic* space cruiser was a computer-generated image created by The Mill. The designs on these pages show some of the initial paintings from which The Mill then designed the *Titanic*. V*oyage of the Damned* was made on location and in the studio, so the cast and crew never actually put to sea (or went into space).

**Passenger Group**
**6-7**

**SHORE LEAVE TICKET**

VALID FOR ONE PASSENGER

For use when travelling on shore.
This ticket remains the property of MAX CAPRICORN CRUISLINERS
and can be withdrawn at any time

# THE ICE WARRIORS

The helmet includes sophisticated communications equipment

Tufts of fur emerge through joints in the armour

The Ice Warrior's voice is a strained hiss in Earth's atmosphere

A sonic disruptor, fitted on the upper wrist, can maim or kill

The huge Ice Warrior towers over humans

The Ice Warriors are originally from the planet Mars. As their name implies, they prefer a cold environment and are susceptible to heat. They are upright reptilian warriors, encased in a shell-like armour so that very little of their actual bodies is visible – or vulnerable to attack. As a species, they have a long tradition of nobility and honour.

The Ice Warriors that the Doctor first encounters have been frozen for centuries beneath a glacier. The later Ice Warriors try to invade Earth and adapt the planet to suit their race. In the far future, they are friendly members of the Galactic Federation, though a group of them wants to return to the belligerent days of their past.

## ICE LORDS

The Martian nobility, sometimes termed Ice Lords, are less heavily armoured, and have a more streamlined helmet.

Higher ranks wear a ceremonial cloak and breastplate, which replaces the full armour of the lower classes. The ornamental belt suggests their 'skin' is a protective suit.

# THE ICE WARRIORS

An ice age grips the world of the future. At Britannicus Base, the Ioniser that holds back the glaciers is barely coping. The Doctor, Victoria and Jamie arrive and learn that an ancient warrior has been found in the glacier.

Revived, Varga (an Ice Warrior) kidnaps Victoria and awakens his crew. The humans, led by Clent, dare not use the Ioniser in case it causes the Martians' spaceship to explode and contaminate the area. The Ice Warriors, realising their world must be long dead, decide to make Earth theirs.

The Doctor gets control of the aliens' ship and its sonic weapons, making the Ice Warriors retreat. Clent is forced to use the Ioniser as a weapon, stopping the glaciers and destroying Varga and his warriors.

Written by
**Brian Hayles**
Featuring
**the Second Doctor,
Jamie and Victoria**
First broadcast
**11 November–16
December 1967
6 episodes**

### THE WARRIORS

The Ice Warriors are led by Varga and his lieutenant, Zondal. There are three other warriors: Rintan, Isbur and Turoc. Knowing that the atmosphere of Mars is (or was) mainly nitrogen with almost no hydrogen or oxygen, the Doctor deduces that the Martians will choke on ammonium sulphide – as indeed Zondal does.

First and foremost, the Martians are warriors. Varga is amused by the strategic naivety of his opponents and laughs with a rasping, coughing sound. When thinking, or possibly sleeping, his head slumps inside his shell like a turtle.

### SONIC WEAPONS

Each of the Warriors has a sonic weapon built into its right forearm. This is fired by clenching the clamp-like fist.

The main armament of the Martian ship is a sonic cannon, which also uses sound waves to destroy all objects in their path.

When Zondal fires the sonic cannon at Britannicus Base, one entire wing of the building is destroyed. Realising the Martians depend on sonic technology, the Doctor is able to adapt their sonic cannon so it works as a weapon against the warriors. The sound waves are trapped and amplified within their helmets.

### THE ICE AGE

The carbon dioxide level in the Earth's atmosphere helps retain the sun's heat. The creation of artificial food means that most arable land has been built over and plants reduced to an absolute minimum. The resulting lack of carbon dioxide has caused a new ice age. Whole countries have been evacuated, and civilisation is close to collapse.

Ionisation is a method of intensifying the sun's heat onto the Earth, into specific areas. But precise control is not easy. Ionisation can produce heat intense enough to melt rock.

## THE SEEDS OF DEATH

Written by
**Brian Hayles**
Featuring
**the Second Doctor,
Jamie and Zoe**
First broadcast
**25 January–1 March
1969
6 episodes**

T-Mat is a system for instantly transporting goods and people. Other forms of transport are now rarely used, and rockets have become obsolete. So when T-Mat Control on the moon stops working, the Doctor, Jamie and Zoe are sent in an antiquated rocket to investigate.

The Ice Warriors have taken over, and plan to use Martian seed pods to sap the oxygen from the air and make Earth like Mars. The Doctor realises that water will destroy the resulting fungus, but an Ice Warrior has been despatched to the Weather Control Station. The Doctor destroys the Warrior and makes it rain, before sabotaging the Martians' homing signal so that their fleet plunges into the sun.

### THE WARRIORS

In overall charge of the invasion is the Grand Marshal. He resembles the Ice Lord Slaar, who leads the raid on the moon. Directing the invasion from his ship, the Marshal speaks without the strained hiss of the Ice Warriors breathing Earth air, since he is in his own atmosphere.

Some Warriors are destroyed using a weapon built from a solar amplifier from the moon's solar-energy store. Focusing dishes attached to a solar power line from the solar amplifier seem to melt the Warriors away so that just a pool of fluid is left on the floor.

### SEED PODS

The Martian seed pods are white spheres that grow and burst, releasing a mist of spores and killing anyone nearby through oxygen starvation. The Ice Warriors send these pods to Earth via T-Mat.

The first developments of fungus are seen as vegetable blight. The large fungus bursts, spreading its spores. Acres of ground are covered in minutes and strong southwesterly winds could spread the disease from London over large parts of Europe, killing crops.

The Doctor manages to destroy the fungus with torrential rain.

### T-MAT

Travelmat Relay (T-Mat for short) is the ultimate form of travel and has superseded old-fashioned rocket ships.

The control centre for the system is on the moon, serving receptions at all major cities on Earth. Travelmat provides an instantaneous means of public travel, sending raw materials and vital food supplies to all parts of the world.

While departure and arrival are from and to specific booths, the Ice Warriors have the controls reset so as to materialise the Doctor in space in order to kill him.

The planet Peladon is being assessed for membership of the Galactic Federation. Delegates from member planets arrive, and the Doctor is mistaken for the Earth delegate. He is wary of the Martian delegate, Izlyr, and his sub-delegate, Ssorg, especially as the Chancellor of Peladon has been killed, apparently by the spirit of the royal beast, Aggedor.

But with Izlyr and Ssorg's help, the Doctor discovers that it is the High Priest Hepesh who wants to prevent Peladon joining the Federation. Hepesh has found an Aggedor creature, thought to be extinct, and trained it to obey him. The Doctor must defeat the King's Champion in single combat and tame Aggedor before he can avert the attempted coup.

Written by
**Brian Hayles**
Featuring
**the Third Doctor and Jo**
First broadcast
**29 January–19 February 1972**
**4 episodes**

### THE FEDERATION

The Galactic Federation is a league of planets and civilisations governed by a shared charter, but retaining local customs and laws where appropriate – for example, for religious ceremonies.

Lord Izlyr is the delegate from Mars, which has presumably been repopulated. Izlyr says the Martians were once a race of warriors, but now reject violence.

Alpha Centauri is a hermaphrodite hexapod with a high-pitched voice, one large eye and six arms. Arcturus resembles a large, tentacled head, kept in a mobile life-support system.

### PELADON

Peladon is a pre-technological medieval planet. Young King Peladon, whose mother was from Earth, rules from the storm-swept Citadel of Peladon – a remote castle built into the side of a desolate mountain.

Hepesh is High Priest of Aggedor, Torbis is Chancellor. King Peladon calls them brothers but this may be a term of affection and common purpose rather than familial relationship. They have been his friends and protectors since he was a boy.

Hepesh fears that becoming a member of the Federation will mean that Peladon will be changed for ever for the worse.

### THE LEGEND OF AGGEDOR

The legend of the curse of Peladon concerns the royal beast of Peladon, now extinct. It is written: 'Mighty is Aggedor, fiercest of all the beasts of Peladon.' Young men would hunt it to prove their courage. Its fur trims the royal garment, its head is the royal emblem.

It is also written that there will come a day when the spirit of Aggedor will rise again to warn and defend his royal master King Peladon. For at that day a stranger will appear in the land, bringing peril to Peladon and great tribulation to his kingdom.

##  THE MONSTER OF PELADON

Written by
**Brian Hayles**
Featuring
**the Third Doctor and Sarah Jane**
First broadcast
**29 March–27 April 1974**
**6 episodes**

Arriving on Peladon fifty years after his previous visit, the Doctor finds it again troubled. Queen Thalira is struggling to keep the trisilicate miners in order as the spirit of Aggedor is apparently angry with them. Alpha Centauri, Federation Ambassador, sends for security forces, and a group of Ice Warriors arrives, led by Commander Azaxyr and his adjutant Sskel.

But Azaxyr is acting on his own initiative, hoping to ship Peladon's valuable trisilicate to the Federation's enemies in Galaxy Five. The Doctor and Sarah Jane manage to unite the court and the miners against the Ice Warriors and expose the technological trickery used to make Aggedor appear and kill the miners.

### AZAXYR'S WARRIORS

Commander Azaxyr assumes control of Peladon when he arrives, imposing martial law. But Azaxyr is not a genuine Federation representative.

He is in fact the leader of a breakaway group of Martians who want to return to their former days of strength and conquest. Azaxyr has betrayed the Federation, but for military glory rather than material wealth. To this end, he has used a human agent and concealed Martian warriors to stir up trouble on Peladon.

For the first time the Martians refer to themselves as Ice Warriors.

### THE FEDERATION

The Federation is at war with Galaxy Five, which staged a vicious and unprovoked attack on them and now refuses to negotiate. Federation technology is based on the amber-like mineral trisilicate. Whoever controls a supply of trisilicate will win the war.

Eckersley is a Federation mining engineer from Earth. He is actually in league with Azaxyr and working for Galaxy Five. His Aggedor projection works by sending an image of the Aggedor statue with a matter projector while a directional heat ray kills miners.

Eckersley's innocent mining associate is one of the mole-like people of Vega – Vega Nexos. He has large eyes with small pupils, and hair-covered legs, arms and face.

## CREATING THE ICE WARRIORS

Writer Brian Hayles originally thought of his Ice Warriors as being closer to human soldiers in medieval-style space armour. It was costume designer Martin Baugh who hit on the idea of a reptilian biped fused into its armoured shell. His initial idea was for a kind of upright crocodile with a Viking-like helmet.

Once the designs were complete, the Ice Warrior suits were made, largely of fibreglass with rubber joints. Despite the joints, they were inflexible, and had to be bolted together with the actor inside. The mouth was made up with latex to appear reptilian. A plan to make the eyes glow behind the tinted glass covers was dropped, as the suits were quite hot enough without putting light bulbs inside them.

The director of *The Ice Warriors*, Derek Martinus, cast Bernard Bresslaw as Varga. He was a very tall actor, best known for his frequent appearances in the *Carry On* series of films. It was Bresslaw who created the distinctive voice of the Warriors. Thinking of how reptilian the costume looked, he experimented with a hissing, lizard-like voice. It was not treated but, because of the problems of acting and speaking in the full make-up and costume, the voices were pre-recorded then played back into the studio. The actors playing the Warriors then synched their lips to the recording. In *The Monster of Peladon*, the pre-recorded Warrior voices were not even spoken by the actors playing the Warriors. They were actually provided by *Doctor Who* producer (and former actor) Barry Letts.

The effect of the Ice Warriors' sonic disruptors was a visual distortion of the target as it is 'hit' by the sound waves. This was achieved by pointing the camera at a sheet of flexible mirrored plastic showing a reflection of the target. When the plastic was pushed gently from behind, so the image was distorted and wobbled.

# THE ISOLUS

The Isolus are empathic beings of intense emotion, similar in appearance to cosmic flowers. They drift through space, with only each other for company.

The Isolus mother jettisons millions of fledgling spores – children – who depend on each other for the empathic link that sustains them. Each child travels inside a pod, riding the heat and energy of solar tides. They take thousands of years to grow to adulthood, so to alleviate their boredom they play together.

Their games involve using their ionic power to create make-believe worlds where they can play, feeding off each other's love and kinship.

The Isolus child that takes over Chloe Webber has been cast adrift from its fellows by a solar flare. Desperate for friendship – for love – it continues trying to create make-believe worlds where it can play.

Stamen forms front of Isolus as it travels through space

Isolus resembles a flower

Isolus absorbs heat and sunlight

Isolus stem forms 'root' system

## CHLOE WEBBER'S MOVING PICTURES

Desperate for friendship and company, the Isolus inside Chloe still tries to create its own worlds. It puts real people – the neighbourhood children – inside the pictures that Chloe draws. They capture the entire audience of the 2012 London Olympics opening ceremony inside a picture. But the Isolus is still lonely, so Chloe then starts to draw the entire world.

The Isolus can also bring Chloe's drawings to life using ionic energy. A crossed-out mistake becomes a ball of graphite scribble that attacks Rose. More frighteningly, a drawing of Chloe's violent father, who recently died, comes to life to threaten Chloe and her mother Trish.

# FEAR HER

The people of Dame Kelly Holmes Close are preparing for the 2012 Olympics, but children are going missing. They are being trapped inside the drawings of 12-year-old Chloe Webber, who has been possessed by a lonely, lost Isolus child, separated from its mother and protective pod.

With the Doctor imprisoned in a drawing, Rose tries to help Chloe and her mother before a picture of Chloe's unpleasant father is brought to life by the Isolus. The Olympic audience disappears from the stadium as Chloe draws it. Then – determined to provide enough friends for the Isolus – she begins a picture of the world. But Rose uses the heat of the Olympic flame to power the pod and reunite the creature with its family.

Written by
**Matthew Graham**
Featuring
**the Tenth Doctor and Rose**
First broadcast
**24 June 2006
1 episode**

### CHARACTER SKETCHES

Chloe's drawings were actually created by 12-year-old Indigo Rumbelow, under the guidance of *Doctor Who* storyboard artist Shaun Williams.

In a number of sequences Chloe had to be seen to be drawing. For these, actor Abisola Agbaje was given versions sketched out in faint pencil, which she could simply draw over. In the completed sequences, it looked as though Chloe was drawing the pictures from scratch.

### THE ISOLUS POD

Each Isolus child travels inside a pod, which is powered by the heat of the stars. When one pod crashes in Dame Kelly Holmes Close, it absorbs heat from the area to convert into power. As a result, the close seems unseasonably cold. The new tarmac laid on the road blisters in the heat from the pod. The pod affects other energy sources, so that cars stop when they pass it.

Rose uses the heat – and love – of the Olympic flame to power up the pod fully and send it back on its journey through the stars.

### CHLOE'S FATHER

Chloe Webber's father died a year ago. Both Chloe and her mother, Trish, were frightened of Mr Webber – Chloe has been suffering nightmares about him, although Trish avoids talking about him. To calm Chloe down, Trish would sing the 'Kookaburra' song to her ('Kookaburra sits in the old gum tree…').

But Chloe has drawn a picture of her father, and hidden it inside her wardrobe. The ionic energy from the Isolus child brings the picture to life as Chloe's fear increases, and the drawing of her dad threatens to come after Chloe and Trish.

## WORD PICTURES

Writer Matthew Graham was originally asked to come up with a story for Series Three of *Doctor Who*, to be broadcast in 2007, but as things turned out, his script was moved forward to become one of the later episodes of the 2006 series. An experienced television scriptwriter, Matthew is best known as the co-creator and lead writer of the BBC series *Life on Mars* and its sequel, *Ashes to Ashes*. There is a strange connection between the two series. When Matthew asked his daughter, Daisy, to come up with a surname for the *Life on Mars* hero Sam, she chose Tyler. It was only later – once Sam Tyler was named – that Daisy told her father she'd suggested the name because the Doctor's companion was Rose Tyler.

Matthew was originally asked to devise a story that was set in a limited location – such as a bunker. This proved restrictive, and instead he brought the Doctor and Rose down to Earth, literally, by wondering what would happen if they turned up in an ordinary street. Even set during the 2012 Olympics, this was more cost-effective than a story set in the past or future.

But right from the start, the story was about drawings that came to life. 'I suggested demonic or possessed children's drawings, pictures where people's eyes follow you round the room. Children's drawings always have big eyes and big hair and stick arms, so what if they move?'

# CREATING THE ISOLUS CHILD

The Isolus child itself also started life as a drawing. Initial concept sketches produced by the *Doctor Who* Art Department were fleshed out into the final, flower-like design and created as animated computer images by effects house The Mill.

## SCRIBBLE CREATURE

One of Chloe's discarded drawings comes to life as a scribble creature, which attacks Rose. The Doctor stops it with his sonic screwdriver.

Back in the TARDIS, he realises it is an animated ball of graphite — made from the same material as the lead of an ordinary pencil. He is able to rub some of it out with an eraser.

The creature has been animated by the same ionic energy the Isolus uses to capture people and imprison them inside Chloe's drawings.

Heavily sunken eyes

Jagrafess needs to keep cool

Like its name, the Mighty Jagrafess of the Holy Hadrojassic Maxarodenfoe is huge. It exists, stretched out across the ceiling and roof of the control room, on Floor 500 of Satellite Five.

It is a vast expanse of flesh, with a sharp-toothed mouth, which communicates with the Editor through his earpiece. Since Satellite Five went online, 91 years before the events of *The Long Game*, the Jagrafess has shaped mankind's development using the satellite's news reports.

By manipulating the news, the Jagrafess is able to develop a climate of fear. It can create an enemy that does not exist, or even use subliminal messaging to affect the economy or change a vote. It is playing a long game, controlling events for its own profit.

The Jagrafess lifespan is about 3,000 years

Unearthly screeching is the only sound the Jagrafess makes

Sharp-toothed mouth extruded from bodily mass

Viscous bodily fluids drip from mouth

### BEHIND THE SCENES

The enigmatic Editor (right) seems to be in charge of Satellite Five, though in fact he answers to the Jagrafess. But even the Jagrafess is not the real power behind the manipulation of the satellite's news reports. It has itself been installed by another, even more deadly and dangerous power to see that humanity follows a set pattern of events. As the Doctor and Rose later discover, the last Dalek survivors of the Time War are actually behind the manipulation of humanity.

 # THE LONG GAME

Arriving on news-broadcasting station Satellite Five, the Doctor, Rose and their new companion Adam discover that broadcasting is not quite what they expected. Journalists channel information through chips embedded in their heads – and Adam soon gets himself a forehead upgrade. The journalists all hope to get promoted to Floor 500, where the Doctor and Rose find that the apparently all-powerful Editor actually works for an alien – the Jagrafess – that is manipulating the broadcasts.

The Doctor realises the Jagrafess needs to be kept cold. He and Rose are captured by the Editor, but they let their new friend Cathica know – and she is able to channel heat up to Floor 500 and destroy the Jagrafess.

Written by
**Russell T Davies**
Featuring
**the Ninth Doctor, Rose and Adam**
First broadcast
**7 May 2005**
**1 episode**

### SATELLITE FIVE

In this time of the Fourth Great and Bountiful Human Empire, Satellite Five is responsible for broadcasting 600 channels of constant news reports. Satellite Five is where news is gathered, written up, packaged and sold. Nothing happens in the Human Empire without going through Satellite Five.

Floor 500 is the Editorial level – where the management is based – and is the place to which everyone else aspires to be promoted. The walls are rumoured to be made of gold. But the reality is very different – it is cold and dilapidated.

### THE EDITOR

Looking like a corporate version of Jack Frost, the Editor lives in the icy environment of Floor 500.

He represents a consortium of banks, working directly with the Jagrafess to maximise the banks' profits. The alien creature's presence means that there is no war or bloodshed, simply a silent occupation, making it a fairly cheap form of government.

When he discovers the truth about the Doctor and the TARDIS, the Editor sees the possibility of controlling humanity for all time.

### ZOMBIES

The Jagrafess controls humanity through computer chips implanted in their heads. This is an extension of the technology the Satellite Five journalists use to gather and broadcast news. Compressed news information is streamed into the brain and the human becomes a part of the analytical software.

The Editor uses drones – animated human corpses – to run his control room on Floor 500. Even though their brains have died, the implanted chips keep working and animate the dead bodies to obey the Editor's commands.

### BEHIND THE HEADLINES

Satellite Five was another computer-generated image created by The Mill, from initial designs by the *Doctor Who* Art Department. On this page you can see some of those initial designs and paintings, which are very close to the final computer-generated images created by The Mill.

Strong, sharp horns

Heavy, armoured battle gauntlets

Scanning device

Heavy, effective armour covers tough hide of Judoon

### INTERROGATION

When hunting down a disguised Plasmavore, the Judoon use highly advanced scanning technology to check that the people at Royal Hope Hospital are human. The scanner emits a blue light and the Judoon take a reading from the device. Once someone is proved to be human, the Judoon use the other end of the same device to mark them on the back of the hand with an X. The ink used is fused with a distinctive compound so it cannot be forged.

The Judoon are a police force available for hire. Other races employ them to carry out inter-planetary law-enforcement tasks on their behalf. A Judoon is hugely powerful, and resembles a large, upright rhinoceros. Arriving in massive vertical spaceships, like huge tower blocks, they can only enforce Galactic Law when specifically invited to do so, or on neutral territory.

Ruthless in the extreme, the Judoon have little interest in other life forms apart from whether they obey the letter of the law. Anyone who opposes them is automatically found guilty of assault and executed.

Plasmavore disguised as old lady called Florence

Internal biology can be changed to match victim's

Bendy drinking straw is used to extract blood from victim

Disguised as an old lady called Florence, the alien Plasmavore takes refuge on Earth when she is hunted by the Judoon. She has been charged with the murder of the Child Princess of Padrivole Regency Nine – a crime she freely admits when captured.

The Plasmavore is a blood-sucking creature that depends on blood to survive. She assimilates an alien's biological make-up through its blood, and so escapes being identified by the Judoon when they scan for non-human life forms. She carries her own drinking straw ready to take blood from whoever is available – the richer and more salty and fatty the blood, the better.

## SLABS

The Plasmavore is protected by two Slabs. These basic slave drones look just like motorcycle couriers, complete with black leather uniforms and crash helmets.

In fact, the Slabs are made of solid leather imbued with simple life and the ability to obey orders from the Plasmavore. The Doctor manages to destroy one of the Slabs, while the Judoon easily deal with the other one.

 # SMITH AND JONES

The Judoon are hunting for a Plasmavore, and have tracked her to the Royal Hope Hospital in London. They use an $H_2O$ scoop to transport the hospital to the neutral territory of the moon, and then hunt for any non-human life forms. The Doctor and his new friend Martha try to evade the Judoon – who will assume the Doctor is their prey if they find him – and unmask the real Plasmavore, disguised as an old lady called Florence.

Cornered, the Plasmavore tries to use the MRI scanner to destroy all other life in the hospital – and on half of the Earth. But having absorbed the Doctor's blood, she registers as non-human and is executed. Safely back on Earth, the Doctor offers Martha a trip in the TARDIS.

Written by
**Russell T Davies**
Featuring
**the Tenth Doctor and Martha**
First broadcast
**31 March 2007
1 episode**

## $H_2O$ SCOOP

The Judoon have access to a range of technology, including universal galactic real-time translation systems, so they can communicate with other life forms – such as humans.

They sometimes use an $H_2O$ scoop, harnessing the inert power of hydrogen, to transport people or entire buildings to neutral space where the Judoon can enforce the law. When the scoop is used it creates what looks like a powerful lightning and thunder storm – but with the rain going up from the ground to the gathering clouds above.

## MAGNETIC PULSE

The Plasmavore plans to destroy the Judoon using a Magnetic Resonance Imaging scanner in the Royal Hope Hospital.

She adapts it to emit a force of 50,000 tesla, enough to fry the brainstem of any living creature within 50,000 miles … including the side of the Earth facing the moon. The Plasmavore will herself be screened from the emission and safe.

Once the Judoon have executed the Plasmavore and left the moon, the Doctor is able to disable the MRI machine by severing a crucial wire.

## MARTHA'S FAMILY

Martha has an older sister, Letitia, and a younger brother called Leo. Her mother and father are Francine and Clive, who have separated.

Francine does not approve of Clive's new – much younger – girlfriend Annalise. This makes Leo's 21st-birthday party rather fraught and the night ends with a family row.

After the party, Martha meets the Doctor again, and accepts his offer of a trip in the TARDIS – which she is astonished to find is much bigger inside than outside!

## MOON LANDINGS

The effects of transporting the Royal Hope Hospital to the moon, and the empty crater it leaves behind in London, were achieved by The Mill using computer-generated images (CGI). The massive Judoon spaceships were also designed and created by The Mill.

The picture above shows the final image of the Judoon marching from their ships across the lunar landscape to the Royal Hope Hospital and passing through the protective shield that keeps the atmosphere in. Below is an early concept painting showing how the hospital might have looked when transported to the moon.

## MAKING MONSTERS

While the Plasmavore is disguised as an old lady, and her deadly Slabs look like motorcycle messengers, the Judoon are obviously an alien race – this is conspicuous even when they are wearing their distinctive helmets. And when the Judoon captain removes his helmet, the alien rhino-like head beneath is revealed.

The impressive animatronic head was designed and created by Neill Gorton's team at Millennium FX. As the captain is the only Judoon to remove his helmet, just one head was needed, and this could be made as impressive as possible.

## THE SHADOW PROCLAMATION

The Doctor first mentioned the Shadow Proclamation when confronting the Nestene Consciousness, and Rose invoked it when trying unsuccessfully to bluff the Sycorax Leader (*The Christmas Invasion*). The Doctor again cited the Shadow Proclamation when dealing with the Isolus Child (*Fear Her*), but it was not until the Doctor and Donna discovered that the Earth had vanished in *The Stolen Earth* that the Doctor revealed the nature of the Shadow Proclamation and turned to it for help.

The Shadow Proclamation is a vast space station that houses the organisation, led by the Shadow Architect. The organisation is dedicated to upholding the conventions and statutes agreed by participating races. Local security, and much of the actual law enforcement, is the responsibility of the Judoon.

A troop of Judoon is stationed permanently at the Shadow Proclamation, and was waiting to arrest the Doctor and Donna when they arrived in the TARDIS.

Shadow Architect is
humanoid, female

Robes denote
office and rank

The most senior official of the
Shadow Proclamation is the
Shadow Architect. It is not known if
the position is elected or appointed.
At the time the Doctor and Donna
go to the Shadow Proclamation
for help, the Shadow Architect
is an elderly pale-skinned female
humanoid, with others of her own
race acting as her staff. It may be
that the post alternates between
different races, or that these pale
female humanoids always fulfil the
role.

Another possibility is that the
question simply does not arise and
the current Shadow Architect has
always been and will always be
the holder of that position.

Attention to poise
and demeanour

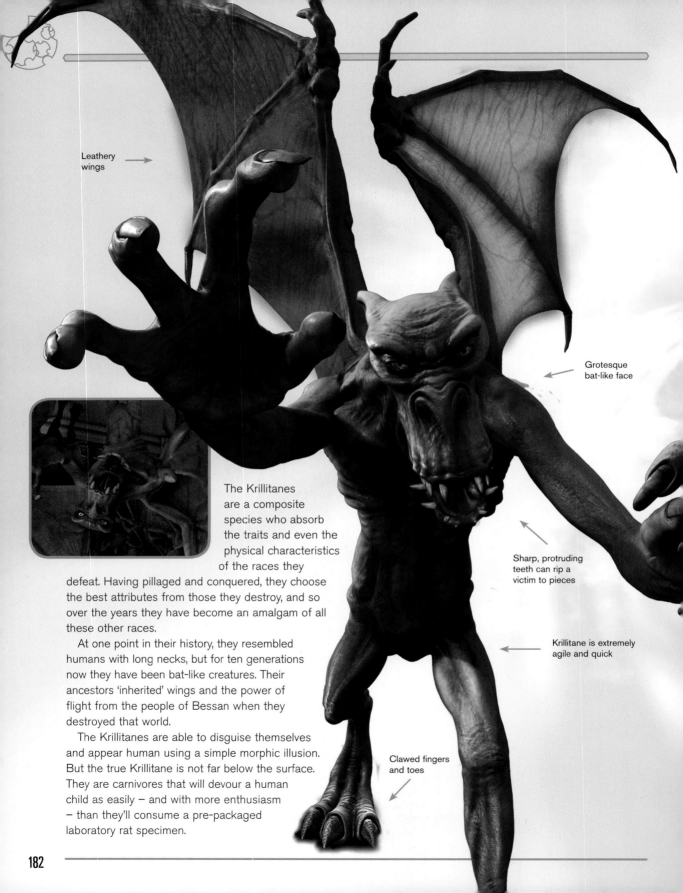

Leathery wings →

Grotesque bat-like face

Sharp, protruding teeth can rip a victim to pieces

Krillitane is extremely agile and quick

Clawed fingers and toes

The Krillitanes are a composite species who absorb the traits and even the physical characteristics of the races they defeat. Having pillaged and conquered, they choose the best attributes from those they destroy, and so over the years they have become an amalgam of all these other races.

At one point in their history, they resembled humans with long necks, but for ten generations now they have been bat-like creatures. Their ancestors 'inherited' wings and the power of flight from the people of Bessan when they destroyed that world.

The Krillitanes are able to disguise themselves and appear human using a simple morphic illusion. But the true Krillitane is not far below the surface. They are carnivores that will devour a human child as easily – and with more enthusiasm – than they'll consume a pre-packaged laboratory rat specimen.

 # SCHOOL REUNION

The Doctor and Rose investigate a school in the middle of a spate of UFO sightings, where exam results have improved dramatically with the arrival of a new head teacher, Mr Finch. With Rose working as a dinner lady and the Doctor as a supply teacher, they meet the Doctor's former companion Sarah Jane Smith, who is also suspicious of events at the school.

In fact Finch is a Krillitane – as are half the staff. They are using Krillitane Oil to enhance the mental capacity of the children in the hope of solving the Skasas Paradigm and gaining control over the universe. The Doctor, Rose, Mickey and Sarah Jane manage to sabotage the plan, and K-9 destroys the store of Oil. The Krillitanes are caught in the blast.

Written by
**Toby Whithouse**
Featuring
**the Tenth Doctor,
Rose, Mickey,
Sarah Jane and K-9**
First broadcast
**29 April 2006
1 episode**

## THE SCHOOL

The Krillitanes have taken over a secondary school by replacing its head teacher and many of the staff. Mr Finch took over Deffry Vale High School three months before the Doctor and Rose's visit, and introduced a new curriculum. This led to a dramatic improvement in the school's results. Despite this success, there is a high turnover of teaching staff, with one teacher being replaced after a winning lottery ticket was pushed through her door.

When Mickey found that over 40 UFO sitings had occurred nearby, he called the Doctor and Rose in to investigate.

## KRILLITANE OIL

The Krillitanes have changed so far from their original form that they now find their own Oil lethally toxic, though it is harmless to humans (and Time Lords). The Oil enhances the mental powers of those who consume it. The chips served at school dinners – definitely not a healthy option – are cooked in the Oil and improve the abilities of some of the pupils to a point where Finch can use them to calculate the Skasas Paradigm.

But the Oil is also highly flammable, and K-9 is able to destroy the school, and the Krillitanes inside, by igniting it.

## THE SKASAS PARADIGM

Also known as the 'God Maker' or the 'Universal Theory', the Skasas Paradigm is the key to the way the universe works. Anyone who unravels it can control the very building blocks of time, space and universal matter. But it takes more than just computational power to crack the Paradigm. It also needs imagination – which is why the Krillitanes are using schoolchildren to work it out.

Once he knows the solution, Finch believes that the universe itself will be like clay in his hands… and he tries to persuade the Doctor to join him.

### BROTHER LASSAR

Brother Lassar is the leader of the Krillitanes who arrive on Earth. In his disguised human form, and calling himself Mr Finch, he has taken over as head teacher of a secondary school. The day after he arrived, half the staff mysteriously fell victim to an especially virulent strain of flu and had to be replaced. Since then there have been other strange events, and even changes to the school dinner menu. But the school's results have improved dramatically, so it seems that the new head teacher is doing something right.

# SCRIPTING THE KRILLITANES

The task of creating new aliens to face the Doctor, Rose and Mickey, and to bring back the popular Sarah Jane Smith and K-9, was given to writer Toby Whithouse. Best known as the creator and author of the popular Channel 4 comedy drama *No Angels*, Toby was approached to write for *Doctor Who* before the first episode of the 2005 series had even aired. Having renewed his acquaintance with both Sarah Jane and K-9 by watching episodes of the classic series, Toby came up with a story called *Black Ops*, set in an army camp and surrounding village. On the suggestion of Russell T Davies, he changed the location to a secondary school, and the story became *School Reunion*.

Like the Gelth, the Reapers and the Jagrafess, the Krillitanes were created entirely as computer-generated images (CGI) by The Mill. These images were then added to the live-action material shot in the studio and on location.

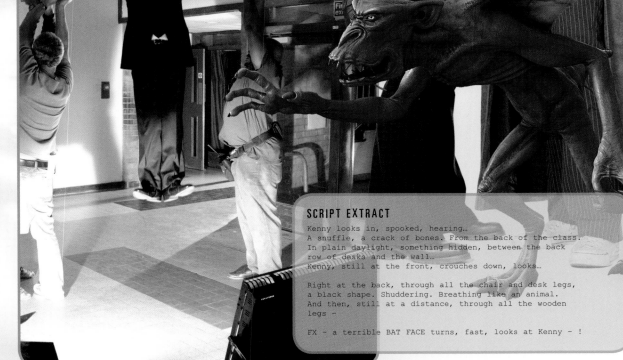

## SCRIPT EXTRACT

Kenny looks in, spooked, hearing…
A snuffle, a crack of bones. From the back of the class.
In plain daylight, something hidden, between the back row of desks and the wall…
Kenny, still at the front, crouches down, looks…

Right at the back, through all the chair and desk legs, a black shape. Shuddering. Breathing like an animal. And then, still at a distance, through all the wooden legs –

FX – a terrible BAT FACE turns, fast, looks at Kenny – !

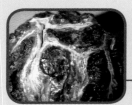

Krynoid grows
from large
gourd-like
plant pod

Tentacles like
branches and
roots

Krynoid does not
need nitrogen to
survive

The Krynoid is a form of
intelligent plant life that
feeds on animals. On
planets where the
Krynoid takes hold,
animal life becomes
extinct. The Krynoid
can infect an animal
with its spores,
causing the 'host'
creature to mutate into
a Krynoid, which retains
some of that host's knowledge,
memory and intelligence. The Krynoid is
also able to transfer some of its power
to the local vegetation, making plant life
hostile and deadly.

No one knows for sure how Krynoid
plant pods travel through space. One
theory is that their planet of origin is
volcanic, and the pods are shot out (in
pairs) by the eruptions.

### TRANSITION STAGES

The first person to be infected with the Krynoid is
Charles Winlett, one of the team that discovers the
Krynoid pods. The scientists put one of the
pods under ultraviolet light and, when it opens,
a shoot emerges, which attacks Winlett.

Winlett's body is taken over by the Krynoid. His
temperature and heart rate drop drastically and
his skin becomes green and blotchy. The Doctor
discovers that Winlett's blood is infected with
plant bacteria and soon his whole body begins
to change into a Krynoid.

Krynoid is
mobile and
seeks out food

 # THE SEEDS OF DOOM

A mysterious alien plant pod is discovered in Antarctica – a Krynoid. It infects one of the expedition team and he mutates. The millionaire plant-collector Harrison Chase learns of the seed pod's existence and is determined to own it. The Krynoid is destroyed, but the Doctor discovers a second pod, which is stolen by Chase's men.

The Doctor and Sarah track them to Chase's country house, where one of his staff is infected and begins to mutate. With the creature beginning to control all plant life, and about to germinate and send out millions of pods, the Doctor has no choice but to let UNIT send in the RAF to bomb the house and destroy the Krynoid.

Written by
**Robert Banks Stewart**
Featuring
**the Fourth Doctor, Sarah Jane and UNIT**
First broadcast
**31 January–6 March 1976**
**6 episodes**

### HARRISON CHASE

Desperate to acquire the Krynoid for his extensive collection of plants, Harrison Chase sends his unscrupulous hitman Scorby to Antarctica to steal the pod.

Once he has a Krynoid, Chase sets out to cultivate it, allowing it to infect one of his scientists – Keeler. Chase is sympathetic to the aims of the Krynoid, feeling humans have neglected the most beautiful parts of nature. He is taken over by the Krynoid as it grows to a giant size, and traps the Doctor and Sarah inside his house. He is finally killed in his own compost machine.

### THE ANTARCTIC BASE

The first Krynoid pod is discovered by scientists based in an Antarctic camp run by the World Ecology Bureau. Chase's henchmen pretend they got lost in their plane, then take the crew hostage and demand the pod. Despite the Doctor's best efforts, they get the second pod and escape, sabotaging the base's power plant so it explodes.

The Doctor and Sarah escape, rescued by a Royal Marine survival team sent in to help. But scientists Stevenson and Moberly have already been killed by the mutating Winlett.

### WORLD ECOLOGY BUREAU

Sir Colin Thackeray is in charge of the World Ecology Bureau, which is based in London. His deputy, a disgruntled man called Dunbar, has told Harrison Chase about the discovery of the Krynoid pod in exchange for money. Though Dunbar later sees the error of his ways, the damage has been done and Chase gets hold of a Krynoid – which later kills Dunbar as he tries to make amends.

Sir Colin Thackeray has heard of the Doctor through his association with UNIT, and later calls in UNIT to help destroy the Krynoid.

When the Doctor is forced to use the TARDIS's Emergency Unit to escape from a volcanic eruption on the planet Dulkis (see page 249), the TARDIS arrives first in a white void and then in what seems to be a forest. The Doctor discovers that the trees are all in the shapes of letters – with lines of trees spelling out sayings and proverbs – and he realises they are in a place where anything is possible: the Land of Fiction. Existing outside the normal space-time dimension, this strange realm is ruled by

the Master of the Land of Fiction, who lives in a citadel on top of a massive cliff. On their way to the citadel, the Doctor and his companions, Jamie and Zoe, meet many fictional characters from novels, fairy tales and mythology – all existing as if they were real in this strange world.

# THE MIND ROBBER

Arriving in the Land of Fiction, the Doctor, Jamie and Zoe meet Gulliver, who tells them of 'the Master', who rules the Land of Fiction. Narrowly avoiding an attack by a unicorn, as well as encounters with Medusa and the Minotaur, they make their way to the citadel. On the way, the Doctor must solve riddles to rescue a trapped Zoe, and do a jigsaw puzzle to replace Jamie's face — when he gets it wrong, Jamie's face changes.

Finally the Doctor meets the Master, an elderly writer enslaved by a computer, the Master Brain, which wants the Doctor to replace the frail Master and help it take over the Earth. The Doctor enlists fictional heroes against the Master's own creations, and the computer is destroyed.

Written by
**Peter Ling**
Featuring
**the Second Doctor, Jamie and Zoe**
First broadcast
**14 September–12 October 1968**
**5 episodes**

### EMERGENCY UNIT

The Emergency Unit shifts the TARDIS out of the space-time dimension — out of reality. It arrives 'nowhere': none of its meters or dials register anything and the scanner is blank.

When images of their homes appear on the scanner screen, both Jamie and Zoe venture outside the TARDIS, despite the Doctor's warnings. In the white void outside the ship, they are menaced by White Robots. The Doctor manages to guide his companions back, but then the TARDIS explodes and they are stranded in a strange forest.

### WHITE ROBOTS

The White Robots that close in on Jamie and Zoe in the void outside the TARDIS serve the Master of the Land of Fiction. They not only exist in the void, but also appear in the Land of Fiction itself, where they protect the controlling computer.

Perhaps the robots were created by the same power that constructed that computer, or perhaps they are also fictional creations that have been made real.

The robot costumes were first used in another 1960s television science fiction series (*Out of the Unknown*, pictured above) — so they are fictional!

### THE MASTER OF FICTION

The Master of the Land of Fiction is actually an elderly human writer who was taken from his desk by the Master Brain when he dozed off on a hot summer's day in 1926. He created 'The Adventures of Captain Jack Harkaway' for *The Ensign*, a boys' magazine, and wrote 5,000 words every week for 25 years — which is why he was selected for his post in the Land of Fiction. His imagination and creativity give life to the inhabitants of the Land, so he cannot leave, but he is nearing death, and the Doctor is an ideal candidate to replace him.

## CREATURE CREATION

The Lazarus Creature, while it had a face that was almost human, was completely computer-generated by The Mill. The face was created from specially taken photographs of actor Mark Gatiss. An early idea was that the creature would change rapidly as it went through various stages of evolution – including a bird and a lizard. But this idea was dropped so that the creature maintained a constant form throughout the episode.

The design of the creature came from the script, and from a sketch (shown above) drawn by Russell T Davies to show what he thought the creature should look like. The result was an impressive and frightening beast that appeared to interact with the (real) actors and environment – in both the LazLabs facility and Southwark Cathedral (actually Wells Cathedral, in Somerset).

Interestingly, the Genetic Manipulation Device in which Lazarus undergoes his change also evolved from something else. It was originally the capsule in which the Doctor and Ida Scott make their descent into the heart of the Impossible Planet. Repainted, and with some minor alterations, the prop was pressed into service once more at LazLabs – again, taking its occupants on a journey through the impossible…

Tail with deadly sting

Face of Lazarus still
recognisable

Enlarged
mandibles

Skeletal arthropod
body

Sharp, spiky forelimbs

Professor Richard Lazarus has always
dreamed of turning back the biological
clock – of becoming younger. He has
invented a Genetic Manipulation Device
which he believes will make him forty
years younger. And, in front of an invited
audience, it seems to
work – Professor Lazarus
emerges from the GMD
looking more like 36 than his
actual 76 years old.

But there is a price. The process
damages his DNA, bringing to the
surface a series of molecules
otherwise dormant in
mankind – bypassed
by evolution. Lazarus is
transformed into a primordial
arthropod creature. Desperate
for sustenance, the creature draws the life energy
from other humans, rampaging through the LazLabs
complex before finally dying in Southwark Cathedral…

## THE LAZARUS EXPERIMENT

Written by
**Stephen Greenhorn**
Featuring
**the Tenth Doctor
and Martha**
First broadcast
**5 May 2007
1 episode**

Taking Martha back home, the Doctor sees part of a news report about Professor Lazarus – who claims he will change what it means to be human. Meanwhile, Martha's sister Tish has been appointed by Lazarus as his head of PR, and gets invitations for her family to Lazarus's demonstration. The experiment seems to work, but soon Lazarus is transformed into a savage primordial monster that craves human life force. He kills his colleague Lady Thaw and goes on the rampage.

The Doctor confronts the creature at Southwark Cathedral. He magnifies the sonic resonance of the cathedral organ, and – disoriented – the Lazarus creature falls to its death from the bell tower.

### THE JONES FAMILY

Martha Jones is the daughter of Clive and Francine (who have now separated), and has a brother and sister. Her brother Leo is 21, with a girlfriend called Shonara and a daughter, Keisha.

Martha's older sister Letitia – Tish for short – works for Professor Lazarus as his Head of Public Relations. After the death of Lazarus, she takes a similar job for Lucy Saxon, wife of prime minister Harold Saxon. But Saxon is in fact the Doctor's old enemy the Master – and life for Tish and her parents is about to get very complicated...

### LADY THAW

An old friend of Professor Lazarus, Lady Thaw is his colleague and benefactor. She also acts as a representative of Harold Saxon, who has invested heavily in Lazarus's work.

At first elated at the apparent success of the Lazarus Experiment, Lady Thaw is soon disappointed to be rejected by her former friend now he is younger. But her disappointment and anger turn to shock and terror as Lady Thaw becomes the first victim of the creature Lazarus has become. It drains the life force from her frail body to sustain itself.

### MR SAXON'S WARNING

Politician, investor, philanthropist... Harold Saxon, principal investor in LazLabs, is in fact the Doctor's old Time Lord enemy the Master. He has already made his plans and ensured that the Doctor will attend the Lazarus Experiment by having Martha's sister Tish appointed LazLabs' Head of PR.

As the Lazarus creature goes on the rampage, one of Saxon's agents gives Martha's mother a warning. He tells her the Doctor is dangerous and convinces Francine that she should betray her daughter's friend to Mr Saxon...

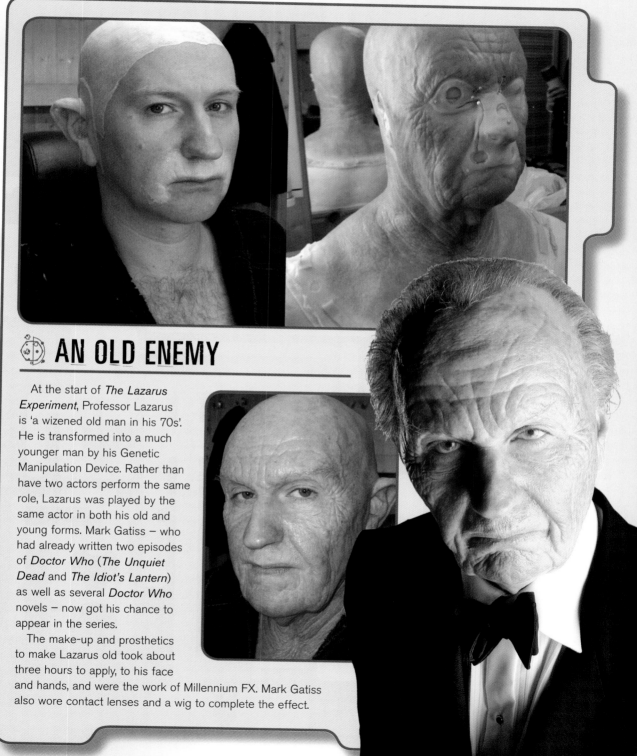

## AN OLD ENEMY

At the start of *The Lazarus Experiment*, Professor Lazarus is 'a wizened old man in his 70s'. He is transformed into a much younger man by his Genetic Manipulation Device. Rather than have two actors perform the same role, Lazarus was played by the same actor in both his old and young forms. Mark Gatiss – who had already written two episodes of *Doctor Who* (*The Unquiet Dead* and *The Idiot's Lantern*) as well as several *Doctor Who* novels – now got his chance to appear in the series.

The make-up and prosthetics to make Lazarus old took about three hours to apply, to his face and hands, and were the work of Millennium FX. Mark Gatiss also wore contact lenses and a wig to complete the effect.

Known as the scourge of the galaxy M87, the Macra are massive crustaceans that depend on gas for their existence, consuming it like food. At one time, they enslaved human colonists, brainwashing them to believe that the gas was valuable. The colonists then unwittingly mined the gas for the Macra, who secretly controlled and regulated the humans' lives.

By the time of the human colonisation of New Earth in the far future, the Macra have devolved into less intelligent, more instinctive creatures, which hunt in a herd. The Doctor encounters them when he is trying to rescue Martha from a traffic jam below the city.

The Macra escaped from New New York Zoo when power was lost and the facility broke down. They made their way to the Undercity, where they found the gas they need to survive. The Macra attack the cars that stray too close purely on instinct and to preserve their territory, as a human might swat at a fly.

Massive pincer-like claws can rip through metal

## MACRA EVOLUTION

When the Doctor first encountered the Macra it was on a future human colony, where the Macra had already become established and taken control. Many years before their regression to unintelligent creatures that act only on instinct and aggression, these early Macra differed from their later form in several ways. Their claws and pincers were more streamlined and they had two smaller claws close to their mouth. The overall shape of the Macra shell was slightly different, and these earlier creatures were spiked with coarse hair.

Over the years, although their shape changed, their bodies evolved and their brains regressed, the Macra retained their aversion to bright light, hiding in the fog and darkness of New New York.

Eyes on stalks
can see in the
dark and below
ground

Ingests
gas to
survive

## EFFECTS EVOLUTION

In the 1960s, visual effects on
television were achieved very
differently from today. Though many of
the same physical effects techniques
were used, in some form or another, the
whole area of computer graphics did
not exist. The first personal computer
was not available until over a decade
after *The Macra Terror* was made, and
the only animation available was, in effect,
cartoon drawings. This was obviously not
an option for *Doctor Who*, and so the original
Macra were built as real, very large, solid props.
(Or, rather – because of the expense – just one
prop! The effect of there being many Macra was
achieved through clever editing.) The Macra prop
was so big and unwieldy that it was fitted to the
back of a van, so it could be moved round the studio.
Its claws and appendages were operated by an actor
inside the Macra.

By the time *Gridlock* was made, digital-effects house
The Mill had already proved how effective a totally
computer-generated creature could be. The Beast
from *The Satan Pit* (see page 30) was achieved
entirely through computer-generated imagery (CGI), and
The Mill rose magnificently to the challenge of creating a
horde of giant crab monsters to threaten the Doctor and
his friends once more.

# THE MACRA TERROR

Written by
**Ian Stuart Black**
Featuring
**the Second Doctor,
Ben, Polly and Jamie**
First broadcast
**11 March–1 April
1967
4 episodes**

The Doctor and his friends arrive on an apparently idyllic colony world. They are welcomed warmly by the colonists, but a voice then speaks to the travellers as they sleep, brainwashing them.

The whole colony is actually controlled by the Macra, who have conditioned the colonists to mine the gas they need to survive. Jamie is sent down the mines – and becomes the first person ever to escape. Ben, meanwhile, is entirely under the influence of the Macra, and even betrays his friends, until the Doctor is able to break his conditioning.

The Doctor manages to expose the truth to the colonists, and the Macra are defeated when the Doctor destroys the gas pumps.

### THE COLONY

The unnamed colony seems idyllic, but underneath this exterior lurks a terrible secret. The 'Controller' is in fact a frail old man, enslaved and controlled himself by the hideous Macra. The colonists have been brainwashed to serve the Macra and mine the gas they need. Anyone who throws off this conditioning, or who is foolish enough to wander out into the colony at night, is killed or taken for 'correction' at the hospital.

Once released from the Macra's mind control, the colonists realise how they have been manipulated.

### THE GAS

The Macra have subverted the colony so that it now exists solely to produce gas for them to survive.

The colonists have been brainwashed to believe that they depend on the gas themselves, and work constantly to mine and refine it.

The colony is located over rock that is rich in a type of salt which generates the gases the Macra need.

These same gases are poisonous to the human colonists, however, who cannot survive for long in the mines without special goggles and breathing masks.

### THE PILOT

In charge of the day-to-day running of the colony, the Pilot is one of the few people who knows the formula of the gas the Macra need. Like everyone else in the colony, he is under the influence of the Macra, and is constantly reciting feel-good phrases such as 'Hard work never hurt anybody', 'Nothing succeeds like success', and 'If at first you don't succeed, try, try again'.

Despite his conditioning, the Pilot's inclination is to be fair and uphold justice in the colony, even before the Doctor shows him the truth about the Macra.

 # GRIDLOCK

The Doctor takes his new friend Martha Jones to New Earth in the year five billion and fifty-three, to show her the far-distant future of humanity. But they arrive in the Undercity, where the citizens struggle to survive in harsh conditions and use patches to heighten their emotions. The whole airborne traffic system is almost at a standstill and Martha is kidnapped by motorists who want to move into the faster 'car share' lane.

Something is stirring in the depths of the Undercity: giant Macra are attacking the cars and dragging away motorists. The Doctor struggles to rescue Martha, but finds himself taken by Novice Hame to meet the Face of Boe, who has a final message to deliver…

Written by
**Russell T Davies**
Featuring
**the Tenth Doctor,
and Martha**
First broadcast
**14 April 2007
1 episode**

### NEW NEW YORK

By the time the Doctor and Martha visit New New York, it is a dying city. The ruling Senate has died – killed by a mutated version of a drug called 'Bliss'. Now the whole city is at a standstill, with traffic gridlocked and taking years to travel just a few miles.

Without power, the Undercity would long since have fallen into the sea, and the Doctor is able to use the last reserves to open the roof of the motorway tunnel. The trapped motorists are able to escape the gridlock to repopulate and revitalise their city.

### THE FACE OF BOE

When the Senate was killed and the city of New New York started to die, it was the Face of Boe who saved it. He sacrificed himself for the city by wiring himself into the city mainframe to keep it running using his own life force.

But the Face is dying from the effort, and is desperate to speak to the Doctor. There is a legend that, when the Face of Boe dies, the sky will crack asunder – which it does for the motorists when the Doctor opens the tunnel roof. It is also said that he will speak one last secret, to a homeless, wandering traveller.

### NOVICE HAME

Once one of the Sisters of Plenitude that ran the huge medical facility outside New New York, Novice Hame now acts as nurse to the dying Face of Boe. She regards this as her penance for past sins, and stays with the Face through the years that he keeps the city alive.

When the mutated virus killed the Senators, the Face of Boe kept Novice Hame safe by shrouding her in protective smoke. He sends her to rescue the Doctor from the gridlock, knowing the Doctor is the only person who can save the city as the Face dies.

## 🌐 BUILDING NEW NEW YORK

As well as the terrifying Macra, digital-effects house The Mill also had to create the images of the New New York skyline. They had already provided views of New New York for the previous year's episode, *New Earth*, and built on this work to create new vistas and backgrounds. Some of the original footage from *New Earth* was reused, playing as scanner images when the Doctor and Martha arrive in the Undercity. The Mill also created the massive traffic jam of air cars on the New New York underground motorway, and added live-action characters, such as the Doctor, to these digital images.

A further challenge was the creation of the vast Senate Chamber, complete with rotting skeletons for the dead senators. Again, these digital images had to be blended with live-action sequences, featuring the Doctor, Martha, Novice Hame and the Face of Boe.

A renegade Time Lord, the Master has been the Doctor's rival and enemy for many years. Once they were friends – they were even at school together. In fact, the two Time Lords – the last two Time Lords – have a lot in common. Both left their home planet of Gallifrey, though while the Doctor wanted to explore the universe, the Master wanted to rule it. A psychopathic megalomaniac, the Master craves power and has no regard at all for the lives of other life forms.

During the Great Time War, the Master – like the Doctor – returned to help his own people against the Daleks. But when the Dalek Emperor took control of the Cruciform, the Master fled. He hid away even from himself – taking on human form, just as the Doctor did when he hid from the Family of Blood. But once he was reborn as the Master, he wasted no time setting out to defeat his old enemy the Doctor…

## TERROR OF THE AUTONS

Written by **Robert Holmes**
Featuring **the Third Doctor, Jo and UNIT**
First broadcast **2–23 January 1971** **4 episodes**

While exiled on 20th-century Earth, the Doctor learns that his old enemy the Master has arrived – and is helping the Nestenes plot to invade Earth (See The Autons, page 17).

## THE MIND OF EVIL

Written by **Don Houghton**
Featuring **the Third Doctor, Jo and UNIT**
First broadcast **30 January–6 March 1971** **6 episodes**

The Doctor is suspicious of Professor Keller's new technique for rehabilitating hardened criminals. Keller is in fact the Master, using an alien mind parasite to sabotage a peace conference and set the world at war…

## THE CLAWS OF AXOS

Written by **Bob Baker & Dave Martin**
Featuring **the Third Doctor, Jo and UNIT**
First broadcast **13 March–3 April 1971** **4 episodes**

Axos comes to Earth – apparently in peace, but actually brought by the Master. Axos offers mankind a wonder-molecule, Axonite, but plans to drain all energy from the planet (see The Axons, page 26).

## COLONY IN SPACE

Written by **Malcolm Hulke**
Featuring **the Third Doctor, Jo and UNIT**
First broadcast **10 April–15 May 1971** **6 episodes**

An Adjudicator sent to resolve a dispute between colonists and the Interplanetary Mining Corporation is actually the Master – hunting for a terrible doomsday weapon concealed on the planet…

## THE DÆMONS

Written by **Guy Leopold**
Featuring **the Third Doctor, Jo and UNIT**
First broadcast **22 May–19 June 1971** **5 episodes**

The Doctor and UNIT are confronted by a creature of immense power that looks like the devil incarnate, which has been summoned by the local vicar – who turns out to be the Master (see The Dæmons, page 78).

## THE SEA DEVILS

Written by **Malcolm Hulke**
⊕ Featuring **the Third Doctor and Jo**
⊕ First broadcast **26 February–1 April 1972** ⊕ **6 episodes**

From an isolated island prison, the Master is reviving intelligent underwater reptiles from prehistory and offering to help them reclaim their planet from the human race (see The Silurians and Sea Devils, page 268).

## THE TIME MONSTER

Written by **Robert Sloman**
⊕ Featuring **the Third Doctor, Jo and UNIT**
⊕ First broadcast **20 May–24 June 1972** ⊕ **6 episodes**

TOMTIT is a new process that manipulates the gaps between particles of time. But its inventor, Professor Thascales, is the Master – who plans to summon Chronos, the terrible creature that destroyed ancient Atlantis…

## FRONTIER IN SPACE

Written by **Malcolm Hulke**
⊕ Featuring **the Third Doctor and Jo**
⊕ First broadcast **24 February–31 March 1973** ⊕ **6 episodes**

Working for the Daleks, the Master is using Ogrons to attack the spaceships of Earth and Draconia and so provoke a war between the two empires (see The Ogrons and Draconians, page 223).

## THE DEADLY ASSASSIN

Written by **Robert Holmes**
⊕ Featuring **the Fourth Doctor**
⊕ First broadcast **30 October–20 November 1976** ⊕ **4 episodes**

Having exhausted all his regenerations, an emaciated, dying Master returns to Gallifrey. He frames the Doctor for the assassination of the Time Lord President…

## THE KEEPER OF TRAKEN

Written by **Johnny Byrne**
⊕ Featuring **the Fourth Doctor, Adric and Nyssa**
⊕ First broadcast **31 January–21 February 1981** ⊕ **4 episodes**

Still searching for a way to extend his life, the Master manipulates the peaceful people of Traken from a statue called Melkur – in fact, his TARDIS. Defeated, he manages to obtain a new body…

## LOGOPOLIS

Written by **Christopher H. Bidmead**
Featuring **the Fourth Doctor, Adric, Nyssa and Tegan**
First broadcast **28 February–21 March 1981** **4 episodes**

Without Logopolis, entropy would take hold and the universe would die…
But the Master sabotages Logopolis and hold the universe to ransom. The
Doctor repairs the damage – but it costs him his life!

## CASTROVALVA

Written by **Christopher H. Bidmead**
Featuring **the Fifth Doctor, Adric, Nyssa and Tegan**
First broadcast **4–12 January 1982** **4 episodes**

A newly regenerated Doctor goes to Castrovalva to recuperate. But the
entire community is a complex space-time trap set up by the Master to
defeat the Doctor. Castrovalva itself doesn't even exist…

## TIME-FLIGHT

Written by **Peter Grimwade**
Featuring **the Fifth Doctor, Nyssa and Tegan**
First broadcast **22–31 March 1982** **4 episodes**

A British Airways Concorde disappears – taken back
to prehistoric times. The Doctor follows to rescue the
passengers and defeat the Master and the Xeraphin…

## THE KING'S DEMONS

Written by **Terence Dudley**
Featuring **the Fifth Doctor, Tegan, Turlough and Kamelion**
First broadcast **15–16 March 1983** **2 episodes**

The Doctor meets King John. But the king is really a
shape-changing android called Kamelion, controlled by the
Master, who plans to sabotage the signing of Magna Carta.

## THE FIVE DOCTORS

Written by **Terrance Dicks**
Featuring **the first five Doctors**
First UK broadcast **25 November 1983** **1 feature-length episode**

The Doctors are taken to Gallifrey's Death Zone, where they have
to fight their way past alien threats to reach the Dark Tower of
Rassilon and discover its secret (see page 60).

## PLANET OF FIRE

Written by **Peter Grimwade**
⊛ Featuring **the Fifth Doctor, Turlough and Peri**
⊛ First broadcast **23 February–2 March 1984** ⊛ **4 episodes**

Kamelion is possessed by the Master, and brings the TARDIS to Sarn. The Master needs Kamelion's help as he has accidentally miniaturised himself while experimenting with his tissue compression eliminator.

## THE MARK OF THE RANI

Written by **Pip & Jane Baker**
⊛ Featuring **the Sixth Doctor and Peri**
⊛ First broadcast **2–9 February 1985** ⊛ **2 episodes**

The Master attempts to join forces with the Rani. She is on Earth to collect a human brain fluid that controls sleep, to keep her subjects docile. The Doctor must defeat them both (see The Rani, page 256).

## THE TRIAL OF A TIME LORD

Written by **Robert Holmes, Philip Martin and Pip & Jane Baker**
⊛ Featuring **the Sixth Doctor, Peri and Mel**
⊛ First broadcast **6 September–6 December 1986** ⊛ **14 episodes**

The Doctor is put on trial by the Time Lords for interfering in the affairs of other races. Help comes from the Master, who appears as an unlikely self-appointed witness for the Doctor's defence!

## SURVIVAL

Written by **Rona Munro**
⊛ Featuring **the Seventh Doctor and Ace**
⊛ First broadcast **22 November–6 December 1989** ⊛ **3 episodes**

The Master is trapped on the planet of the Cheetah People. Infected by the environment, he is slowly becoming one of the feline race. His only hope of escape is the Doctor…

## DOCTOR WHO – THE TV MOVIE

Written by **Mathew Jacobs**
⊛ Featuring **the Eighth Doctor, Grace and Chang**
⊛ First UK broadcast **27 May 1996** ⊛ **1 movie-length episode**

The Doctor is summoned to collect the remains of the Master, who has been executed by the Daleks. But the Master is not dead, and he steals a human body in San Francisco at the end of the millennium…

 # UTOPIA

With Captain Jack clinging to the outside, the TARDIS takes the Doctor and Martha to the very end of the universe – and the planet Malcassairo. Here, under the guidance of Professor Yana, a small group of human survivors has constructed a huge rocketship to take them in search of Utopia. Utopia was said to be out towards the Wildlands of space – beyond the Condensate Wilderness and close to the Darkmatter Reefs.

But the arrival of the Doctor and his friends awakens old memories – an old personality – hidden deep within Professor Yana's mind… Reborn as the Doctor's ancient enemy the Master, he kills his companion Chantho and steals the Doctor's TARDIS – regenerating into a younger form…

Written by
**Russell T Davies**
Featuring
**the Tenth Doctor, Martha and Captain Jack**
First broadcast
**16 June 2007**
**1 episode**

## THE FUTUREKIND

Futurekind are the mutated savages that the human race might become if it degenerates. They have fanged teeth, paint their bodies, and hunt anything they can eat. The Doctor, Martha and Captain Jack arrive to witness a manhunt and are soon caught up in it themselves, but they manage to save the man being chased.

The human survivors on Malcassairo shelter inside a huge silo, where they have built their rocketship. But as the ship departs, leaving the Doctor, Captain Jack and Martha behind with the Master, the Futurekind break in…

## CHANTHO

Last survivor of the insectoid Malmooth race on the distant planet of Malcassairo far in the future, Chantho is Professor Yana's assistant in the rocketship project. She adores Yana and will not leave Malcassairo without him. Every time she speaks, she prefixes each sentence with 'Chan' and ends it with 'Tho'.

Chantho is present when Yana opens his pocketwatch and is reborn as the Master. The Master has no qualms about killing his former friend. But Chantho's dying act is to shoot the Master – forcing him to regenerate into a new body.

## HIDING FROM THE TIME WAR

When the Dalek Emperor took control of the Cruciform in the Great Time War, the Master fled. He disguised himself as a human, using a Chameleon arch to lock his memories and personality away. Reborn as Yana, he believes he was found as a child on the coast of the Silver Devastation, with only a fobwatch…

It may be coincidence, or destiny, that the message the dying Face of Boe gives the Doctor is: 'You Are Not Alone' – the initials of which spell YANA. Or, if Captain Jack really becomes the Face of Boe, then perhaps it is a deliberate clue…

### THE MASTER REBORN

After being shot by his erstwhile companion Chantho, the Master regenerates into a younger form. The effect of the regeneration looked just like the regeneration from the Ninth to the Tenth Doctor (and the Tenth Doctor's later regeneration).

In the case of the Master, footage of actor Derek Jacobi as the older, Professor Yana incarnation of the Master was recorded first. This was then mixed with footage of the younger Harold Saxon incarnation of the Master played by actor John Simm. With digital effects for the fiery glow added by The Mill, the illusion is complete – and the Master regenerates into a new body at last…

The Master calls the aliens he brings to Earth 'the Toclafane', but the Doctor knows that this is a name from Time Lord mythology.

The Toclafane are technologically advanced spheres, each about the size of a football, speaking in sing-song voices like naughty children. They hover and fly through the air and can emit pulses of energy as well as using knives and cutting tools that slide out from their round casings.

They appear to be mechanical, but when Martha manages to open a Toclafane sphere she discovers that inside is a withered, disembodied human head plugged into the mechanisms. This is what the human race will become in order to survive on Utopia trillions of years in the future. They have been brought back to the present day by the Master to conquer the Earth and rule over their own ancient ancestors.

## FULLY ROUNDED DESIGN

These design drawings show how the Toclafane spheres open and how they deploy their weaponry. All except one of the Toclafane themselves were computer-generated images created by The Mill.

**FINGERS DEPLOYED**

**ATTACK MODE**

## THE SOUND OF DRUMS and LAST OF THE TIME LORDS

Written by
**Russell T Davies**
Featuring
**the Tenth Doctor,
Martha and Captain Jack**
First broadcast
**23–30 June 2007
2 episodes**

New Prime Minister Harold Saxon is in fact the Master, who returned to Earth in the Doctor's TARDIS 18 months before the Doctor met Martha. 'Saxon' assassinates his cabinet, and then claims to have made contact with benevolent aliens – the Toclafane. He sets up a meeting with them on the *Valiant* attended by himself and the President of the USA.

But it's a trap. The Toclafane kill the President, then billions of them appear to wipe out a tenth of the Earth's population. For a year, the Master rules Earth, building a fleet of war rockets to conquer other worlds. He holds the Doctor prisoner, ageing him into a small wizened creature… It is up to Martha to organise resistance and mobilise the people of Earth.

### THE VALIANT

A huge flying aircraft carrier designed by the Master and under the command of UNIT, the *Valiant* is the venue for the first meeting between the human race and the alien Toclafane in the early years of the 21st century.

While the *Valiant* is usually kept in high-altitude flight, even when being serviced and repaired, it is brought close to ground level during the attempted Sontaran invasion (see The Sontarans, page 288).

The *Valiant* is later destroyed during the initial Dalek attack in *The Stolen Earth* (see page 122).

### FACING THE VORTEX

Before a Time Lord novice entered the Academy on Gallifrey, the young child was made to look into the Untempered Schism. This was a rip in the fabric of space and time – a view into the awesome and terrible beauty of the Time Vortex itself…

Different novice Time Lords reacted in different ways to the experience. Some it inspired to greatness, some it drove insane. It was the catalyst that eventually persuaded the Doctor to flee Gallifrey. The Master was driven mad by the experience – forever hearing an insistent drumbeat inside his damaged mind…

### WHO IS MR SAXON?

Harold Saxon is a myth. The Master gave himself a fictional background – a childhood, schooling, a degree from Cambridge University, athletic prowess, a successful business career before entering politics… He even wrote a novel, *Kiss Me, Kill Me*. While working on this book he met his future wife – Lucy Saxon.

One of the few people unaffected by the Master's mesmeric influence was journalist Vivien Rook, who discovered that Harry Saxon had no real past. When she tried to warn Lucy, who already knew the truth, the Master had her killed.

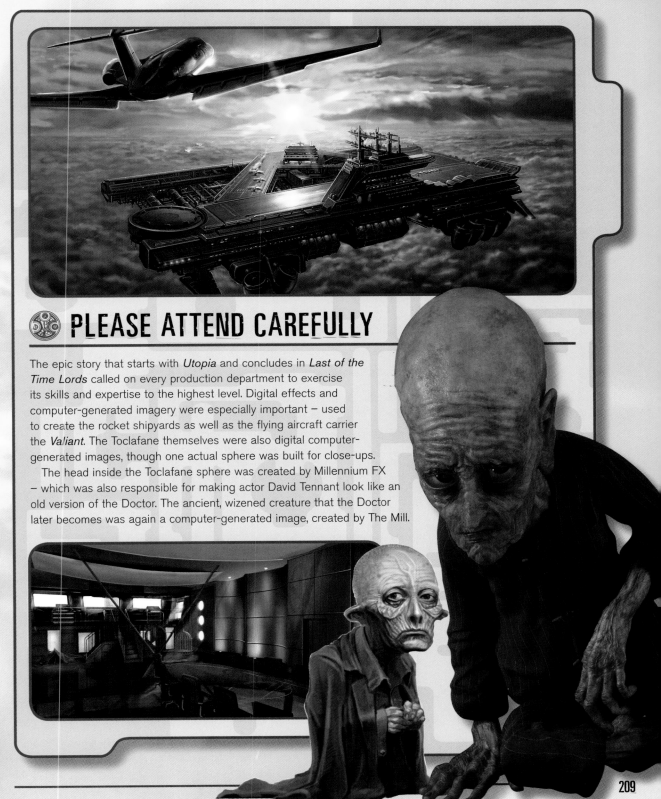

## PLEASE ATTEND CAREFULLY

The epic story that starts with *Utopia* and concludes in *Last of the Time Lords* called on every production department to exercise its skills and expertise to the highest level. Digital effects and computer-generated imagery were especially important – used to create the rocket shipyards as well as the flying aircraft carrier the *Valiant*. The Toclafane themselves were also digital computer-generated images, though one actual sphere was built for close-ups.

The head inside the Toclafane sphere was created by Millennium FX – which was also responsible for making actor David Tennant look like an old version of the Doctor. The ancient, wizened creature that the Doctor later becomes was again a computer-generated image, created by The Mill.

Midnight is a planet of contrasts. The landscape is beautiful – the rocks and mountains are made of diamonds, glittering under a blazing sun. But the sun is X-tonic, emitting raw galvanic radiation. Any living thing – carbon-based, or hydrogen-based, even silicates or gas-beings – exposed to its light for just a fraction of a second without protection, will burn up. Vaporise.

The only place where life can survive is inside the amazing Leisure Palace, a fantastic complex of large glass bubbles on the surface of Midnight. It is a luxury hotel and health resort built out of X-tonic-resistant materials and shipped to Midnight in pre-constructed sections. The windows are made from reinforced finito-glass that is over four metres thick. Facilities include swimming pools, gyms, shops, bars, and also the famous antigravity restaurant (bibs provided). You can witness the beauty of Midnight's surface at closer hand on an organised tour – safely shut away inside an armoured Crusader vehicle.

But there are rumours – stories of a shadow glimpsed against the diamond rocks… Of a dark shape seen running across the glittering landscape… Of an entity that can eat its way into the brain and take over the speech of its host… That can steal your voice, and then maybe your thoughts… Creeping into your head, whispering in your mind, turning you against your friends…

 # MIDNIGHT

Leaving Donna to relax at the Leisure Palace, the Doctor goes on the Crusader 50 tour. But the vehicle breaks down en route to the Sapphire Waterfall. The stranded passengers and crew hear a knocking from outside. Yet nothing can survive on the surface of Midnight – or can it?

The knocking stops, but one of the passengers, a woman called Sky, has been possessed by something and repeats everything anyone says. Soon she is speaking at the same time as the others. She fixes on the Doctor as her target and pre-empts his speech before stealing his voice completely…

The Midnight Entity is destroyed by the tour Hostess – who ejects herself and Sky out of the vehicle to be vaporised in the X-tonic sunlight…

Written by
**Russell T Davies**
Featuring
**the Tenth Doctor and Donna**
First broadcast
**14 June 2008**
**1 episode**

### THE SAPPHIRE WATERFALL

Although the planet's surface is lethal, it is possible to view Midnight's spectacular bejewelled landscape for short periods through finito-glass. Organised tours visit some of the most spectacular sights.

One of these is the famous Sapphire Waterfall. The sapphire itself is actually a massive compound silica with iron pigmentation, which slowly shatters as it reaches the Cliffs of Oblivion on the Multi-Faceted Coast…

The round-trip journey from the Leisure Palace takes eight hours in the Crusader 50. On-tour entertainment is provided.

### CRUSADER 50 PASSENGERS

The Crusader 50 can carry up to 24 passengers, but the trip to the Sapphire Waterfall is rather undersubscribed. The passengers trapped with the Doctor include Mrs Sky Sylvestry – who is possessed by the Midnight Entity.

Also on board are Professor Winfold Hobbes – an expert on Midnight – and his student assistant Dee Dee Blasco. Hobbes is making his 14th trip to the Sapphire Waterfall. The final passengers are the Cane family – Biff and his wife Val are on holiday with their (bored) teenage son, Jethro.

### THE CRUSADER 50 CREW

The vehicle's driver is Joe, although most of the systems – including navigation and detour-planning – are automatic. The trainee mechanic is Claude, who has no idea what has caused the engine failure that strands them. Both Joe and Claude are killed when the drive-cabin is ripped from the main vehicle.

The Hostess is responsible for the safety and comfort of the passengers. The Doctor is mortified to realise that no one aboard knows the name of the woman who saves them all at the cost of her own life…

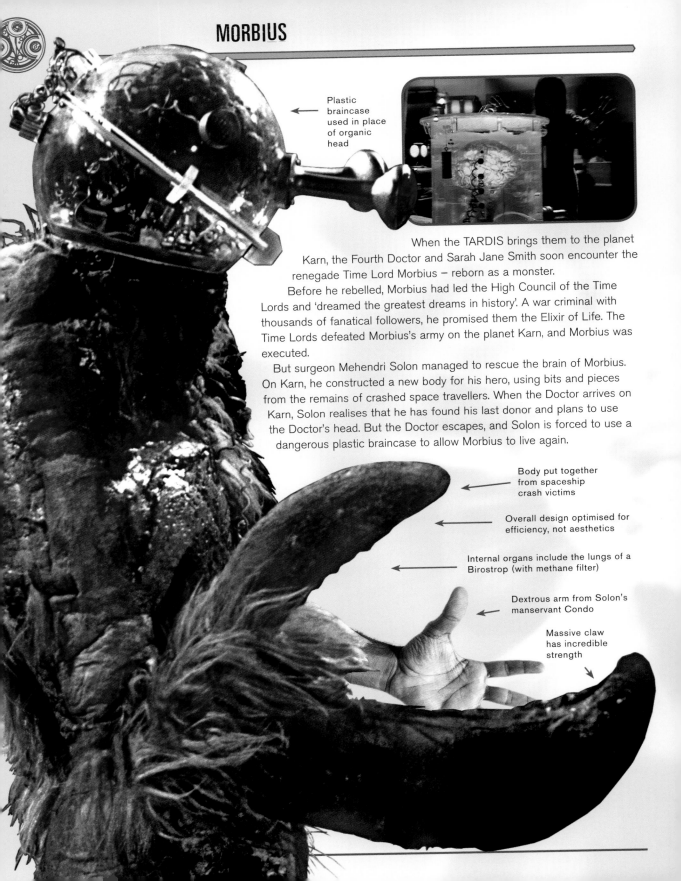

Plastic braincase used in place of organic head

When the TARDIS brings them to the planet Karn, the Fourth Doctor and Sarah Jane Smith soon encounter the renegade Time Lord Morbius – reborn as a monster.

Before he rebelled, Morbius had led the High Council of the Time Lords and 'dreamed the greatest dreams in history'. A war criminal with thousands of fanatical followers, he promised them the Elixir of Life. The Time Lords defeated Morbius's army on the planet Karn, and Morbius was executed.

But surgeon Mehendri Solon managed to rescue the brain of Morbius. On Karn, he constructed a new body for his hero, using bits and pieces from the remains of crashed space travellers. When the Doctor arrives on Karn, Solon realises that he has found his last donor and plans to use the Doctor's head. But the Doctor escapes, and Solon is forced to use a dangerous plastic braincase to allow Morbius to live again.

Body put together from spaceship crash victims

Overall design optimised for efficiency, not aesthetics

Internal organs include the lungs of a Birostrop (with methane filter)

Dextrous arm from Solon's manservant Condo

Massive claw has incredible strength

 # THE BRAIN OF MORBIUS

The TARDIS is drawn to the planet Karn, where the renegade Time Lord Morbius was executed. The Doctor and Sarah Jane meet Solon, who drugs the Doctor, planning to take his head for the creature he has made to house the salvaged brain of Morbius. Before Solon can operate, the Doctor is 'rescued' by the Sisterhood of Karn. They believe he has been sent by the Time Lords to steal their Elixir of Life, and plan to execute him.

The Doctor manages to convince the Sisterhood that Solon has kept Morbius's brain. Solon is forced to use an artificial braincase, but static electricity builds up in the cranial cavity, driving Morbius mad. Fleeing from the Sisterhood, he falls over a cliff to his death.

Written by
**Robin Bland**
Featuring
**the Fourth Doctor and Sarah Jane**
First broadcast
**3–24 January 1976**
**4 episodes**

### THE SISTERHOOD

The Sisterhood worship the Flame of Life which provides them with the Elixir that gives them immortality. They are led by Maren, who was already old when the Elixir was discovered. The Sisters live for ever, and have formidable mental powers -- which they use to crash passing spaceships onto the surface of the planet in case they have come to Karn to steal the Elixir.

Until Morbius, only the Time Lord High Council knew of the Elixir and since the Time of the Stones the Sisterhood have shared the Elixir with them.

### CONDO

Solon rescued his servant Condo from the wreck of a Dravidian Starliner. He told Condo he had to amputate his arm to save his life after the crash. But in fact, Solon has given the arm to the creature he has created to house the brain of Morbius.

Condo is loyal, but lacking in mental ability. He is highly emotional – falling in love with Sarah Jane when she is blinded, and threatening to kill his master when Solon offers him to the Sisterhood.

When he discovers what Solon has done with his arm, he is enraged and Solon is forced to shoot him.

### MORBIUS'S REBELLION

As Time Lord President, Morbius tried to go against their most basic philosophy and rule other peoples and other worlds. He raised an army from other races, promising them the gift of eternal life to be provided by the Elixir of the Sisterhood of Karn.

Morbius and his army were finally defeated on Karn by the Time Lords. Tried as a criminal, Morbius was executed by vaporisation, his body dispersed to the nine corners of the universe. But, somehow, Solon managed to rescue his brain…

## VISITING NEW EARTH

By the year five billion and twenty-three, with the original Earth abandoned and destroyed when the sun expanded, the human race has adopted a planet in the galaxy M87 as 'New Earth' – a new home, to satisfy humanity's nostalgia for the old planet.

In many ways, New Earth resembles the original. There is water, blue sky… and corruption. But there are also several moons, and apple-grass grows in the meadows. The massive new mega-cities – like New New York (actually the fifteenth version of the city) – sprawl across the planet's surface.

The Catkind Sisters of Plenitude run the planet's most advanced medical facility, just outside New New York.

# NEW EARTH

Written by
**Russell T Davies**
Featuring
**the Tenth Doctor
and Rose**
First broadcast
**15 April 2006
1 episode**

Arriving on New Earth in response to a message the Doctor receives on his psychic paper, the Doctor and Rose visit a huge hospital complex run by the Catkind Sisters of Plenitude. The message is from the Face of Boe, who seems to be dying, despite the help of the Sisters.

Rose meets another old acquaintance – Cassandra – alive and well, and out for revenge. While Cassandra implants her consciousness inside Rose's body, the Doctor discovers that the miracle treatments the Sisters offer come at a price – a price the Doctor believes is too great. The Doctor must battle to restore Rose to her own body, and to save the hospital from the infected 'patients' that the Sisters have created.

### OTHER WORLDS

Rose has been to several alien worlds with the Doctor. In *Boom Town* she mentions Grajick Major, the Glass Deserts of San Kaloon and Justicia (which also features in the novel *The Monsters Inside*). She tells Mickey about Woman Wept – a world that has a continent shaped like a lamenting woman, where the sea froze in a second. Among other worlds the Doctor has mentioned to Rose is Barcelona – a planet where the dogs have no noses, so just how *do* they smell?

### THE PATIENTS

The Sisters of Plenitude hide a terrible secret. In the Intensive Care Unit of the hospital they store sick patients. But these are not people who have caught diseases or been taken ill. They are specially grown humans who have been infected with every known disease, making them living incubators for the cures the Sisters use. Because they are the carriers of the diseases, they do not die from them. The Sisters have experimented with clonemeat and biocattle, but human flesh is the only environment in which the diseases can be cultivated successfully.

The patients are kept in individual sealed booths, fed with pipes bearing nutrients and oxygen... and more disease. They are perpetually unconscious, created only to be ill – the ultimate research laboratory. They are not as insensitive and ignorant as the Sisters believe. But the policy of Matron Casp is to incinerate any of these patients who show signs of real, thinking life.

Once released by Cassandra, the patients want only to be loved – to be wanted, to be hugged. But in the sterile atmosphere, their very touch is fatal, and it is up to the Doctor to devise a cure while staying away from them long enough to administer it...

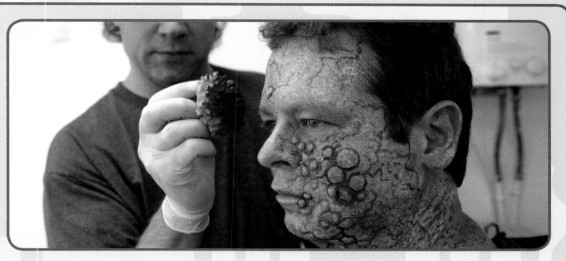

 # INFECTING THE PATIENTS

The infected Patients kept in the 'Intensive Care' Unit by the Sisters were created using a combination of prosthetics and conventional make-up techniques. While they were to appear horrific, the Patients are tragic, sympathetic characters in the story and not really monsters as such, so they needed to appear grotesque without being overtly monstrous.

Another consideration the production team had was that, given the age range of the audience, they did not want the make-up to be too horrific or extreme for younger and more sensitive viewers. So the initial design ideas were toned down to avoid showing blood or open wounds, or too much gory red. Getting the right balance and making the Patients frightening without being horrific was a difficult challenge, but one that the prosthetics, make-up and costume design teams rose to magnificently, as the images on this page show.

## SCRIPT EXTRACT

FX: WIDE SHOT, the Doctor and Rose's gantry just one level of many; rows above, rows below, connected by metal staircases. Booth after booth after booth, very Borg ship.

CUT TO the Doctor, using the sonic screwdriver on a booth's locking bolt. Click!, and he heaves the door open.

The PATIENT is a sick Human. Wearing a simple, dirty-grey tunic. Every inch of skin is flaky, mottled, dirty, wet. Immobile, but the eyes are alive, scared.

# THE HOSPITAL

The huge medical facility outside New New York is run by the Sisters of Plenitude. They are Catkind who have taken a lifelong vow to help others and to minister to and heal the sick. Humanity poses a challenge for them, as humans are afflicted with so many diseases.

Within the hospital, the Sisters can miraculously cure even the most virulent and previously untreatable diseases and conditions. These include:

**Petrifold Regression** – in which the patient literally turns to stone

**Marconi's Disease** – treated on New Earth using a unique cell-washing cascade

**Pallidome Pancrosis** – which usually kills the victim within ten minutes.

There is even a unit specialising in nano-dentistry. But the one thing the Sisters of Plenitude cannot cure is old age.

And, as the Doctor discovers, the treatments the Sisters administer are based on a terrible, dark secret that festers at the heart of their hospital…

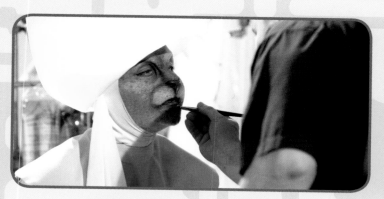

## MAKING THE SISTERS

The original designs for the faces of the Sisters of Plenitude were painted over photographs of the actresses chosen to play the roles. Millennium FX made the final masks, based on an agreed design, using a process that punches tiny filaments of flock-like material through a thin latex face mask. They took a mould of each actress's face, and individually tailored the masks to fit.

The finished products were then fixed in position and blended with make-up to create the final impressive appearance of the cat people. The masks themselves were so thin and delicate that they could only be used once – the process of removing the mask at the end of the day in effect destroyed it. So a new mask was needed for each character every day.

### SCRIPT EXTRACT

NUNS – The SISTERS OF PLENITUDE – glide to and fro, in flowing cream robes and formal headgear, their faces concealed behind veils…

SISTERS are hurrying towards him, led by MATRON CASP. As she approaches, she lifts her veil. The Sisters are CATS; beautiful, but with that cool feline archness, too.

# OGRI

A silicon life form from the planet Ogros in Tau Ceti, the Ogri are sentient rocks. They feed on the amino acids and proteins that exist in the swamps on Ogros, the nearest equivalent on Earth being blood.

Brought to Earth by the villainous Cessair of Diplos, several Ogri have become part of the mysterious stone circle called the Nine Travellers, which explains why there are now more than nine stones in all. The Ogri have been active for a while – crushing the unfortunate Doctor Borlaise, who surveyed the stones in 1754.

Cessair keeps the Ogri fed with blood from ritual sacrifices of animals – and humans. As well as absorbing blood poured onto them, the Ogri suck the blood out of anyone who touches them, including two unfortunate campers. The Doctor believes that the Ogri have entered into Earth mythology, with the giants Gog and Magog, and the term 'ogre' all deriving from their name.

Ogri is made of heavy stone

Mistaken for part of the Nine Travellers, a stone circle

Blood can be absorbed through surface

## THE MEGARA

The two Megara who put the Doctor – and later Cessair – on trial appear as flashing, swirling lights. They are justice machines, but with living cells at their core, and they act as combined judge, jury and – if necessary – executioner. Although the Doctor is acting in their interests, by releasing them to complete their duties, the Megara are literal-minded and put him on trial for this misdemeanour.

Being telepathic, the Megara can assess the level of truth in a witness's statement, but are not permitted to read memories to obtain evidence unless the witness is incapable through loss of consciousness, death, or natural stupidity.

# THE STONES OF BLOOD

The Doctor, Romana and K-9 have been sent to find the six segments of the Key to Time for the White Guardian. Tracing a segment to Earth, they meet Professor Rumford, who is studying a strange stone circle. Several of the stones are actually alien Ogri, being fed on blood by a cult that worships a goddess known as the Calleach. The Doctor discovers that the Calleach is, in fact, the alien Cessair of Diplos.

When Romana is taken to a prison ship in hyperspace, the Doctor follows and releases the Megara to try Cessair for her crimes. The Doctor is put on trial, but convinces the Megara that Cessair is guilty. He retrieves the Great Seal of Diplos – the third segment of the Key to Time.

Written by
**David Fisher**
Featuring
**the Fourth Doctor, Romana and K-9**
First broadcast
**28 October–18 November 1978**
**4 episodes**

## PROFESSOR RUMFORD

Professor Emilia Rumford is an expert on Bronze Age sites and is surveying the Nine Travellers. Stubborn and determined, she is initially sceptical of the Doctor and Romana's theories and suggestions. Only after she has been chased by one of the Ogri and found hidden portraits of the various aliases of Cessair of Diplos, does Professor Rumford begin to believe them.

When the Doctor follows Romana into hyperspace, he trusts Professor Rumford and K-9 to operate the equipment that can bring them both back.

## CESSAIR OF DIPLOS

Charged with both murder and the theft of the Great Seal of Diplos, Cessair was kept on a prison ship in hyperspace, to be taken back to Diplos for trial by the Megara justice machines. But Cessair escaped to Earth and assumed a number of identities over the 4,000 years she lived there. Before masquerading as Vivien Fay, Cessair had previously been Mother Superior of the Little Sisters of St Gudula, the reclusive Mrs Trefusis, the Brazilian widow Senora Camara, and the 'wicked Lady Morgana Montcalm', who is said to have murdered her husband on their wedding night.

Tried and found guilty by the Megara following the Doctor's intervention, Cessair is sentenced to perpetual imprisonment – becoming one of the stones in the Nine Travellers. The Ogri she had taken are returned home.

##  GOING IN CIRCLES

As a location for *The Stones of Blood*, the *Doctor Who* production team used a real stone circle – the Rollright Stones, near Chipping Norton in the Cotswolds. Although steeped in legends and myths of its own, the stone circle was not quite what was needed: to become the Nine Travellers, a fake 'altar' stone, as well as two uprights with a plinth, were added, along with the Ogri stones themselves.

There were also several versions of the Nine Travellers. Some scenes – involving the Doctor's near-sacrifice, and the Calleach, for example – were shot in the studios at BBC Television Centre, on a specially constructed replica of the circle. Because the location material was shot on videotape rather than film (which was usually used for location filming), the match between the two is perfect and it's difficult to tell which is which.

An added complication was that, while the Nine Travellers are in the middle of deserted moorland, there is a road running past the Rollright Stones. So visual effects designer Mat Irvine made a model that was used for long shots of the entire circle.

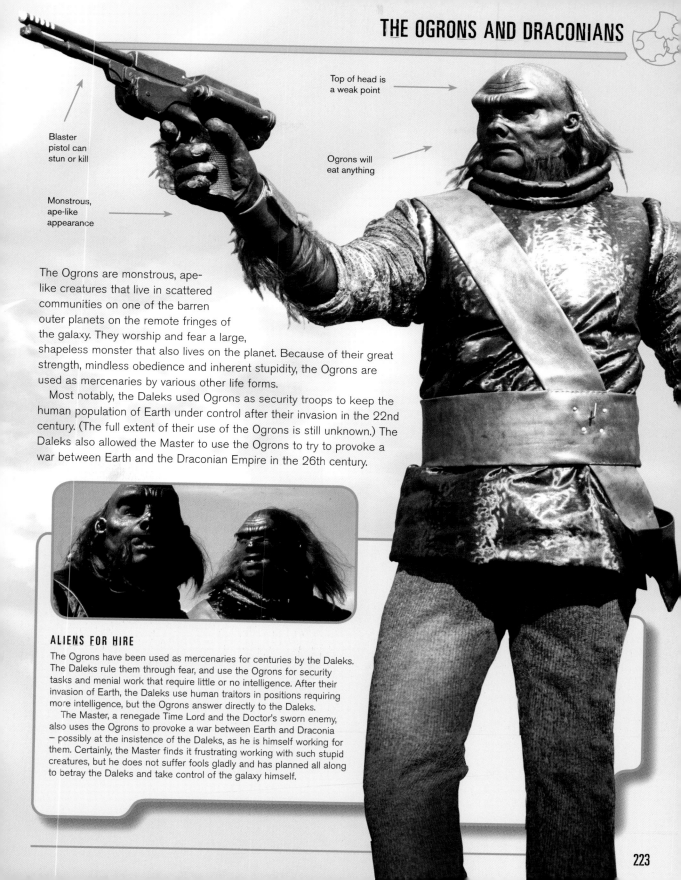

Top of head is
a weak point

Blaster
pistol can
stun or kill

Ogrons will
eat anything

Monstrous,
ape-like
appearance

The Ogrons are monstrous, ape-like creatures that live in scattered communities on one of the barren outer planets on the remote fringes of the galaxy. They worship and fear a large, shapeless monster that also lives on the planet. Because of their great strength, mindless obedience and inherent stupidity, the Ogrons are used as mercenaries by various other life forms.

Most notably, the Daleks used Ogrons as security troops to keep the human population of Earth under control after their invasion in the 22nd century. (The full extent of their use of the Ogrons is still unknown.) The Daleks also allowed the Master to use the Ogrons to try to provoke a war between Earth and the Draconian Empire in the 26th century.

## ALIENS FOR HIRE

The Ogrons have been used as mercenaries for centuries by the Daleks. The Daleks rule them through fear, and use the Ogrons for security tasks and menial work that require little or no intelligence. After their invasion of Earth, the Daleks use human traitors in positions requiring more intelligence, but the Ogrons answer directly to the Daleks.

The Master, a renegade Time Lord and the Doctor's sworn enemy, also uses the Ogrons to provoke a war between Earth and Draconia – possibly at the insistence of the Daleks, as he is himself working for them. Certainly, the Master finds it frustrating working with such stupid creatures, but he does not suffer fools gladly and has planned all along to betray the Daleks and take control of the galaxy himself.

Reptilian humanoids, the Draconians have an empire that rivals and borders that of Earth. Since the terrible war in the 26th century, there has been an uneasy truce between the humans and the Draconians – or 'dragons' as the Earth forces nicknamed them.

The Draconians are ruled by a hereditary emperor, and are a race steeped in honour and tradition. They do not lie, and females are not permitted to speak in the presence of their 'betters', such as the emperor.

There is a legend of a man who came to Draconia during the time of the fifteenth Emperor and saved the Draconians from a great plague that threatened to wipe them out. He came in a strange ship called the TARDIS, and his name was the Doctor.

Traditional greeting is: 'My life at your command.'

Robes are ornate rather than practical

Raised shoulders designate a nobleman

Scaly, reptilian skin

## THE WAR

In 2520, the empires of Earth and Draconia met. The clash of two such different cultures threatened to be a violent one, and so a conference was arranged: two unarmed ships would meet in space. But the Earth ship was damaged in a neutron storm, and as it drifted, helpless, the Draconian ship arrived – a battle cruiser that failed to answer any of the humans' communications.

By a brilliant act of ingenuity, the Earth commander, Williams, destroyed the battle cruiser before it could open fire. The war that followed was a terrible mistake. It was not until twenty years later that Williams discovered the Draconian ship was unarmed and its comms system had been destroyed in the same storm that damaged his ship.

Eventually peace was restored and there were trade treaties and even cultural exchanges between Earth and Draconia … until it seemed to both sides that the other was, again, taking the offensive.

#  DAY OF THE DALEKS

Sir Reginald Styles, the key diplomat at a vital peace conference, is attacked by a man who fades away like a ghost before he can kill Styles. Called in by UNIT to protect Styles, the Doctor and Jo discover that freedom fighters from a future Earth, which the Daleks have invaded, are travelling back in time to try to kill Styles. They believe he sabotaged the conference so that war broke out – all but wiping out humanity and allowing the Daleks to invade, but the Doctor realises that this isn't so.

Escaping from a terrifying, Dalek-dominated world of the future he hurries back to save the peace conference. But the Daleks send a taskforce after him to make sure the peace delegates are exterminated...

Written by
**Louis Marks**
Featuring
**the Third Doctor, UNIT and Jo**
First broadcast
**1–22 January 1970**
**4 episodes**

#  FRONTIER IN SPACE

The Doctor and Jo arrive on a cargo ship as it is attacked. While the human crew, hypnotised by the Master, see the attackers as Draconians, the Doctor and Jo see them as they really are – Ogrons. Jo is accused of being a Draconian agent and imprisoned on Earth, while the Doctor is sent to a penal colony on the moon.

They are both rescued – by the Master – who takes them prisoner, but his ship is intercepted. The Doctor persuades the Draconians that the Master, not the humans, is to blame for attacking their ships. The Master escapes to the Ogrons' planet, but the Doctor follows him – to find that the Master has been provoking war on behalf of the Daleks!

Written by
**Malcolm Hulke**
Featuring
**the Third Doctor and Jo**
First broadcast
**24 February–31 March 1973**
**6 episodes**

# OMEGA

The mask was designed to protect Omega from the corrosive effect of the singularity light beam that powers his world, but the corrosion has already taken place, and beneath the mask he does not exist

Omega is arguably the first-ever Time Lord

Antimatter Gell Guards are directed by Omega's will

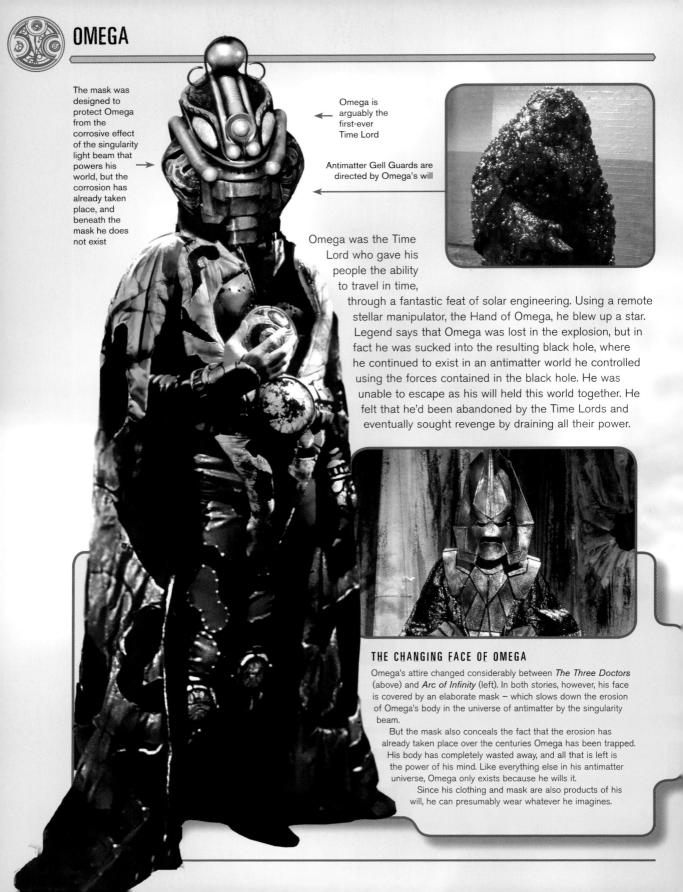

Omega was the Time Lord who gave his people the ability to travel in time, through a fantastic feat of solar engineering. Using a remote stellar manipulator, the Hand of Omega, he blew up a star. Legend says that Omega was lost in the explosion, but in fact he was sucked into the resulting black hole, where he continued to exist in an antimatter world he controlled using the forces contained in the black hole. He was unable to escape as his will held this world together. He felt that he'd been abandoned by the Time Lords and eventually sought revenge by draining all their power.

## THE CHANGING FACE OF OMEGA

Omega's attire changed considerably between *The Three Doctors* (above) and *Arc of Infinity* (left). In both stories, however, his face is covered by an elaborate mask – which slows down the erosion of Omega's body in the universe of antimatter by the singularity beam.

But the mask also conceals the fact that the erosion has already taken place over the centuries Omega has been trapped. His body has completely wasted away, and all that is left is the power of his mind. Like everything else in his antimatter universe, Omega only exists because he wills it.

Since his clothing and mask are also products of his will, he can presumably wear whatever he imagines.

# THE THREE DOCTORS

With their power over time being drained away through a mysterious black hole, the Time Lords send the first two incarnations of the Doctor to help the third investigate. The First Doctor is trapped in a 'time eddy', able only to advise, but the Second and Third Doctors travel through the black hole and battle the renegade Time Lord Omega in a world of antimatter. Omega wants the Doctor to take his place so he can escape from his world. But the Doctors discover that only Omega's will lives on and he cannot leave.

Using the Second Doctor's recorder, which has not been converted into antimatter, the Doctors destroy Omega and his world – granting him the only freedom he could ever have.

Written by
**Bob Baker & Dave Martin**
Featuring
**the First, Second and Third Doctors, Jo and UNIT**
First broadcast
**30 December 1972 –20 January 1973**
**4 episodes**

# ARC OF INFINITY

Omega has somehow managed to survive. In a further attempt to escape, Omega plans to 'bond' with a Time Lord and assume his form in the real universe. To achieve this, he needs the bio-data of a specific Time Lord – the Doctor. To prevent Omega's escape, the Time Lords try to execute the Doctor, but he escapes and unmasks the traitor in the High Council of Time Lords who has been helping Omega.

The Doctor travels to Amsterdam, where he confronts Omega – who is now in the Doctor's form. But the transition is unstable, and Omega's body is deteriorating. Despite feeling sympathy for his old adversary's predicament, the Doctor and his friends are able finally to defeat Omega.

Written by
**Johnny Byrne**
Featuring
**the Fifth Doctor, Nyssa and Tegan**
First broadcast
**3–12 January 1983**
**4 episodes**

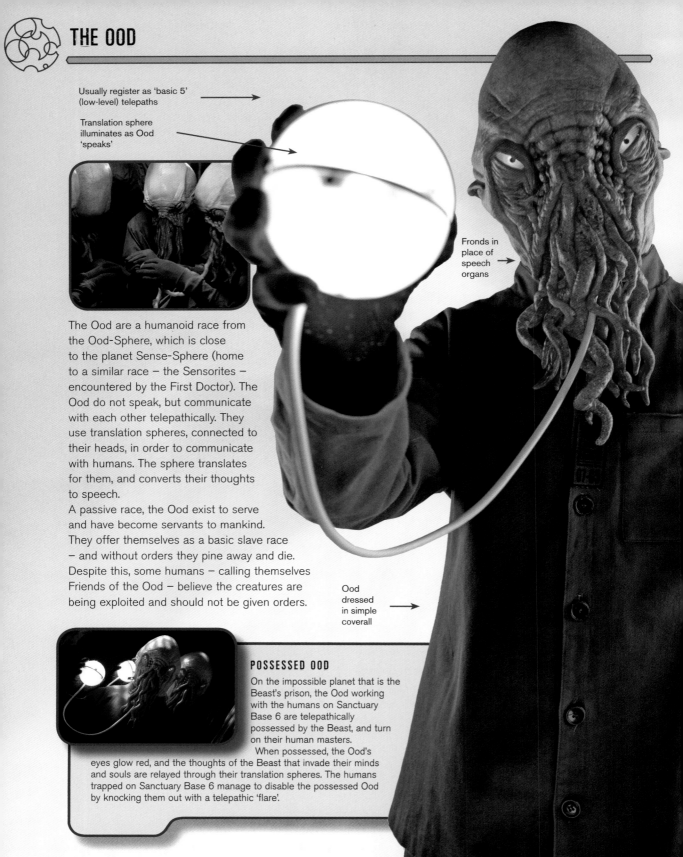

# THE OOD

Usually register as 'basic 5' (low-level) telepaths

Translation sphere illuminates as Ood 'speaks'

Fronds in place of speech organs

The Ood are a humanoid race from the Ood-Sphere, which is close to the planet Sense-Sphere (home to a similar race – the Sensorites – encountered by the First Doctor). The Ood do not speak, but communicate with each other telepathically. They use translation spheres, connected to their heads, in order to communicate with humans. The sphere translates for them, and converts their thoughts to speech.

A passive race, the Ood exist to serve and have become servants to mankind. They offer themselves as a basic slave race – and without orders they pine away and die. Despite this, some humans – calling themselves Friends of the Ood – believe the creatures are being exploited and should not be given orders.

Ood dressed in simple coverall

## POSSESSED OOD

On the impossible planet that is the Beast's prison, the Ood working with the humans on Sanctuary Base 6 are telepathically possessed by the Beast, and turn on their human masters.

When possessed, the Ood's eyes glow red, and the thoughts of the Beast that invade their minds and souls are relayed through their translation spheres. The humans trapped on Sanctuary Base 6 manage to disable the possessed Ood by knocking them out with a telepathic 'flare'.

## THE OOD BRAIN

The truth about Red Eye, and about the Ood themselves, is only revealed when Friends of the Ood finally succeed in infiltrating and sabotaging Ood Operations on the Ood-Sphere.

When the Doctor and Donna arrive on the Ood-Sphere, the Red Eye is taking hold and more and more Ood are turning hostile. But when the Doctor examines 'raw' Ood before they are prepared for sale, he finds that, instead of the interface device for communication, the Ood naturally have a second brain – a hind-brain – which they hold in their hands. Ood Operations remove this before selling the Ood – in effect mentally crippling the creatures and making them willing slaves.

Realising that a creature with a separate forebrain and hind-brain could not survive without a third component in their makeup, the Doctor discovers a secret carefully guarded by the owners of Ood Operations for two centuries – an enormous brain which connects all the Ood together in telepathic harmony. Or rather, it used to – until it was found beneath the northern glacier on the Ood-Sphere, and a psychic barrier was set up to break the connection between the Brain and the Ood…

## ⬡ PLANET OF THE OOD

Written by
**Keith Temple**
Featuring
**the Tenth Doctor
and Donna**
First broadcast
**19 April 2008
1 episode**

The Doctor and Donna's arrival on the icy Ood-Sphere coincides with a visit from the chief executive of Ood Operations, Klineman Halpen. He is concerned that the incidence of 'Red Eye' among the Ood is increasing, and sales are dropping off. Unknown to Halpen, a Friends of the Ood agent has managed to lower the psychic barrier round the Ood Brain hidden in 'Warehouse 15' — causing the Red Eye plague.

Halpen has been secretly fed Ood-graft by his servant Ood Sigma, and finally mutates into an Ood himself. Freed from docile slavery, Oodkind are once more connected to their main Brain and to each other. Free at last — to make their own choices, and to sing.

### OOD OPERATIONS

Set up by the Halpen family to exploit the Ood commercially, Ood Operations has been selling Ood as servants across three galaxies for more than two centuries. The company remains in the control of the Halpen family and continues to keep secret the true nature of the Ood and the existence of the main Ood Brain.

But sales are falling, and the company has been infiltrated by Friends of the Ood — their agent Doctor Ryder turns the psychic barrier down to its minimum setting, allowing the Brain to communicate with the Ood...

### CHIEF EXECUTIVE KLINEMAN HALPEN

Chief Executive of Ood Operations, Klineman Halpen is responsible for exploiting and selling the Ood. Ruthless and determined to make money, he has kept the true nature of the Ood secret and exploited the creatures for profit.

The Halpen family has owned and controlled the company since they discovered the Ood Brain beneath the Northern Glacier of the Ood-Sphere. They moved the brain to Warehouse 15.

But Ood Sigma has been replacing Halpen's hair tonic with Ood-graft — making Halpen mutate into an Ood himself.

### OOD SIGMA

Personal Ood Assistant to Chief Executive Halpen, Ood Sigma seems to be the perfect servant. But he is planning for the liberation of his people, and working towards the day when they will be free. He has replaced Halpen's hair tonic with Ood-graft, which Halpen takes regularly (worried he is going bald). The result is that Klineman Halpen slowly mutates into an Ood.

When the psychic barrier round the Ood Brain is finally deactivated, Ood Sigma, like all his fellow Ood, is once again free to sing...

# BRINGING THE OOD TO LIFE

Originally, the Slitheen were to be with the humans on Sanctuary Base 6, but as the scripts for *The Impossible Planet* and *The Satan Pit* developed, it was felt that a new race of aliens would fit the story better. These episodes were the last to be made in the 2006 series of *Doctor Who*, so budgets were tight. It was up to Millennium FX to produce as many Ood as possible, as cheaply – and quickly – as they could. The fact that the Ood have no visible mouths, are all identical, and wear simple coveralls, helped keep costs down.

Millennium FX made 12 Ood, though computer graphics made it seem that there were more. One of the masks had animatronics built in so that it could change expression. Millennium FX also provided the Ood translation spheres, which lit up when the actor pressed a switch on the back. The Ood ended up being every bit as impressive and 'eerily elegant' as the scripts described them.

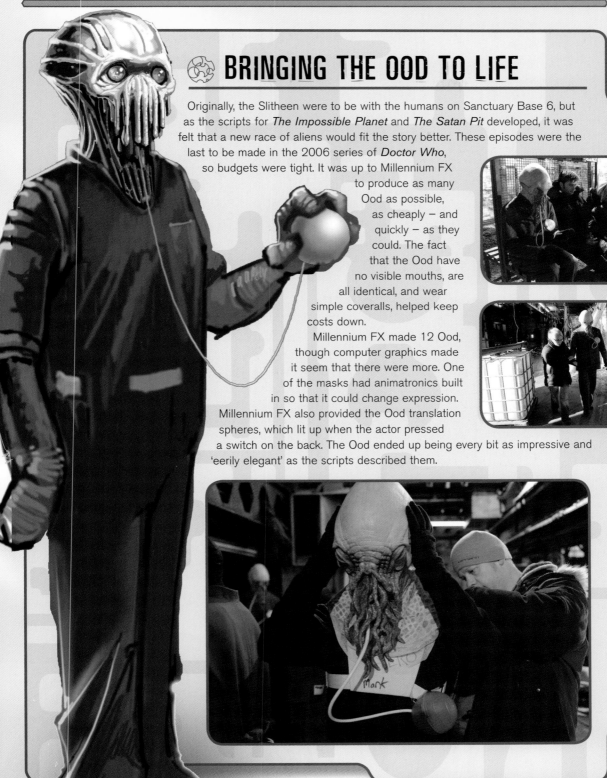

## THE OOD-SPHERE

The snow-covered environment of the Ood-Sphere was actually created in late August, when there was a distinct lack of snow at the location used in South Wales.

To create the illusion of a cold, icy environment, a combination of physical and digital effects was used. Fake snow – largely made from shreds of paper – was used to cover the location. For long shots and to create the impressive snowy vistas of the Ood-Sphere, The Mill added digital matte paintings (DMPs) of the alien landscape.

The Mill also provided the Ood Operations base, Halpen's rocket ship, the giant claw that is used to attack the Doctor, the red eyes of the Ood, the Ood Brain itself (and the psychic barrier surrounding it) and multiplied the number of Ood to make it seem there were more than a dozen.

 ## BECOMING AN OOD

Another key sequence that required a physical effect as well as the expertise of digital-effects house The Mill was the final transformation of Chief Executive Halpen into an Ood. The physical aspects of the transformation consisted of actor Tim McInnerny removing a prosthetic scalp specially sculpted by the Millennium FX company. Beneath the fake scalp was an Ood head…

This effect was enhanced digitally, with the Mill adding the fronds that spew from Halpen's mouth.

The first version of the transformation was a view from the front as the fronds emerge. But this was later reshot from the side so the fronds were seen in profile. For this final version, a stand-in was used instead of Tim McInnerny – 'Best Boy' electrician Peter Chester making his TV debut!

## PLATFORM ONE

When the Earth is finally destroyed by the expanding sun, five billion years in the future, Platform One affords the best view of the event.

The gravity satellites that have protected the deserted Earth from the fire of the sun for millennia have been switched off after funding ran out, and various life forms are gathering to watch 'Earthdeath' (followed by drinks in the platform's Manchester Suite).

Platform One is run by the Steward, an ever-polite and diplomatic blue-skinned Crespallion, determined to ensure that the Earthdeath event goes to plan and that his important guests are well catered for and at ease. He is assisted by a staff of uniformed, diminutive blue-skinned humanoids. But when the Ninth Doctor and his new friend Rose Tyler arrive, a saboteur is already at work: Lady Cassandra – claiming to be the last pure-blood Earth human – is using spindly metal robot spiders to attack the Platform's systems so it will be destroyed when the sun expands.

Cassandra herself is by this time – after years of cosmetic and enhancement surgery, and genetic (and gender) manipulation – little more than a thin piece of skin stretched across a metal frame. Her brain resides in a nutrient tank at the base of the frame (see page 38).

The Doctor is able to save the Platform and thwart Cassandra's plans. But the Earth is destroyed on schedule, burning up as the sun swells to engulf it…

### PLATFORM ART

An immense amount of design work went into the realisation of Platform One. Before the computer-generated model of the space station and its shuttle craft could be started, the whole platform was rigorously designed. Everything was defined – down to where the shuttles would dock, and how the structure of the station would appear glimpsed through windows in the Manchester Suite.

The drawings and painting here show show some of that work and the painstaking amount of detail put into Platform One by both the *Doctor Who* Art Department and effects house The Mill.

## THE END OF THE WORLD

Written by
**Russell T Davies**
Featuring
**the Ninth Doctor
and Rose**
First broadcast
**2 April 2005
1 episode**

The Doctor and Rose join the guests on Platform One to witness the final end of the planet Earth as it is burned away by the expanding sun, five billion years in our future. But not all the guests visiting the Platform are there merely as sightseers. With robotic spiders systematically sabotaging the Platform and the number of deaths steadily rising, it is up to the Doctor and Rose to discover the truth and unmask the culprit.

The Doctor restores Platform One's systems then confronts the villain – the last human, Lady Cassandra. The station is now so hot that Cassandra's stretched skin-body dries out and snaps. Although the Doctor and Rose don't know it, they will meet Cassandra again (see *New Earth*).

### TARDIS TRANSLATION

Almost everywhere the Doctor goes, from ancient Earth to civilisations in the far future, he can understand the language – and the local life forms can understand him. The Doctor explains to Rose that she can understand the aliens on Platform One because the TARDIS telepathic field translates their languages so that she hears English.

Rose is not happy to discover that the TARDIS in effect gets inside her head to translate the alien and foreign languages, though this is not an aspect of the process the Doctor has considered before.

### UNIVERSAL TELEPHONE

The Doctor adapts Rose's mobile phone so it will work across time and space. The first calls Rose makes is to her mum, Jackie. In fact, Jackie gets the call the day before the events of *Rose*, and she believes that her daughter is calling from nearby.

The Doctor later 'upgrades' a phone for his next companion, Martha Jones. After she has left the Doctor, Martha uses her phone to call him and ask him to come and help (see *The Sontaran Stratagem*). Donna Noble is also able to use her phone from the TARDIS, and the Doctor upgrades Barclay's phone in *Planet of the Dead*.

### PSYCHIC PAPER

In this story, we see the Doctor use his 'slightly psychic' paper for the first time. The paper shows people what the Doctor wants them to see (or what they expect) – in this case the Doctor and Rose's invitation to Platform One to witness the Earthdeath event.

The Doctor uses his psychic paper on many occasions, as do his companions. Captain Jack Harkness has his own psychic paper in *The Empty Child*, while Rose is unable to deceive Torchwood operatives who are trained to be immune to its effect in *Army of Ghosts*.

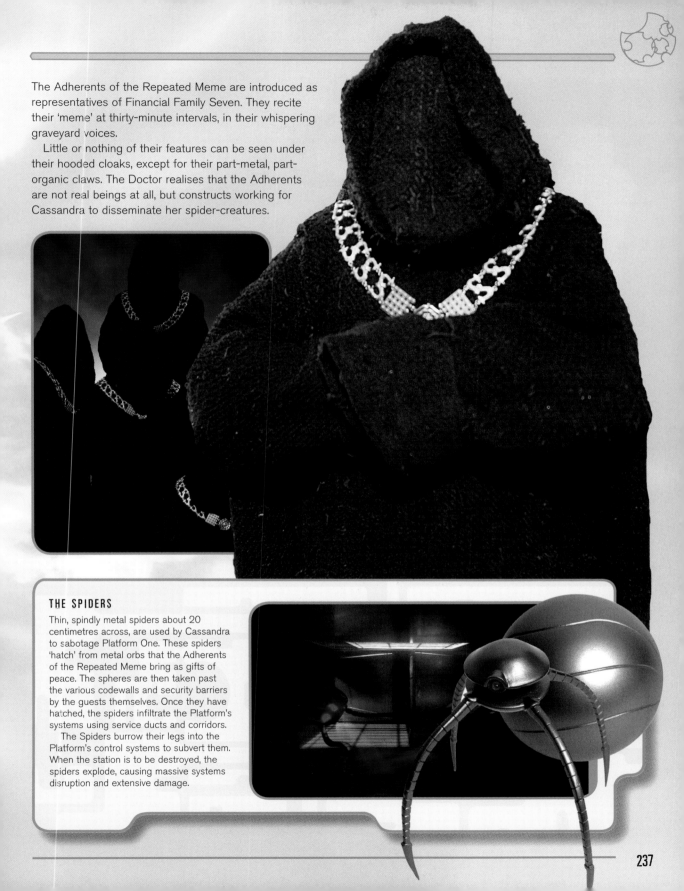

The Adherents of the Repeated Meme are introduced as representatives of Financial Family Seven. They recite their 'meme' at thirty-minute intervals, in their whispering graveyard voices.

Little or nothing of their features can be seen under their hooded cloaks, except for their part-metal, part-organic claws. The Doctor realises that the Adherents are not real beings at all, but constructs working for Cassandra to disseminate her spider-creatures.

### THE SPIDERS

Thin, spindly metal spiders about 20 centimetres across, are used by Cassandra to sabotage Platform One. These spiders 'hatch' from metal orbs that the Adherents of the Repeated Meme bring as gifts of peace. The spheres are then taken past the various codewalls and security barriers by the guests themselves. Once they have hatched, the spiders infiltrate the Platform's systems using service ducts and corridors.

The Spiders burrow their legs into the Platform's control systems to subvert them. When the station is to be destroyed, the spiders explode, causing massive systems disruption and extensive damage.

Heads sprout shoots and leaves

Humanoid features, but grown from wood

Bark instead of skin

Wooden hands are very dextrous

The Forest of Cheem is a collective of 'Trees' – humanoid creatures grown from wood, sprouting branches and leaves. Jabe, Lute and Coffa represent the Forest on Platform One for the viewing of the End of the World.

It is traditional for the Trees of the Forest to offer cuttings from their relatives as peace-offerings and gifts. The more revered and illustrious the relative, the greater the value of the gift.

They do not revere or understand technology – Jabe refers to the mainframe that controls Platform One as 'the metalmind' and her own personal digital assistant as a 'metalmachine'.

The Trees have massive forests on many planets – making them rich as investors in land. Earth is important to them as so many of their species evolved from trees from Earth. Jabe, for example, is a direct descendant of a tropical rainforest.

# FROM THE PLATFORM ONE GUEST LIST

Information about each of the guests invited to witness the End of the World was given to the Steward. Reproduced here is the information about visitor Jabe and the Forest of Cheem. Extract translated by Russell T Davies.

The origins of the Forest of Cheem go all the way back to the Middle Blue Period of the Planet Earth. In the Fifth Calendar Year of 111222/9967, an area of land across the equator, approximately 500 miles long and 3 miles wide, was sold at auction, to alleviate the Earth's terrible debts. But while other victims of this illegal auction suffered terribly – Brazil and its five billion occupants were sold to the Deathsmiths of Goth, there to be experimented upon in bizarre and terrible ways – the Equatorial Patch was bought by the wise and wonderful Brothers of Hame. The Brotherhood, descendants of the legendary Halldons, consisted of genetic experts, dedicated to enhancing the universe with new forms of life. The Equatorial Patch was isolated on the Panjassic Asteroid Field, cultivated, fostered, nurtured, and its evolution gently accelerated. The evolutionary journey of a billion years was compressed into a mere three hundred. First, the rainforest achieved a level three sentience. Within two generations, the first treeforms were beginning to take shape, moulded in the bark, with arms reaching from treetops. It is written that: 'The wind in the branches became a single, harmonious voice.' Twenty years later, having been cradled in wombs of vine and sap, the treeforms were walking. Language and community and compassion came soon after.

Two hundred years after the start of the experiment, the Forest had named itself, taking the title Cheem from its word for water. It existed on the groves of the Asteroid Field as a separate theocracy, and soon resented the control of the ever-watchful Brotherhood. Minor skirmishes broke out when the Forest tried to assert its own evolutionary rights, and demanded an end to the Brotherhood's experiments. But the Brotherhood had learnt from early mistakes in genetic acceleration, and soon granted the forest complete independence.

Then the path of the Forest takes a shadowy turn, the stuff of mythology. It is said that, as one, every treeform heard the Great Calling. The entire race boarded their barkships and fled the Asteroid Field, in the course of one night. They travelled to the far edges of the universe, and out of recorded history. What they saw there, what they learnt, is never spoken of. Some say the Forest met God; some say the Forest killed God; some say the Forest is God. But no treeform will ever discuss the Great Calling, its origin or its consequences. Nevertheless, the Forest returned from the depths of space, after an absence of five thousand years, with a wisdom and grace unparalleled in Fit Five civilisations. They have ascended to join the Higher Species. It is said that treeforms now walk in the most hallowed of halls. And while legends persist of a mighty, invisible Time War, it is said that the Forest alone observed the secret battle, and wept.

Now, as humanity's seed dissipates, and the Forest of Cheem's roots spread to all civilised worlds, the treeforms are treated with reverence, wherever they go.

Selected from the Forest's younger branches, out of the Caven Hol Arboretum, the Treeform Jabe Ceth Ceth Jafe is boarding Platform One to represent her species, at the End of the World. The Corporation owning all Platforms and Associated Venues would like to welcome Jabe and her consorts, and hopes that she has an unforgettable, life-changing experience.

The Moxx of Balhoon is a diminutive blue-skinned creature, supported by and transported on an antigravity chair. He represents the solicitors Jolco and Jolco. His speech is terse and to the point.

Saliva may be projected from mouth in formal spitting

Distinctive blue skin

Legs not strong enough to support full weight of body

# SECURITY PROCEDURES

Involving any Cith, Moxx or Grame of Balhoon. Legislated by Russell T Davies.

The Moxx is part of the Rack Fen Jackovittie Rab Mol Mol 'feh' Mol Tassic Conglomerate, part of the Hanamacat Pel Jadrabone, part-associated with the Raccidane Hoblomeer, but independent of the Roc Maff Payteen Six. Genetic Code Registration 5.6.9.222.0.

The Moxx is blue. He travels on an antigravity chair. His accepted form of formal greeting is to spit. In an emergency, if his bodily fluids are not replaced by the chair's internal filter every 25 minutes, then the Moxx has been known to sweat glaxic acid. In this case, do not touch the Moxx. He will be grateful if you point out the problem. He might even reward you with coins of solid blick. Or perhaps a song. His favourite song is 'Yap Cap Forward Bigga Toom Toom Toom'.

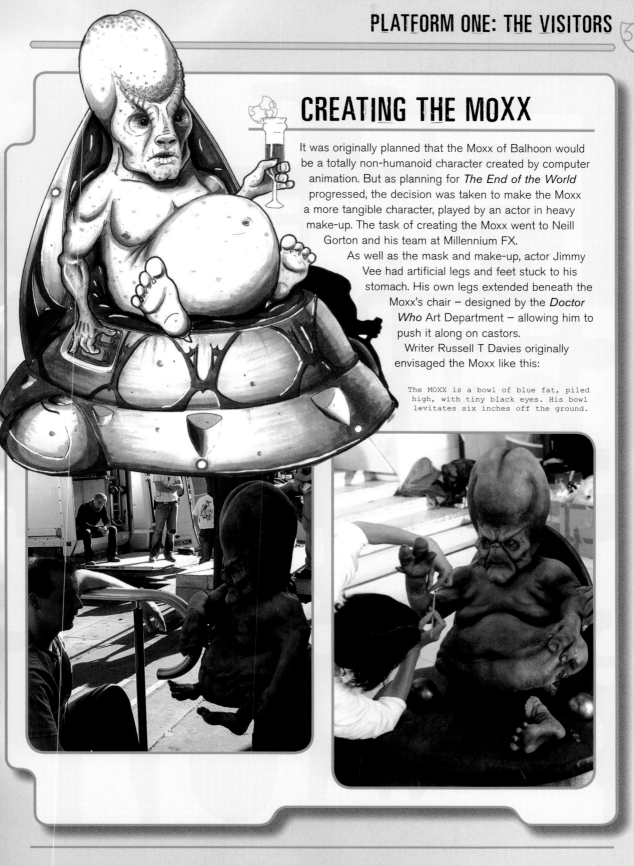

# CREATING THE MOXX

It was originally planned that the Moxx of Balhoon would be a totally non-humanoid character created by computer animation. But as planning for *The End of the World* progressed, the decision was taken to make the Moxx a more tangible character, played by an actor in heavy make-up. The task of creating the Moxx went to Neill Gorton and his team at Millennium FX.

As well as the mask and make-up, actor Jimmy Vee had artificial legs and feet stuck to his stomach. His own legs extended beneath the Moxx's chair – designed by the *Doctor Who* Art Department – allowing him to push it along on castors.

Writer Russell T Davies originally envisaged the Moxx like this:

```
The MOXX is a bowl of blue fat, piled
high, with tiny black eyes. His bowl
levitates six inches off the ground.
```

# AN INVITE TO THE END

To swell the number of guests on Platform One, the *Doctor Who* design teams created several 'extra' aliens to appear in the background of crowd scenes in the Manchester Suite. Introductions to these aliens were added back into the script after they had been designed.

Although created for just a day's shooting, the pictures on these pages show the care and attention to detail that goes into even the smallest part of each episode of *Doctor Who*.

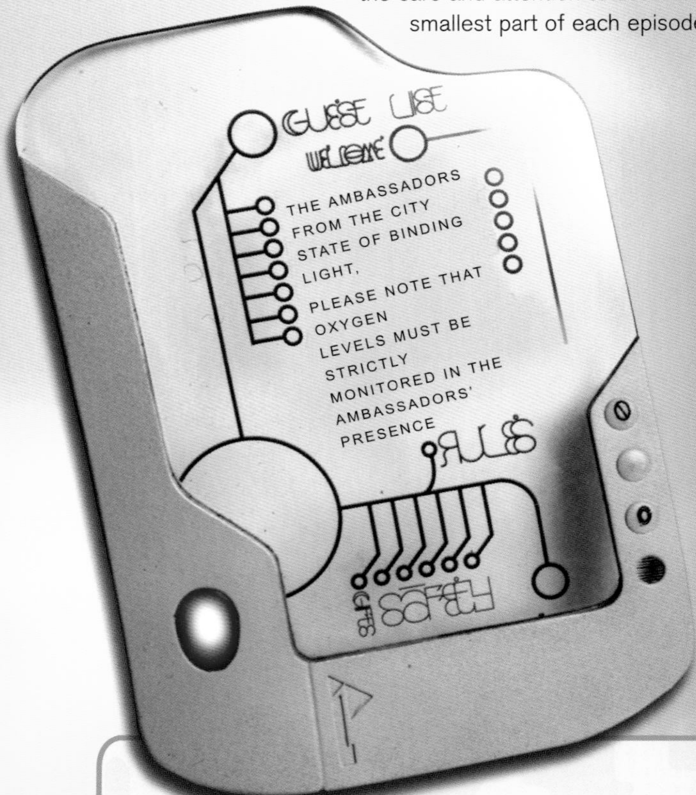

GUEST LIST

WELCOME

THE AMBASSADORS FROM THE CITY STATE OF BINDING LIGHT,

PLEASE NOTE THAT OXYGEN LEVELS MUST BE STRICTLY MONITORED IN THE AMBASSADORS' PRESENCE

RULES

SAFETY

### ALSO INVITED...

From the exalted clifftops of Rex Vox Jax, the inventors and copyright holders of hyposlip travel systems, the Brothers Hop Pyleen

Cybernetic hyperstar Cal 'Spark Plug' MacNannovich and his entourage

Mr and Mrs Pakoo

Chosen scholars of Class Fifty-Five from the University of Rago Rago Five Six Rago

### THE STEWARD

Although Platform One is entirely automated, its
day-to-day running is supervised by the Steward, an
ever-polite and diplomatic blue-skinned humanoid
determined to ensure that Earthdeath goes to plan and
that his important guests are well catered for and at
ease. He is responsible for everything that happens in
the 'Maximum Hospitality' environment.

The Steward is assisted by a staff of uniformed,
diminutive blue-skinned humanoids who scurry about
Platform One ensuring everything runs smoothly and
who may only speak when given permission to do so.

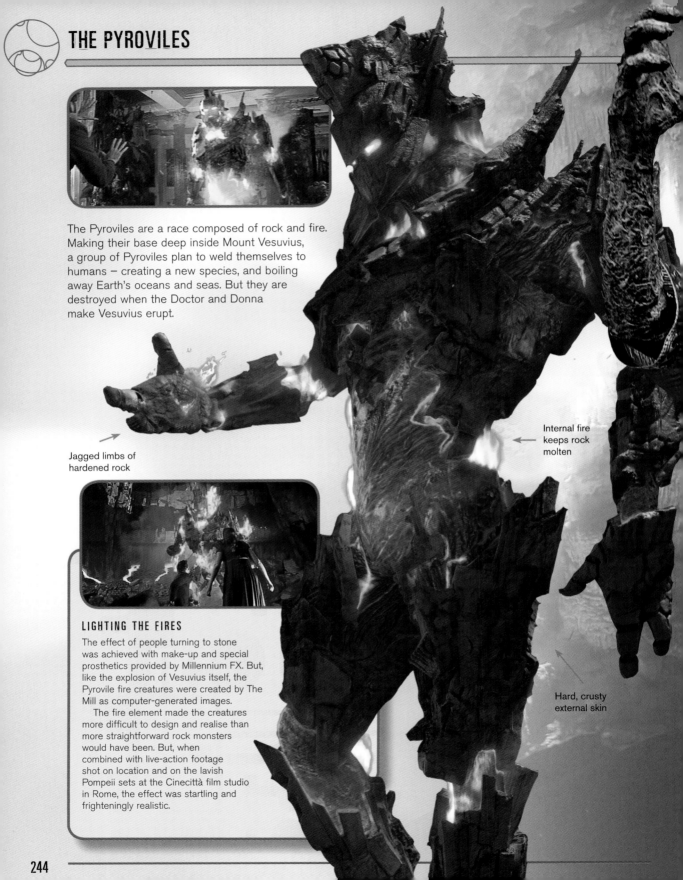

# THE PYROVILES

The Pyroviles are a race composed of rock and fire. Making their base deep inside Mount Vesuvius, a group of Pyroviles plan to weld themselves to humans – creating a new species, and boiling away Earth's oceans and seas. But they are destroyed when the Doctor and Donna make Vesuvius erupt.

Jagged limbs of hardened rock

Internal fire keeps rock molten

## LIGHTING THE FIRES

The effect of people turning to stone was achieved with make-up and special prosthetics provided by Millennium FX. But, like the explosion of Vesuvius itself, the Pyrovile fire creatures were created by The Mill as computer-generated images.

The fire element made the creatures more difficult to design and realise than more straightforward rock monsters would have been. But, when combined with live-action footage shot on location and on the lavish Pompeii sets at the Cinecittà film studio in Rome, the effect was startling and frighteningly realistic.

Hard, crusty external skin

## 🌀 VOLCANO DAY

Faced with the task of recreating ancient Pompeii, the *Doctor Who* team actually went to Italy – though not to Pompeii itself. Instead, they spent two days in 2007 shooting on the lavish studio sets used for the HBO TV series *Rome*. Parts of the studio were damaged by fire before the *Doctor Who* team arrived, but luckily the areas used for Pompeii were unaffected.

The footage shot in Rome was combined with location and studio work from much closer to the programme's Cardiff home, but the end result was a totally believable ancient Roman environment.

Combined with The Mill's stunning digital effects for the Pyrovile creatures and the eruption of Vesuvius, Pompeii became a tour-de-force of spectacular design.

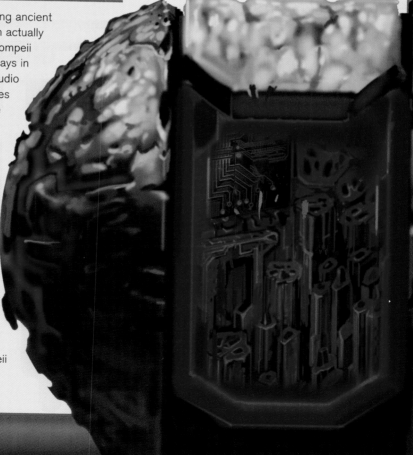

# QUARKS

The Quarks are the robot servants of the Dominators – the so-called Masters of the Ten Galaxies. The Dominators' mission is to colonise other planets, taking prisoners back to their home planet as slaves (to make more Quarks available for the war effort). Short, brutal robots, the Quarks have weaponry built into their folding arms, and powerful sensor equipment. They are powered by ultrasound, and can exchange power between themselves, as well as use their arm-sockets to power other equipment.

Quarks speak in a high-pitched voice and communicate with each other using beeps and squeals – for example, a double-beep indicates confirmation of an order.

Sensor equipment

Arms fold away into body

Weaponry and power relays inside arms

## THE DOMINATORS

The ship that lands on the planet Dulkis is commanded by two Dominators – Navigator Rago and Probationer Toba. Their task is to enslave the population of Dulkis and create a fuel source for the Dominators' space fleet.

Rago, the senior Dominator, is intelligent and analytical. He is used to his commands being obeyed, and barely tolerates Toba's frequent insubordination. Toba has a taste for death, unmitigated by the responsibility or experience of command. He is confident and impulsive enough to try to rebel against Rago, and is defeated only because the Quarks are programmed to obey the more senior Dominator.

 # THE DOMINATORS

The TARDIS lands on the Island of Death on Dulkis. The Dulcians have renounced war after seeing the horrors of their nuclear testing on the island – but now the cruel Dominators have arrived, with their deadly Quarks. Using the background radiation on the island to refuel their ship, they plan to enslave the Dulcians and drill into the planet to blow up a seed device that will turn it into a radioactive fuel dump for their fleet.

While Jamie and his friend Cully fight against the Quarks, the Doctor and Zoe rescue the Dulcians forced to clear drilling sites for the bore holes. The Dominators deploy their device, but the Doctor intercepts it and smuggles it aboard their ship, which is destroyed.

Written by
**Norman Ashby**
Featuring
**the Second Doctor, Jamie and Zoe**
First broadcast
**10 August–7 September 1968**
**5 episodes**

## DULKIS

When he last visited the planet, the Doctor found Dulkis so peaceful he did not want to leave. Dulkis is ruled by a council, of which Senex is Director.

The Seventh Council initiated research – 172 years earlier – that culminated in the test detonation of an atomic bomb on the 'Island of Death'. After this, all further research was prohibited and the island preserved as a museum and a warning for future generations. There is a survey unit on the island monitoring radiation and students visit regularly to be shown the horror of its effects.

## CREATING THE QUARKS

Although attributed to 'Norman Ashby', *The Dominators* was actually scripted by writers Mervyn Haisman and Henry Lincoln. But when the story was cut back from six to five episodes, and the first designs of the Quarks arrived, Haisman and Lincoln were not pleased – they removed their names from the project and used a pseudonym. The Quarks remain an iconic *Doctor Who* monster, though, and battled the Doctor in several 1960s comic strips. Pictured here is one of costume designer Martin Baugh's initial concept paintings.

# THE RACNOSS

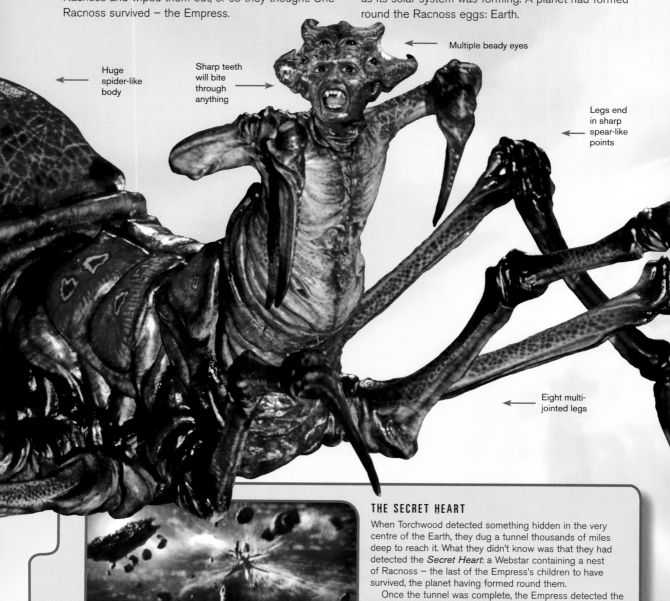

The Racnoss are huge creatures that came from the Dark Times, billions of years ago. They were born hungry and devoured everything – even whole planets. The Fledgling Empires went to war against the Racnoss and wiped them out, or so they thought. One Racnoss survived – the Empress.

In hibernation, she drifted in her Webstar spaceship to the very edge of space. There, awakened at last from her slumbers, she sought the last of her subjects and found they had escaped into the orbit of a new star, just as its solar system was forming. A planet had formed round the Racnoss eggs: Earth.

Multiple beady eyes

Huge spider-like body

Sharp teeth will bite through anything

Legs end in sharp spear-like points

Eight multi-jointed legs

## THE SECRET HEART

When Torchwood detected something hidden in the very centre of the Earth, they dug a tunnel thousands of miles deep to reach it. What they didn't know was that they had detected the *Secret Heart*: a Webstar containing a nest of Racnoss – the last of the Empress's children to have survived, the planet having formed round them.

Once the tunnel was complete, the Empress detected the *Secret Heart* reaching out across space to find her, billions of years after they were separated. The Empress returned to awaken her people. But she hadn't bargained on the Doctor being there when it happened.

# THE RUNAWAY BRIDE

Donna Noble is at her own wedding when she suddenly fades away…
and reappears inside the TARDIS. The Doctor realises that Donna is being
chased by the Roboforms he encountered before the Sycorax invasion
– again disguised as sinister Santas.

Donna has been dosed with deadly Huon particles so that she will revive
the dormant children of the Empress of the Racnoss, who now controls
the Roboforms. But the Doctor uses explosive baubles from the deadly
Christmas trees to flood the Empress's underground base, drowning the
Racnoss. The Empress appears to die when her Webstar spaceship is
destroyed by an armoured tank.

Written by
**Russell T Davies**
Featuring
**the Tenth Doctor
and Donna**
First broadcast
**25 December 2006
1 feature-length episode**

### DONNA NOBLE

Life seems to be coming together for
Donna Noble. She has a good job at
security firm H.C. Clements, and is about
to marry her fiancé Lance. But Donna has
been dosed with deadly Huon particles to
turn her into the key to the rebirth of the
hideous Racnoss.

Transported to the TARDIS, Donna
needs the Doctor's help to discover the
truth – and defeat the Empress. Chased
by sinister Santas and attacked by deadly
Christmas trees, Donna decides to stay
at home and turns down the Doctor's
invitation to travel with him.

### LANCE BENNETT

Head of Human Resources at H.C.
Clements, Lance has formed an alliance
with the Empress of the Racnoss. He will
provide the key to release her children
– and that key is Donna, dosed with Huon
particles in her coffee. Lance even agrees
to marry Donna to make sure she cannot
escape from him.

The Empress has promised to show
Lance the universe, but she betrays him
– using him, instead of Donna, as the
key, force-feeding him Huon liquid and
dropping him through a shaft to the
centre of the Earth.

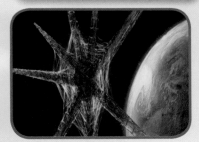

### THE WEBSTAR

The spaceships of the Racnoss are their
Webstars – giant star-shaped structures
of intricate web material. As the Empress
prepares for her children to emerge from
the centre of the Earth, where they are
in hibernation inside their own ancient
Webstar, her craft descends. It shoots out
bolts of deadly energy that will reduce the
human race to nothing more than food.
The Empress's children will be hungry
when they emerge…

But the Empress has used all the ship's
energy to release the children and it is
shot down by blasts from a tank.

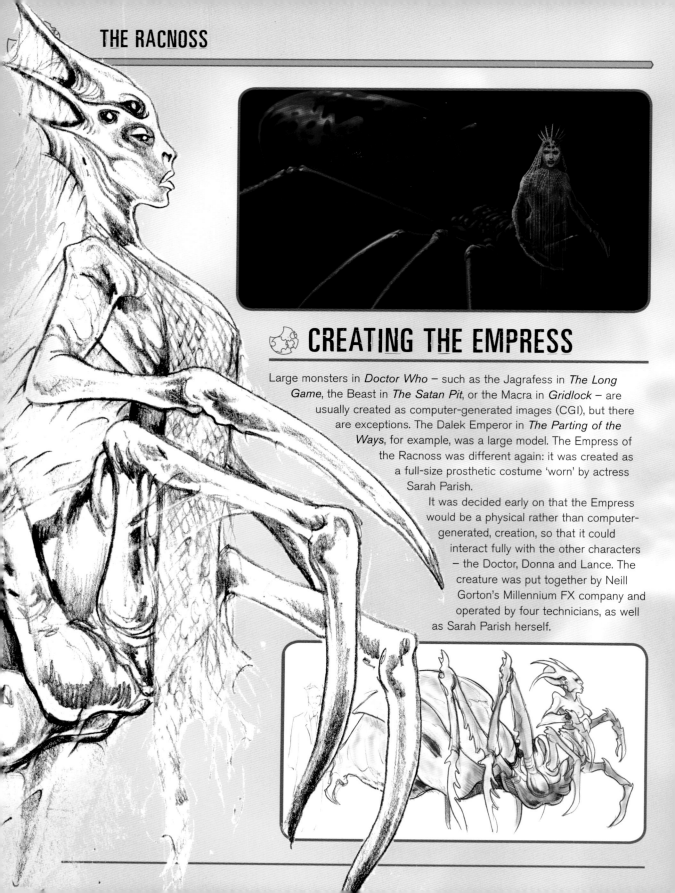

## CREATING THE EMPRESS

Large monsters in *Doctor Who* – such as the Jagrafess in *The Long Game*, the Beast in *The Satan Pit*, or the Macra in *Gridlock* – are usually created as computer-generated images (CGI), but there are exceptions. The Dalek Emperor in *The Parting of the Ways*, for example, was a large model. The Empress of the Racnoss was different again: it was created as a full-size prosthetic costume 'worn' by actress Sarah Parish.

It was decided early on that the Empress would be a physical rather than computer-generated, creation, so that it could interact fully with the other characters – the Doctor, Donna and Lance. The creature was put together by Neill Gorton's Millennium FX company and operated by four technicians, as well as Sarah Parish herself.

The final creature was very different from the original ideas supplied by the *Doctor Who* Art Department. Millennium FX made a large clay model of the Empress, and from this worked out how to build the full-size creature. Sections were modelled in clay, or sculpted in polystyrene, then finished in fibreglass. The final creature was so large it could not be completely assembled in the company's workshops – and the first time the entire creature was put together was on location ready for filming.

Weighing half a tonne, the Empress was operated like a giant puppet worked by control rods. Sarah Parish balanced as if on a see-saw, so that she could move the body up and down simply by shifting her weight slightly. She spent hours in make-up before being slid into the body of the grotesque creature, lying like a figurehead at the front of a ship. The upper body and front 'arms' of the Empress were the actor's own – everything else was part of the huge, car-sized rig built by Millennium FX.

##  FOLLOW THAT CAB!

One of the most impressive and exciting sequences in *The Runaway Bride* is where Donna is driven off in a taxi by a sinister Santa. Although set in London, only a small part of the chase was actually shot on the M4 – the rest was done on a link road in Cardiff. Many of the shots were achieved 'on the run' using a rolling roadblock – a cordon of police cars moving along the road while the *Doctor Who* production team worked in the cleared space between them.

The sequence took a huge amount of planning and preparation, and combined live-action stunt driving, computer-generated images (CGI – mainly of the TARDIS), and even live shots of David Tennant as the Doctor being hung over the road!

The pictures on this page show how the stunning, finished effect was planned and achieved.

# THE RANI

The Rani is a renegade Time Lord. She is a brilliant chemist, as well as being adept in other areas of science. She was exiled by the Time Lords after one of her experiments on mice turned them into monsters, resulting in an unfortunate incident with the President's cat. In the Doctor's opinion, the Time Lords should never have exiled the Rani, but locked her in a padded cell instead.

Ruler of planets such as Miasimia Goria and later Lakertya, the unscrupulous Rani sees their inhabitants merely as subjects for her experiments.

Beautiful but deadly

The Rani dresses glamorously when not in disguise

### THE RANI'S TARDIS

The Rani's TARDIS, unlike the Doctor's, can still disguise itself to blend in with its surroundings using its Chameleon Circuit. Disguised as a cupboard in *The Mark of the Rani*, it appears as a reflective pyramid in *Time and the Rani*.

The Doctor opens the Rani's TARDIS with his own TARDIS key, but the internal design is different from the Doctor's TARDIS – it is dark, with a round console. It is linked to a Stattenheim remote control. The Doctor is able to sabotage the Rani's TARDIS by resetting the navigational system and velocity regulator.

# THE MARK OF THE RANI

The Doctor and Peri arrive in Killingworth, where George Stephenson is organising a meeting of the greatest British thinkers and engineers. The Master is seeking revenge on the Doctor, who abandoned him to die on the planet Sarn. The Master also plans to take control of the great thinkers and manipulate them to turn Earth into a power base. But the Rani is in Killingworth, too. She is extracting fluid from people's brains, making them unnaturally aggressive.

The Doctor manages to sabotage the Rani's TARDIS, so that she and the Master are trapped inside it when it suffers time spillage – alongside an embryo tyrannosaurus, which starts to grow…

Written by
**Pip & Jane Baker**
Featuring
**the Sixth Doctor
and Peri**
First broadcast
**2–9 February 1985
2 episodes**

# TIME AND THE RANI

The Rani attacks the TARDIS, causing the Doctor to regenerate. She has taken over the planet Lakertya with alien Tetraps as her henchmen. Using the combined talents of various geniuses she has taken from throughout history – including Einstein and, she hopes, the Doctor – the Rani plans to create a time manipulator. She has built a missile to fire at an asteroid composed of strange matter, creating a chain reaction to power the device. As a side effect, the peaceful people of Lakertya will be destroyed, but the Rani isn't about to let a little thing like genocide put her off. The newly regenerated Doctor recovers in time to help Mel thwart the Rani's plans, and the Rani is captured by the Tetraps.

Written by
**Pip & Jane Baker**
Featuring
**the Seventh Doctor
and Mel**
First broadcast
**7–28 September 1987
4 episodes**

Robot's eyes glow red when it has been reprogrammed to kill

Stylised human features may cause 'robophobia' in sensitive people

Robot's class indicated by plate

The robots that the Fourth Doctor and Leela find operating a huge Sandminer on a distant planet are stylised humanoids, identified by type and number, programmed to obey the human crew and perform menial tasks. Each Voc-class robot has over a million multi-level constrainers, which prevent it from being able to harm humans. But, as the Doctor and Leela discover, someone has learned how to override these constraints and the robots have got more than cleaning on their minds.

The robots are controlled by a silver Super Voc, in this case SV7. It controls the other robots, acting as their coordinator and relaying all commands.

The golden Voc robots, all numbered with a V prefix, are intelligent, with a degree of self-control. They can also speak, and have a certain amount of initiative.

The dark-coloured Dum robots are single-function robots used for simple labour tasks. They are all numbered with a D prefix and cannot speak.

Robot can detach components – for example, hand can be removed

Humans use robots to perform all menial and service tasks from crewing Sandminers to giving massages

 # THE ROBOTS OF DEATH

The Doctor and Leela arrive on a Sandminer where the crew believe them to be responsible for a murder. The alternative – that one of the robots on board is responsible – is too terrible to contemplate. But also on board is an undercover operative from the mining company and a disguised robot detective, D84. They are looking for mad scientist – and 'boring maniac' – Taren Capel, who has threatened to reprogram robots to kill people and take over the world.

With most of the crew dead, and the robots now in open rebellion, Taren Capel finally reveals himself - and the Doctor, Leela and D84 are forced to take drastic action.

Written by
**Chris Boucher**
Featuring
**the Fourth Doctor and Leela**
First broadcast
**29 January–19 February 1977**
**4 episodes**

### THE SANDMINER

Storm Mine Four travels over the vast desert, extracting valuable ores and minerals from the shifting sands. The Sandminer is commanded by Uvanov. The human crew includes: Pilot Toos; Chief Mover Poul (an undercover agent for the company, who has robophobia); the impetuous Mover Borg; Chief Fixer Dask; Cass; Kerril; Zilda; and government meteorologist Chub.

While the robots can mine without human supervision, their lack of instincts means they are less efficient at tracing and following ore streams.

### TAREN CAPEL

Raised by robots from birth, Taren Capel believes that it is his mission to free his 'brother' robots from human bondage. He has taken the place of a member of the Sandminer's crew in order to convert robots to kill humans. When he orders the death of a human, Capel hands the robot a corpse marker to place on the body.

The robots identify humans in their command circuit by voice. When Taren Capel's voice is altered by helium, SV7 does not recognise him and, obeying his command to 'kill all humans', kills Capel.

### D84

D84 is a disguised Voc or Super Voc working with Poul to check whether Taren Capel is aboard the Sandminer. While the robots are said not to have feelings, D84 strikes up a relationship with the Doctor and ultimately sacrifices himself to destroy the converted robots.

The Doctor is able to create a 'final deactivator' tuned into Taren Capel's robot command circuit. Wounded by a Laserson Probe wielded by one of Capel's homicidal robots, D84 activates the device, destroying all of Capel's robots except SV7.

# SANTA ROBOTS

The Doctor first encountered the Roboforms soon after he regenerated into his current form, and described them as 'pilot fish' arriving in the wake of the Sycorax spaceship (*The Christmas Invasion*). Exactly where the Pilot Fish Roboforms come from is still not clear, but they seem to crave energy – power to keep them going. They are controlled remotely and have now come under the influence of the Empress of the Racnoss. She uses the Roboforms, still disguised as a Santa band, to hunt for Donna, but the Doctor is able to override her control.

Santa mask hides robotic features beneath

Red camouflage disguise suit for concealment

### HERE COMES SINISTER SANTA

While the Santa masks used in *The Christmas Invasion* were made to look as if the Roboforms were wearing false beards, the masks for *The Runaway Bride* were a single, fibreglass piece that was big enough to fit over the new gold-coloured robot heads worn by the actor. The heads were also made from fibreglass.

In both *The Christmas Invasion* (page 306) and *The Runaway Bride* (page 251), the Doctor is menaced by Roboform Christmas trees. Placed at Donna's wedding reception, presumably by Lance with the help of the Santa Roboforms, these trees are decorated with exploding baubles.

Baubles and decorations are deadly explosives

Trees are operated by Santa Roboforms using remote control

Leaves are miniature scythes with razor-sharp edges

# SCAROTH

Jagaroth are humanoid in shape

Distinctive alien skin ripples and twitches

Scaroth has many human guises, including Captain Tancredi

Jagaroth's true face (usually concealed behind tight-fitting mask)

Cravat conceals bottom of human face mask

Skin beneath bodysuit is similar texture to head

The Doctor describes the Jagaroth as a 'vicious, callous, warlike race'. They existed millions of years ago, and all but one of the Jagaroth were killed when their spaceship exploded while trying to take off from prehistoric Earth.

Scaroth was the pilot of that ship, and the only survivor; splintered into 12 aspects of himself, scattered throughout Earth's history and living independent but connected lives – each aspect is identical, but none is complete.

Scaroth claims he helped Man discover fire, invent the wheel, map the heavens and build the pyramids… always working to advance human evolution to a point where the technology he needs is available to his self furthest in the future – Count Scarlioni, in Paris, 1979.

## THE JAGAROTH SPACESHIP

For *City of Death*, visual effects designer Ian Scoones was keen to develop the design of primeval Earth for his model shot of the Jagaroth spaceship exploding, rather than match his model to a studio set. He created a detailed picture of what he intended to build and, in agreement with set designer Richard McManan-Smith, built a large, detailed model.

*City of Death* opens with an impressive shot of the primeval landscape, culminating with the appearance of Scaroth's spider-like spaceship. This sequence, including the spaceship taking off, 'warping' and then exploding, was one of the most impressive model sequences achieved on *Doctor Who* up until that time, and remains just as spectacular today.

# THE CAVES OF ANDROZANI

Androzani Minor is the only source of valuable spectrox, and the army is trying to defeat Sharaz Jek and his android rebels who hold the mines. The Doctor and Peri arrive in the middle of the conflict and are infected with raw spectrox, which is deadly. They are captured by the army and sentenced to death, but are rescued by the enigmatic Sharaz Jek.

While the Doctor struggles to find a cure for their deadly infection, the political manoeuvring reaches a critical point. The Doctor manages to escape the carnage and rescue Peri, but back in the TARDIS he only has enough antidote to cure her. She wakes to find the Doctor near death. As she watches, his features blur and change…

Written by
**Robert Holmes**
Featuring
**the Fifth Doctor
and Peri**
First broadcast
**9–16 March 1984
4 episodes**

### ANDROZANI MINOR

Androzani Minor, unlike its larger neighbour Androzani Major, is uncolonised. It is a desert world with a core made of superheated mud that erupts from time to time, with very little warning. Sharaz Jek was caught in one of these mudbursts, after Morgus gave him faulty detection equipment.

The caves of Androzani Minor are infested with bats, and reptilian carnivores exist in the planet's magma, leaving it only to hunt for food. The bats create the spectrox nests, which are the source of the valuable spectrox liquid.

### MORGUS

Morgus is the chairman of the Sirius Conglomerate on Androzani Major. Since he controls what little spectrox there is available, it is in his interest to keep the war going – to keep the price of spectrox high – so he is supplying guns to Jek in return for more spectrox.

Fearing that his duplicity has been discovered, Morgus assassinates the president and goes to Androzani Minor to find Jek's spectrox. He is betrayed by his secretary and becomes a fugitive. His only hope is to find the spectrox, but instead he is killed by Jek.

### SPECTROX

Refined spectrox is one of the most valuable substances in the universe – a few drops taken daily are enough to hold back the ravages of time.

Raw spectrox is so toxic to humans that it causes spectrox toxaemia, fatal within a few days of skin contact. First a rash develops, followed shortly by cramps and spasms. Finally the thoracic spinal nerve is slowly paralysed, before thermal death point is reached.

The only known cure, discovered by Professor Jackage, is to drink the milk of the queen bat.

# SIL AND THE MENTORS

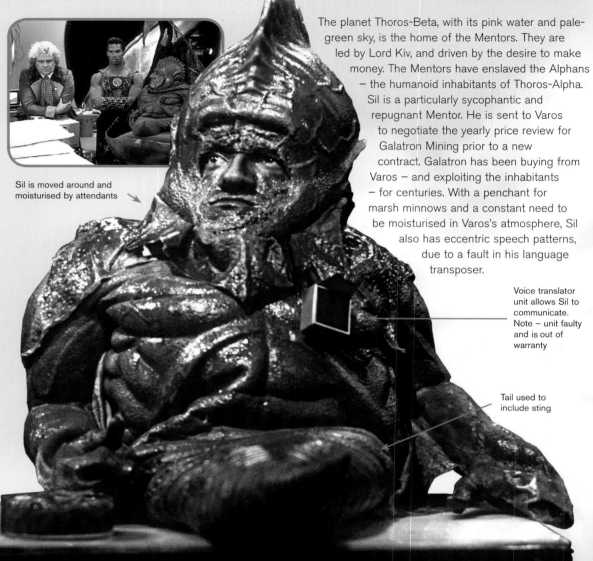

Sil is moved around and
moisturised by attendants

The planet Thoros-Beta, with its pink water and pale-
green sky, is the home of the Mentors. They are
led by Lord Kiv, and driven by the desire to make
money. The Mentors have enslaved the Alphans
– the humanoid inhabitants of Thoros-Alpha.
Sil is a particularly sycophantic and
repugnant Mentor. He is sent to Varos
to negotiate the yearly price review for
Galatron Mining prior to a new
contract. Galatron has been buying from
Varos – and exploiting the inhabitants
– for centuries. With a penchant for
marsh minnows and a constant need to
be moisturised in Varos's atmosphere, Sil
also has eccentric speech patterns,
due to a fault in his language
transposer.

Voice translator
unit allows Sil to
communicate.
Note – unit faulty
and is out of
warranty

Tail used to
include sting

## VAROS

Varos is in the constellation of Cetes and is the only known source of the
rare ore Zeiton-7. Over two hundred years ago it was a prison colony for
the criminally insane, and now the descendants of the officer elite still hold
power. The Governor is chosen at random from 12 senior officers and must
propose solutions to Varos's problems. These are then put to a public vote
and the Governor is subjected to a potentially lethal cell bombardment if he
fails to gain enough popular support.

Torture and execution are carried out in the Punishment Dome. The whole
dome is covered by cameras. Varos sells tapes of what happens in the
Punishment Dome, as well as broadcasting the events, to divert questions
and thoughts of discontent and revolution.

 # VENGEANCE ON VAROS

The TARDIS 'stalls' and only has enough power to get to Varos – a former prison planet that is the sole source of the valuable Zeiton-7 needed for repairs. The TARDIS arrives in the Punishment Dome, and the Doctor and Peri find themselves trying to escape the tortures and challenges of the Dome on live television.

Meanwhile, the fair but strict Governor of Varos tries to negotiate a higher price for Zeiton-7 with Sil, a representative of the Galatron Mining Corporation, who has led the Varosians to believe that Zeiton-7 is worthless. The Doctor and Peri join forces with rebel leader Jondar to help the Governor break free of dependence on Sil and the Mentors.

Written by
**Philip Martin**
Featuring
**the Sixth Doctor and Peri**
First broadcast
**19–26 January 1985**
**2 episodes**

# THE TRIAL OF A TIME LORD: MINDWARP

The Doctor is put on trial by his own people, and the events of *Mindwarp* form part of the evidence against him…

Tracing a high-tech weapon to Sil's home planet of Thoros-Beta, the Doctor and Peri find a sea monster biologically upgraded to operate sophisticated machinery, and a creature that is part-man, part-wolf. Human scientist Crozier is experimenting on the native Alphans for the Mentor leader Kiv, to find a way for him to survive as his brain grows too big for his body. With the Doctor suffering the after effects of a mind-control machine – and apparently cooperating with the Mentors and turning on Peri – events seem set to play out to a tragic conclusion…

Written by
**Philip Martin**
Featuring
**the Sixth Doctor and Peri**
First broadcast
**4–25 October 1986**
**4 episodes**

# SILURIANS AND SEA DEVILS

Millions of years ago, the Earth was inhabited by intelligent reptiles. But when a small planet was detected approaching Earth, they thought it would draw away the atmosphere and create a global catastrophe. To avoid extinction, they built huge hibernation chambers, where they slept through the crisis. They would be awakened when the atmosphere returned.

But the small planet never drew away the Earth's atmosphere, and so the reptiles never woke. Instead the planet was captured by Earth's gravity and became its moon. The various groups of reptiles that have awoken since – called Silurians and Sea Devils by the people who first encountered them – regard the Earth as their planet, and humans as upstart apes to be destroyed.

Third eye can stun or kill. It can operate Silurian devices, and burn through rock

Unlike other reptiles, Silurians and Sea Devils walk upright

Amphibious Sea Devil can live underwater or on land

Combined snout and mouth

# THE SILURIANS

The Doctor and UNIT investigate mysterious power failures at a research centre beneath Wenley Moor. They discover that a nearby colony of Silurians is drawing off the power to revive more Silurians, who plan to wipe out mankind with a deadly plague. The Doctor manages to find a cure for the disease, but the Silurians take over the research centre and prepare to destroy the Van Allen Belt, which shields Earth from the harmful radiation of the sun. If they succeed, humankind will die, but reptiles will thrive. The Doctor defeats the Silurians, who retire into hibernation, believing that the centre's reactor is about to explode. Against the Doctor's wishes, the Brigadier destroys the Silurian base.

Written by
**Malcolm Hulke**
Featuring
**the Third Doctor,
Liz and UNIT**
First broadcast
**31 January–14
March 1970
7 episodes**

## MONSTER PET

The Silurians are able to control their pet dinosaurs using a signalling device that emits a high-pitched warble. The same device can also be used to summon other Silurians and gain access to their base.

The first contact with the Silurians comes when two cavers are attacked by the dinosaur, which is then called off by the Silurians. One of the men is killed, the other – Spencer – degenerates into a nervous condition brought on by the shock. Delirious, he draws on the sickbay wall – his pictures are similar to ancient cave paintings, but include images of Silurians.

## THE PLAGUE

When primitive apes used to raid their crops, the Silurians killed them with a poison. The Silurians release this poison to create a plague that will wipe out the human race – descendants of those apes.

Once infected, the victims develop pustules, then their skin becomes discoloured. Finally, they fall unconscious and die.

The Silurians are sure the humans are too primitive to develop a cure, and they are right – it is the Doctor who finds a solution, despite a Silurian attempt to stop him.

# THE SEA DEVILS

Written by
**Malcolm Hulke**
Featuring
**the Third Doctor and Jo**
First broadcast
**26 February–1 April 1972**
**6 episodes**

When the Doctor and Jo visit the Master in his island prison, they find that ships have disappeared mysteriously in the area. Visiting the nearby naval base, the Doctor examines a charred lifeboat and concludes that the problem centres on an abandoned sea fort. There, they encounter a Sea Devil. A navy submarine sent to investigate beneath the fort fails to return.

The Master has made contact with the Sea Devils, encouraging them to take over the naval base. He intends to help them reawaken sleeping reptiles all over the world. But the Doctor booby-traps the Master's reactivation device. The two Time Lords escape from the Sea Devil base in the captured submarine moments before the device explodes.

## HMS SEASPITE

The naval base HMS *Seaspite*, is commanded by Captain John Hart. He is in charge of the adaptation of the sea fort for use as a SONAR testing station. The submarine, under Commander Ridgeway, is fitted with experimental SONAR equipment, which Hart hopes will detect the Sea Devils.

Captain Hart also calls on an air-sea rescue helicopter, a hovercraft, a diving vessel, and a taskforce of naval vessels that depth-charge the Sea Devil base.

## THE MASTER'S IMPRISONMENT

Captured by UNIT, the Master has been imprisoned indefinitely. There were calls for him to be executed, but the Doctor pleaded for clemency and now the Master is the only prisoner in a castle on an isolated island. The prison is patrolled by armed guards and protected by CCTV and minefields.

The prison's governor is Colonel Trenchard, a weak-minded man who has fallen under the Time Lord's influence. Under the Master's direction, Sea Devils take over the prison – releasing the Master and killing Trenchard.

# 🌐 WARRIORS OF THE DEEP

The Doctor, Tegan and Turlough arrive in the underwater Seabase Four in 2084. The world is divided into two belligerent power blocs, and the base is on constant alert – always ready to fire its deadly proton missiles.

But a group of Silurians and Sea Devils attacks the base. Using a deadly, bio-engineered underwater creature called a Myrka, they gain control of the base and prepare to launch the missiles. They plan to provoke a war that will wipe out humanity, but leave the Earth undamaged for them to take over. By linking directly to the base weapons systems, the Doctor is able to stop the launch. The Silurians and Sea Devils are killed with hexachromite gas, which is deadly to reptiles.

Written by
**Johnny Byrne**
Featuring
**the Fifth Doctor,
Tegan and Turlough**
First broadcast
**5–13 January 1984
4 episodes**

### EVOLVING TO SURVIVE

In *Warriors of the Deep*, the physical appearance of both the Sea Devils and the Silurians has changed significantly since the Doctor's previous encounters with them.

The Sea Devils now wear Samurai-style body armour in place of the garments made of netting which they were wearing in *The Sea Devils*.

The Silurians have 'shells' protecting their torsos. Their third 'eye' now illuminates when they speak, rather than – as in *The Silurians* – when they focus their mental energies.

### SEABASE FOUR

Seabase Four is one of several undersea bases that both power blocs use to monitor each other and detect and respond to any aggression. The base is heavily armed with proton missiles, which wipe out human life while leaving the environment relatively undamaged.

To eliminate any danger of computer error, missile-launch is controlled by a specially conditioned human whose mind can interface with the weapons system. But Seabase Four has been infiltrated by enemy agents, who have their own ideas about launching the missiles.

### THE MYRKA

The Myrka is a large reptile with stubby forearms. It is a bio-engineered creature, which has been bred by the Silurians as a living weapon. It is capable of electrifying its victims simply by touching them and can function both on dry land and underwater.

It appears invulnerable to the weapons available on Seabase Four. But it is unused to light since it lives in the depths of the ocean, and the Doctor deduces that it can be destroyed by exposure to certain wavelengths of light. He kills it with an ultraviolet converter.

# THE SLITHEEN

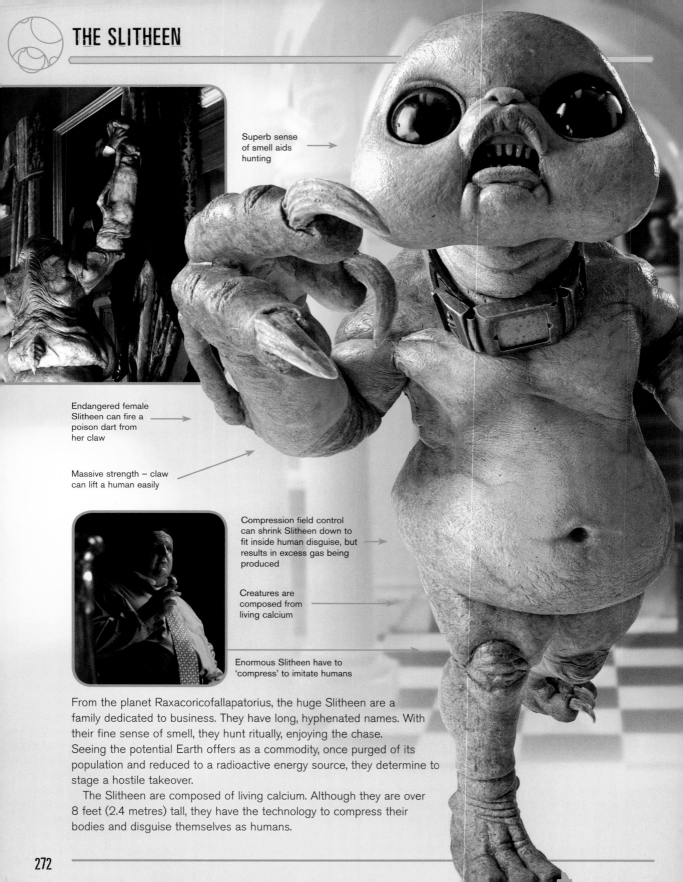

Superb sense of smell aids hunting

Endangered female Slitheen can fire a poison dart from her claw

Massive strength – claw can lift a human easily

Compression field control can shrink Slitheen down to fit inside human disguise, but results in excess gas being produced

Creatures are composed from living calcium

Enormous Slitheen have to 'compress' to imitate humans

From the planet Raxacoricofallapatorius, the huge Slitheen are a family dedicated to business. They have long, hyphenated names. With their fine sense of smell, they hunt ritually, enjoying the chase. Seeing the potential Earth offers as a commodity, once purged of its population and reduced to a radioactive energy source, they determine to stage a hostile takeover.

The Slitheen are composed of living calcium. Although they are over 8 feet (2.4 metres) tall, they have the technology to compress their bodies and disguise themselves as humans.

## INFILTRATION!

To disguise themselves as humans, the Slitheen squeeze into artificial human bodysuits, sealed with a hidden zip across the forehead. They use a compression field – controlled by a device worn around the neck – to make their bodies fit inside the suits. Being so large, they can only shrink down far enough to impersonate very large people.

As a side effect of the compression field, gas is released – meaning that the disguised Slitheen have to make embarrassing bodily noises in order to vent it. The gas, caused by calcium decay, smells of bad breath. When the suit is opened, pent-up energy is released with electrical flashes round the zip and blue electrical discharges from the bodysuit.

## ALIENS OF LONDON and WORLD WAR THREE

Written by
**Russell T Davies**
Featuring
**the Ninth Doctor, Rose, Mickey and Jackie**
First broadcast
**16–23 April 2005**
**2 episodes**

The Doctor returns Rose to Earth just in time to witness a spaceship crash into the Thames. The press reports that First Contact has been made with an alien race – a body is found in the wreckage.

But as experts gather at Downing Street and the Prime Minister disappears, the Doctor begins to suspect that not all is as it seems. Has there really been a crash-landing? Or is this all part of a dastardly ploy by aliens who are already on Earth, and whose plans for the planet are nearing completion? Trapped in the Cabinet Office, the Doctor and Rose, together with Harriet Jones (MP for Flydale North), must decide whether to risk everything in a last-ditch bid to save the Earth.

### HARRIET JONES

MP for Flydale North, Harriet Jones is concerned to put a proposal to the Cabinet for Cottage Hospitals not to be excluded from becoming Centres of Excellence. Her own mother is being cared for in the Flydale Infirmary.

She describes herself as a 'lifelong backbencher … not one of the babes'. But the Doctor knows that she will be elected Prime Minister for three successive terms and become the architect of Britain's golden age. He will meet her again in *The Christmas Invasion* and she gives her life to contact him in *The Stolen Earth*…

### MISSING PERSON

The Doctor takes Rose home to the Powell Estate the day after she left. Except he's made a mistake and Rose has actually been gone a whole year.

Rose's mum Jackie believes that Rose has been murdered by Mickey. Though in fact Mickey is the only person who knows that Rose left with the Doctor – but that's hardly a reliable alibi. Rose tells Jackie she's been travelling with the Doctor, but Jackie is less than impressed. It is not until she is attacked by a Slitheen that she begins to trust the Doctor – and Mickey, who saves her life.

### APPEARING AS THEMSELVES

*Blue Peter* presenter Matt Baker and the BBC's then Political Editor Andrew Marr appear as themselves in this story. Other famous people featured in later episodes include: newsreader Huw Edwards (*Fear Her*); Derek Acorah, Alistair Appleton, Trisha Goddard and Barbara Windsor playing Peggy Mitchell (*Army of Ghosts*); Sharon Osbourne, Ann Widdecombe and pop group McFly (*The Sound of Drums*); Nicholas Witchell (*Voyage of the Damned*); Kirsty Wark (*The Sontaran Stratagem*); and Paul O'Grady and Richard Dawkins (*The Stolen Earth*).

## PIGS IN SPACE

As part of their deception, the Slitheen create a fake alien life form out of an ordinary farmyard pig. They dress it in a spacesuit and leave it to be found in the crashed ship. The pig is taken to Albion Hospital, where it is examined by Toshiko Sato, working undercover for Torchwood. The pig has been augmented with Slitheen technology – it stands on its hind legs, and its brain has been 'wired up' and had components added to convince 'Doctor' Sato that it is no hoax.

Despite the Doctor's attempts to befriend it, the terrified pig flees and is shot by soldiers guarding the hospital.

## ALIENS ARE HERE!

A spaceship crash-landing in the River Thames after colliding with the clock tower that houses Big Ben at the Palace of Westminster seems to signal the arrival of aliens on Earth. As the Doctor points out to Rose, the crash-landing is perfect – from the angle of descent to the colour of the trailing smoke.

But the Doctor soon realises that the crash is too perfect. The crash has been staged by the Slitheen to draw attention away from their ship in the North Sea and to lure the world's experts on extraterrestrial incursion to London.

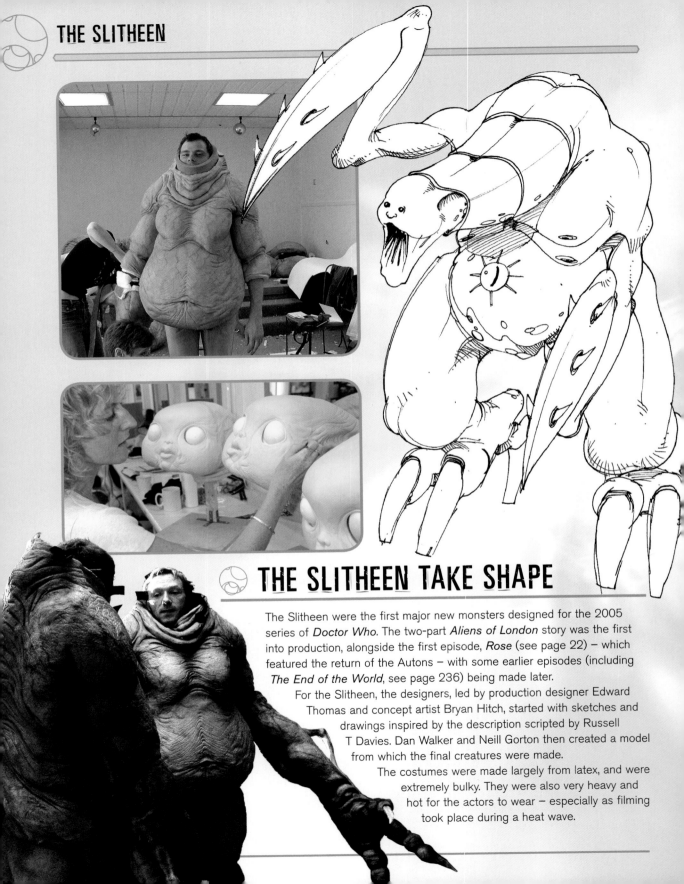

## THE SLITHEEN TAKE SHAPE

The Slitheen were the first major new monsters designed for the 2005 series of *Doctor Who*. The two-part *Aliens of London* story was the first into production, alongside the first episode, *Rose* (see page 22) – which featured the return of the Autons – with some earlier episodes (including *The End of the World*, see page 236) being made later.

For the Slitheen, the designers, led by production designer Edward Thomas and concept artist Bryan Hitch, started with sketches and drawings inspired by the description scripted by Russell T Davies. Dan Walker and Neill Gorton then created a model from which the final creatures were made.

The costumes were made largely from latex, and were extremely bulky. They were also very heavy and hot for the actors to wear – especially as filming took place during a heat wave.

# COMPUTING ALIENS

For some sequences, having an actor in a Slitheen costume was not practical. In particular, the suits were not designed for rapid movement – the heads 'waggled' if the actor inside tried to run – so the various chases in 10 Downing Street in *World War Three* had to be carefully planned.

Sometimes clever editing and rapid intercutting made it appear that Slitheen were hurrying through corridors when in fact they were hardly moving. On other occasions, computer-generated Slitheen were added to 'clean' images of the background and animated to show the creatures moving at speed.

Another complicated sequence was the Slitheen shedding of their human guise. Rather than having an actor in a Slitheen costume inside a human costume, the actor wore an all-over bodysuit marked with black crosses to give reference points to the animators. The actors inside the 'human suits' were then replaced in post-production with computer-generated Slitheen apparently squeezing out of their human guise (above).

# THE FAMILY SLITHEEN

Extract from *Jane's Book of Planets*, translated by Russell T Davies.

The world of Raxacoricofallapatorius is a beautiful place. Wild and yet graceful poppito trees blow in the cinnamon breeze; white marble temples sit atop cliffs of sapphire and chalk; endless burgundy oceans crash around spectacular ice-caves at the four poles.

The indigenous species, the Raxacoricofallapatorians, are civilised, elegant and proud. With skins of living calcium, and the wonders of slipstream compression technology at their disposal, they have a strict code of government, which educates their children in the disciplines of poetry, mathematics and democracy, from the day they are hatched.

Of course, every paradise has its serpent. The shame of Raxacoricofallapatorius is the Family Slitheen, descendants of the original Huspick Degenerate, cousins to the Blathereen and Rackateen, born far away from the main planetary continent on the Islands of Hisp. Over many centuries, the Slitheen established themselves as a criminal clan, infiltrating all levels of government, and subtly controlling the planet's off-world distribution of the valuable spice, Offich. They became so deeply embedded in government that they threatened to tarnish their entire species with their crimes.

But in the Great Purge of Yon:556, the Slitheen were exposed, shamed, and arrested en masse. Many fled their homeworld. The entire clan – every cousin, step-sister, half-mother and fiancée – thought to number more than 550, was tried and found guilty, in perpetuity. Justice is harsh on Raxacoricofallapatorius. The surviving Slitheen have been given the death sentence in their absence, with no chance of appeal. Should a Slitheen ever return to the homeworld, they would be taken to the largest cliff-top temple, the Palace of Enforced Atonement. There, a thin solution of acetic acid would be

prepared. Watched by thousands of spectators in the open-air amphitheatre, all chanting the Dawn Prayer 'Oh Deliver Us Weeping And Shamed', the Slitheen would be lowered into the cauldron, slowly, and boiled. The solution would be tempered so that only the outer skin dissolves; the inside of the Slitheen would fall into the solution, to become soup. And for fifteen to twenty seconds, it is thought, the Slitheen would still be alive. A living soup. The resulting liquid would then be drunk by the priests and ministers of Raxas Prime. To date, not one Slitheen has yet returned home.

Deprived of a homeworld, it is said that the Family has degenerated still further. Early attempts to make profits out of drug-running, arms-dealing and chizzle-waxing were thwarted by the local star-system's police force, the Wrarth Warriors. Scattered across the off-world archipelagos, and with their bank accounts frozen, the Slitheen have had to resort to ever more desperate measures to make money. But they have declared that they will survive, and return home one day. No matter what the cost.

 # BOOM TOWN

Written by
**Russell T Davies**
Featuring
**the Ninth Doctor, Rose,
Captain Jack and Mickey**
First broadcast
**4 June 2005
1 episode**

The TARDIS needs to refuel, so the Doctor lands it over the wound left by the time rift in Cardiff. But also in Cardiff is a surviving Slitheen – Blon Fel Fotch Passameer-Day Slitheen – in her disguise as Margaret Blaine, now Mayor of Cardiff. She is planning to open the Rift and use the power that would be released to escape. Knowing that this would destroy the world, the Doctor, with the help of Rose, Jack and Mickey, captures the Slitheen. But if they return her to Raxacoricofallapatorius, she will be executed.

Margaret holds Rose hostage, but looks into the heart of the TARDIS and reverts to a Slitheen egg – which the Doctor decides to take home so she can have another chance at a more enlightened life…

## THE SARAH JANE ADVENTURES

The Doctor's former companion Sarah Jane Smith has encountered the Slitheen several times. In her own spin-off television series, *The Sarah Jane Adventures*, Sarah is helped by K-9, her adopted son Luke and his friends to investigate strange and weird events.

In one of their first adventures, they discover a plot by the Slitheen centred on Luke's school. In a later adventure, the Slitheen are out for revenge – and have finally perfected their human disguises so that they don't have to appear as fat people.

Sarah and her friends have encountered many other foes, including a Sontaran and the Trickster. It was one of the Trickster's Brigade – a Time Beetle – that distorted the events of Donna's life in *Turn Left*.

Sarah travelled with the Doctor in his third and fourth incarnations, but has also met the Tenth Doctor – first in *School Reunion* where they defeated the Krillitanes, and later in *The Stolen Earth* and *Journey's End*, where she helped him defeat Davros and the Daleks.

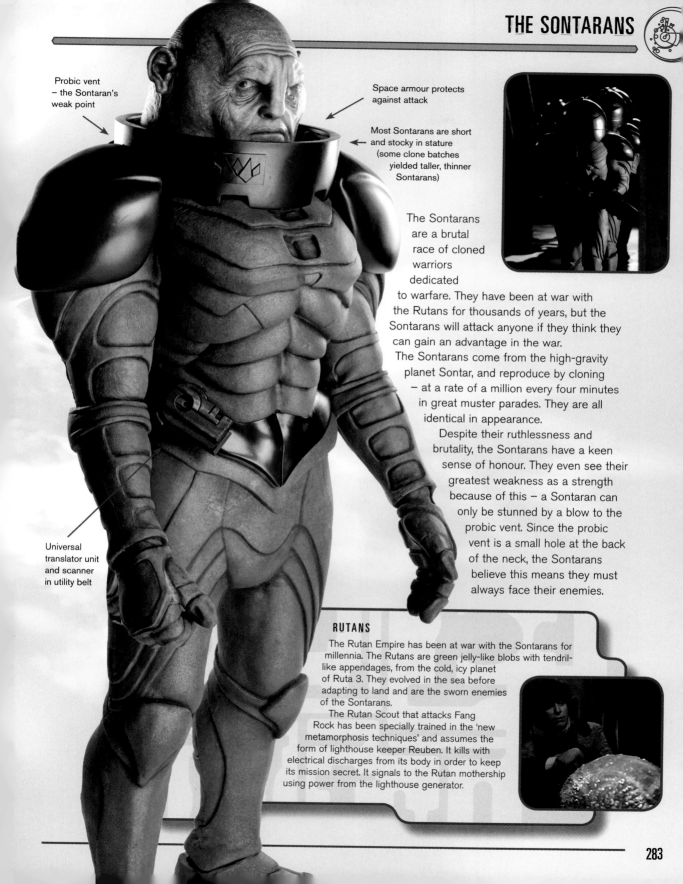

Probic vent
– the Sontaran's
weak point

Space armour protects
against attack

Most Sontarans are short
and stocky in stature
(some clone batches
yielded taller, thinner
Sontarans)

The Sontarans
are a brutal
race of cloned
warriors
dedicated
to warfare. They have been at war with
the Rutans for thousands of years, but the
Sontarans will attack anyone if they think they
can gain an advantage in the war.
The Sontarans come from the high-gravity
planet Sontar, and reproduce by cloning
– at a rate of a million every four minutes
in great muster parades. They are all
identical in appearance.
Despite their ruthlessness and
brutality, the Sontarans have a keen
sense of honour. They even see their
greatest weakness as a strength
because of this – a Sontaran can
only be stunned by a blow to the
probic vent. Since the probic
vent is a small hole at the back
of the neck, the Sontarans
believe this means they must
always face their enemies.

Universal
translator unit
and scanner
in utility belt

## RUTANS

The Rutan Empire has been at war with the Sontarans for
millennia. The Rutans are green jelly-like blobs with tendril-
like appendages, from the cold, icy planet
of Ruta 3. They evolved in the sea before
adapting to land and are the sworn enemies
of the Sontarans.
The Rutan Scout that attacks Fang
Rock has been specially trained in the 'new
metamorphosis techniques' and assumes the
form of lighthouse keeper Reuben. It kills with
electrical discharges from its body in order to keep
its mission secret. It signals to the Rutan mothership
using power from the lighthouse generator.

 # THE TIME WARRIOR

Written by
**Robert Holmes**
Featuring
**the Third Doctor,
Sarah Jane and UNIT**
First broadcast
**15 December 1973
–5 January 1974
4 episodes**

A Sontaran commander, Linx, crash-lands in medieval England. He offers a local robber baron, Irongron, advanced weapons in exchange for shelter and help repairing his spaceship. But Linx needs more sophisticated help, and kidnaps scientists from the 20th century. The Doctor and journalist Sarah Jane Smith travel back in time to find the scientists, and help Sir Edward of Wessex combat Irongron.

Linx kills Irongron as the Doctor and Sarah Jane sneak into the castle and send the scientists home, but Linx has already completed his repairs and is ready to blast off. As Linx prepares to leave, Sir Edward's archer, Hal, hits him in the probic vent with an arrow.

## ROBOT KNIGHT

As well as providing breach-loading rifles for Irongron and his men, Linx constructs a robot knight. When Irongron asks if it kills, Linx tells him: 'It does nothing else, and it cannot be killed.'

The knight is operated from a control box, which is damaged when it is shot away with an arrow and the knight goes out of control. Irongron knocks its head off with an axe, and it still 'walks' after falling over. Linx suggests he will make a new knight that will perhaps obey Irongron's voice. The Doctor later disguises himself as this voice-controlled robot.

## SONTARAN EQUIPMENT

Linx's ship is equipped with an osmic projector (or frequency modulator), which he uses to bring back scientists from the 20th century. The Doctor says that Linx's spherical scoutship is, like its owner, incredibly powerful for its size.

As well as having the translation device on his belt, the Sontaran is armed. He uses a cylindrical gun to knock Irongron's sword away and later to burn his axe handle. The weapon can also stun or kill living beings. Linx is later able to mesmerise Sir Edward's squire and Sarah Jane so they answer his questions.

## STAKING A CLAIM

When Linx arrives on Earth, he immediately claims the planet for the Sontaran Empire. He plants a rod in the ground which opens to reveal the Sontaran flag. Linx then speaks the words of the declaration:

'By virtue of my authority as an officer of the Army Space Corps, I hereby claim this planet, its moons and satellites, for the greater glory of the Sontaran empire…'

Irongron and his followers, watching this curious ritual, are unaware they have just been annexed.

# THE SONTARAN EXPERIMENT

The Doctor, Harry and Sarah Jane arrive on Earth in the far future and find it a barren wasteland, destroyed by solar flares. A group of stranded space travellers from an Earth colony are being observed by Field Major Styre, a Sontaran who is using some of them to assess human strengths. His report is the precursor to a Sontaran invasion of this part of the galaxy.

The Doctor challenges Styre to single combat and, while the Sontaran is distracted, Harry sabotages his energy supply. Weakened, Styre tries to re-energise himself, but the energy feeds on him instead and he is killed. The Doctor then persuades the Sontaran Grand Marshal that the humans now know their invasion plans, and the attack is called off.

Written by
**Bob Baker & Dave Martin**
Featuring
**the Fourth Doctor,
Sarah Jane and Harry**
First broadcast
**22 February
–1 March 1975
2 episodes**

## ABANDONED EARTH

Although it has become strategically important to the Sontarans (in an effort to gain an advantage over the Rutans), Earth has been abandoned by humanity. When it was threatened by solar flares, some humans left to found colonies out in space, while others were selected to go into cryogenic suspension aboard a giant space 'Ark' called Nerva (adapted from Nerva Beacon – see *Revenge of the Cybermen*, page 58). The humans who remained behind went into underground shelters, but perished in the solar flares.

## STYRE'S ROBOT

Styre is assisted in his experiment by a robot. Powered by a terulian drive, the robot is resistant to the colonists' weapons, and can shoot out ropes to capture them and hold them immobile. It moves rapidly, even on rough terrain.

The Doctor is able to disable the robot using his sonic screwdriver.

 # THE INVASION OF TIME

Written by
**David Agnew**
Featuring
**the Fourth Doctor,
Leela and K-9**
First broadcast
**4 February–
11 March 1978
6 episodes**

The Doctor returns to Gallifrey, but Leela is concerned that he is acting strangely. It seems he has betrayed his people, the Time Lords, to the Vardans – aliens who can travel along any broadcast wavelength. This means that, in effect, they can read thoughts.

The Doctor is actually trying to persuade them to materialise fully so he can defeat them. This done, however, the Doctor discovers that the Sontarans were behind the Vardan invasion – and a battle group of the Sontaran Special Space Service, led by Commander Stor, arrives to take control of Gallifrey. The Doctor lures the Sontarans into the TARDIS, and eventually defeats them using a forbidden Demat gun.

### THE VARDANS

The Vardans can travel along any form of broadcast wavelength – even the TARDIS scanner – and materialise at the end of it. They are telepathic, able to read thoughts (including encephalographic patterns), which is why the Doctor has to shield his thoughts. They are humanoid but, until they properly materialise, they appear as shimmering silver shapes. K-9 detects the coordinates of their source planet as vector 3 0 5 2 alpha 7, 14th span. He is able to use modulation rejection to eject the Vardans from Gallifrey, and the Doctor plans to time loop their planet.

### PRESIDENTIAL INVESTITURE

Invested as President, the Doctor is 'crowned' with a circlet giving him access to the Matrix, the repository of all Time Lord knowledge. Gold Usher announces:

'It is my duty and privilege, having the consent of the Time Lords of Gallifrey, to invest you as President of the Supreme Council. Accept therefore the Sash of Rassilon. Accept therefore the Rod of Rassilon. Seek therefore to find the Great Key of Rassilon… I invest you Lord President of the Supreme Council. I wish you good fortune and strength. I give you the Matrix.'

### HORROR OF FANG ROCK

The Fourth Doctor and Leela arrive in the early 20th century on Fang Rock – a tiny island with only a lighthouse on it. One of the keepers is missing, and another claims that the 'Beast of Fang Rock' has now returned. But this beast is actually a Rutan scout – surveying Earth for possible use as a base against the Sontarans. Although the keepers and the survivors of a shipwreck are killed, the Doctor manages to destroy the Rutan mothership by converting the lighthouse for use as a giant laser-like beam to shoot the craft down.

 # THE TWO DOCTORS

The Second Doctor and Jamie investigate time-travel experiments at Space Station Camera. The Sixth Doctor arrives after a Sontaran attack to discover everyone dead, except Jamie. The Doctor realises his earlier self is being held close to Seville by the Sontarans, in league with misguided scientist Dastari, and two Androgums, Shockeye and Chessene.

The Sontarans, under Group Marshal Stike, want to discover the secret of time travel by experimenting on the Doctor. When this fails, Dastari tries to turn the Doctor into an Androgum so he will reveal the secret. Meanwhile, the Sontarans plan to kill Dastari, Shockeye and Chessene – but are themselves tricked and destroyed by Chessene.

Written by
**Robert Holmes**
Featuring
**the Sixth Doctor and Peri, & the Second Doctor and Jamie**
First broadcast
**16 February– 2 March 1985**
**3 episodes**

## ANDROGUMS

The Androgums work as servitors on Space Station Camera, doing all the station maintenance. Androgum law states that the gratification of pleasure is the sole motive for action. Androgums are incredibly strong – the Doctor says Shockeye could break both him and Jamie in half with one hand.

Chessene's karm name is Chessene o' the Franzine Grig. She has been enhanced by nine operations performed by Dastari. Shockeye's karm name is Shockeye o' the Quawncing Grig. He is the Station Chef and is keen to taste human meat.

## CLONING SONTARANS

The Sontarans were created by prolific *Doctor Who* writer Robert Holmes. In response to script editor Terrance Dicks's request for a story set in medieval times, Holmes wrote his outline as a citation for Commander Linx, addressed to 'Terran Cedicks' and describing Linx's brave conduct in the events of *The Time Warrior*.

Holmes was reportedly not happy with the notion of writing a pseudo-historical story. He said he was dragged kicking and screaming into it. He boasted that he got his own back later when he was script editor by dragging Terrance Dicks kicking and screaming onto a lighthouse – by having him write *Horror of Fang Rock*, which ironically featured the Sontarans' mortal enemy the Rutans.

 # THE SONTARAN STRATAGEM and THE POISON SKY

Written by
**Helen Raynor**
Featuring
**the Tenth Doctor,
Donna, Martha
and UNIT**
First broadcast
**26 April–3 May 2008
2 episodes**

Martha calls the Doctor back to Earth to help investigate ATMOS – a navigation and anti-pollution system installed in 400 million cars. UNIT raids the ATMOS factory, and the Doctor discovers the Sontarans are planning to use ATMOS to emit a gas that will suffocate all humans. The gas will create ideal conditions for Earth to become a clone world – where the Sontarans can create millions of cloned troops.

While UNIT take on the Sontaran troops, the Doctor uses an atmospheric converter to burn off the deadly gas and destroy the Sontaran Warship. Though a single Sontaran escapes, he is eventually defeated by Sarah Jane Smith (in *The Sarah Jane Adventures: The Last Sontaran*).

### LUKE RATTIGAN

Teenage technology genius Luke Rattigan invented the Fountain Six Search Engine when he was just 12 years old. He became a millionaire almost overnight, and later opened the Rattigan Academy.

But Rattigan is now in league with the Sontarans. In return for his help producing and distributing the ATMOS system, the Sontarans have promised to lead him and his gifted students to a new planet, Castor 36… But the Sontarans have no intention of helping Rattigan. Betrayed and disillusioned, Rattigan destroys the Sontaran Warship.

### CLONED MARTHA

The Sontarans create a clone of Martha, 'programmed' to use UNIT technology and abort codes to prevent the countries of Earth launching a counter-attack against the Sontarans. But the Doctor knows at once that the fake Martha is a clone – he can tell from her behaviour and even the way she smells.

The clone dies once the real Martha is released from the Sontaran cloning equipment. But she has enough of Martha's true personality and feelings to give the the Doctor vital information about the Sontaran plans before she expires.

### UNIT

The Unified Intelligence Taskforce is responsible for Operation Blue Sky – the raid on the ATMOS factory. The UNIT section deployed is commanded by Colonel Mace, who gives Martha Jones operational control for the raid.

The UNIT force manages to avoid the worst effects of the ATMOS gas by blowing it away using the massive engines of UNIT's flying aircraft carrier *Valiant*. Colonel Mace and his troops then fight off the Sontaran invaders, with air support from the *Valiant*, giving the Doctor time to defeat them.

## MAKING UP SONTARANS

For *The Sontaran Stratagem* and *The Poison Sky*, ten Sontaran troopers were created — all played by actors just five feet tall. In addition, two 'full' Sontarans were created complete with masks — General Staal and Commander Skorr. The masks were designed by Millenium FX and sculpted from foam rubber and applied so that the actors had some freedom of expression through the mask.

The Sontaran costumes were recoloured a distinctive deep blue (rather than the dark gunmetal grey of previous Sontarans). Insignia were added to the uniform collars, and the battle armour — also provided by Millennium FX — had a most robust, sculpted look to it. In all, it took each actor about three hours in make-up and costume fitting to become a Sontaran.

### SCRIPT EXTRACT

From the shadows steps SONTARAN GENERAL STAAL; short, stocky, strong, in full uniform, including domed helmet. A strutting, formal, military General through-and-through, complete with swagger stick.

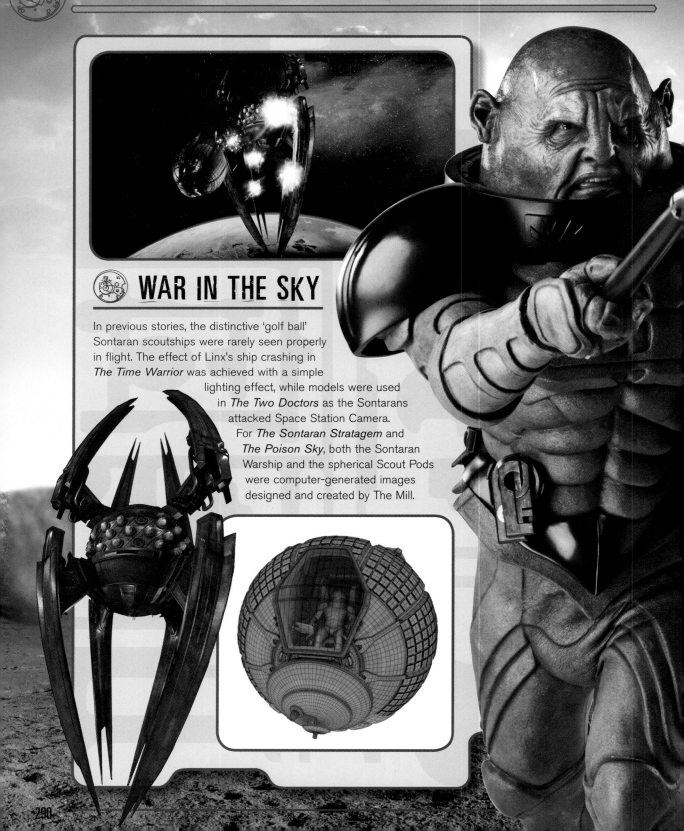

## WAR IN THE SKY

In previous stories, the distinctive 'golf ball' Sontaran scoutships were rarely seen properly in flight. The effect of Linx's ship crashing in *The Time Warrior* was achieved with a simple lighting effect, while models were used in *The Two Doctors* as the Sontarans attacked Space Station Camera. For *The Sontaran Stratagem* and *The Poison Sky*, both the Sontaran Warship and the spherical Scout Pods were computer-generated images designed and created by The Mill.

# STINGRAYS AND TRITOVORES

Creature resembles
a stingray

Mouth will crush
and consume
anything

Exoskeleton is made
of metal and acts
as a Faraday Cage
inside wormholes

### VOICES OF THE DEAD

Carmen and Lou are two of
the passengers on the bus
when it goes through the
wormhole to San Helios.
Lou tells the Doctor that
they do the lottery every
week – and every week they
win £10. This is because Lou's wife Carmen is
slightly psychic. This ability is enhanced by San
Helios's alien suns. Carmen can
sense the approaching Stingray
swarm, and hear the voices of
the dead of San Helios crying
out to her.
 She can also see something of
the Doctor's future – and warns
him that his song is
ending. 'It is returning
through the dark,'
she tells him. 'He
will knock four
times…'

UNIT refers to them as 'Stingrays',
but the swarm of creatures
that devastated San Helios and
many other worlds, turning them
to barren deserts, bear only a
superficial resemblance to real
stingrays.
 The creatures eat anything
and everything, swarming in their
billions. They fly at tremendous
speed, encircling the
worlds they
ravage
with such
velocity that
they open a
wormhole to take them to
their next feeding ground – another planet.
 They eat metal, extruding it into their exoskeletons
– so that they have metal bones. Their metal
exoskeletons enable them to survive journeys through
the wormholes.

# STINGRAYS AND TRITOVORES

The Tritovores are an insectoid race from the Scorpion Nebula. They resemble giant, humanoid flies. A technologically advanced species, with well-developed space flight based on Crystal Nucleus power, they trade with other races and planets for the waste products they feed on.

Communicating in their own chirping speech, the Tritovores can translate other alien languages so they can understand it. But the technology is not two-way.

Insectoid features

Bristling, dark hair covers body

Flight suit for space travel

 # PLANET OF THE DEAD

Written by
**Russell T Davies and
Gareth Roberts**
Featuring
**the Tenth Doctor and
Christina**
First broadcast
**11 April 2009
1 episode**

Tracing a small wormhole in space, the Doctor takes the bus. But when the wormhole grows in size, the whole bus falls through it to the planet San Helios. With help from the other passengers, particularly Christina, the Doctor struggles to get the bus moving so they can return through the wormhole. But a swarm of voracious creatures that resemble stingrays is flying across the planet, devouring everything in its path – and has created the wormhole to take them on to their next feeding ground: Earth.

The Doctor and Christina are helped by two stranded Tritovores whose ship has crashed, and the Doctor manages to get the bus back to Earth. UNIT close the wormhole before the whole Stingray swarm can follow.

### SAN HELIOS

The planet San Helios in the Scorpion Nebula has three suns and a population of a hundred billion. The largest city is San Helios City, a beautiful conurbation of ziggurats and walkways shining in the light of the suns. That is, until the Stingrays arrive. They devastate San Helios, eating everything in their path and reducing the entire planet to one vast desert... Then they create a wormhole to move on to their next feeding ground.

But the Doctor shifts the wormholes so that from now on the creatures will feed on uninhabited planets.

### SORVIN AND PRAYGAT

Travelling to San Helios to arrange a trading agreement, Sorvin and Praygat were ten miles up when their drive system stalled (colliding with Stingrays), and their ship crashed into the desert that San Helios had become. Stranded, they thought at first that the passengers of the 200 – the bus – had come to destroy them. But they soon realised their mistake and worked with the Doctor and Christina to find a way of escaping from the planet.

But some Stingrays had got into the ship when it crashed, and both Sorvin and Praygat were killed when they attacked...

### UNIT

The UNIT team that investigates the wormhole is headed by Captain Magambo. Her technical advisor is Doctor Malcolm Taylor – a technical genius who analyses the wormhole.

Both are impressed and delighted to be working with the Doctor – even if it is only over the phone. Malcolm in particular is rather overwhelmed. But when Magambo wants to close the wormhole to stop the Stingrays getting through, it is Malcolm who ensures it is kept open long enough for the Doctor and his friends to return safely.

# CRIME LADY

Lady Christina de Souza is a thief. She doesn't need the money, but she loves the challenge and the excitement. But the police are after her – Detective

Inspector McMillan and Sergeant Dennison have been after Lady Christina for a while. They know she's behind many of the most ambitious and daring art thefts of recent years, but so far she has eluded them.

When she steals the ancient gold Cup of Athelstan, she gets more excitement than she bargained for. With McMillan and Dennison hot on her heels, she is forced to escape in a bus. And no sooner has she boarded than the Doctor follows – tracking the growing wormhole that will take the bus and all its passengers to another world in another sky.

Christina adapts quickly to the new and dangerous environment, and takes charge. But she soon realises how much she needs – and trusts – the Doctor. Before long, she is putting her criminal skills to good use to get the vital Crystal Nucleus system that the Doctor needs. After they return to Earth, the Doctor helps Christina evade the police, and she escapes in the flying bus.

### THE CUP OF ATHELSTAN

Lady Christina's latest prize is the ancient Cup of Athelstan, valued at £18 million. She steals it from the International Gallery, where it has been kept safely for 200 years, secure behind a sophisticated electronic alarm system and under armed guard. That doesn't stop Christina from lowering herself from the domed roof of the gallery to steal it and leave behind her trademark waving cat statuette.

The ancient cup is made of gold, and was given to the first King of Britain by Hywel, King of the Welsh. Despite its value, the Doctor knows life is even more precious. He destroys the cup to get the bus working and save the lives of Christina and the other passengers.

# ANOTHER WORLD IN ANOTHER SKY

The production of *Planet of the Dead* called on all the various skills and expertise of the *Doctor Who* team. Creating the planet of San Helios involved both studio work, shooting inside a real double-decker bus, and travel abroad to find a genuine desert environment. Lighting, and the addition of extra suns in the sky completed the illusion.

The two alien races in this story were created in very different ways. The Stingrays were computer-generated images, designed and created by The Mill. Particularly challenging were the sequences where three Stingrays escape through the wormhole and battle against UNIT.

The Tritovores were a combination of costume, make-up and prosthetics – overseen by Neill Gorton and his team at Millennium FX.

## SCRIPT EXTRACT

FX SHOT: CU on the dot-of-light PROBE, against blue sky – then it swoops down – INTO A SWARM! A blizzard of STINGRAY-LIKE CREATURES in flight. They're grey but with a metallic exo-skeleton glinting in the sun. BOLTS OF LIGHTNING shoot through the swarm, like it's generating electricity. FX SHOT: CU on a STINGRAY. Snapping red O-shaped mouth.

# SUTEKH AND THE MUMMIES

Mask covers Osiran jackal-like head →

Eyes glow when Sutekh uses his immense mental powers →

Osiran costume and style formed the basis for Ancient Egyptian design ↙

From the planet Phaester Osiris, Sutekh is the last survivor of the Osirans – a devious and cunning race. He is a force for evil who destroyed his own planet and was finally caught on Earth by the surviving Osirans, led by Horus. Once defeated, Sutekh was imprisoned beneath a pyramid in Egypt, unable to move. The power source for his prison was the Eye of Horus, housed in another pyramid on Mars.

But when Egyptologist Marcus Scarman finds Sutekh's 'tomb', the last surviving Osiran is able to use his immense mental powers to control Scarman and make him use Osiran service robots to build a missile that will destroy the Pyramid of Mars and free Sutekh from his ancient bonds.

Sutekh is unable to move until the Eye of Horus is destroyed →

## THE OSIRANS

Seven thousand years ago, Sutekh (also known as Set or Seth) destroyed his own planet, Phaester Osiris, and left a trail of havoc across half the galaxy. Horus and the 740 other surviving Osirans finally cornered Sutekh in ancient Egypt, where their conflict became the basis for the ancient Egyptians' myths and religion.

With no vocal capability, mummies nod to signify understanding of their orders

Bandages prevent corrosion of internal parts

Mummy is actually an Osiran service robot

Sutekh's mummy servants are actually Osiran service robots. Their bindings are chemically impregnated to protect them from damage and corrosion. They are activated and controlled by servants of Sutekh using an ancient ring, which draws power from Sutekh's tomb. Sutekh himself and Marcus Scarman can control the mummies directly by mental force. The instructions are relayed into a pyramid in the small of the mummy's back, but an etheric impulse projected along the right wavelength can block this control.

Incredibly strong, the mummies can strangle or crush people to death

## WRAPPING UP

The costumes for the mummies were designed by Barbara Kidd, and were in several separate pieces – pre-wrapped arms and legs (in two pieces), with the head worn like a helmet and two main body sections. The actors were able to see out through a slit covered by a thin bandage. They found moving through the woods especially tricky because of the uneven ground.

Instructions and power are channelled to a pyramid-shaped device located in the small of the mummy's back

 # PYRAMIDS OF MARS

Written by
**Stephen Harris**
Featuring
**the Fourth Doctor
and Sarah Jane**
First broadcast
**25 October–15
November 1975
4 episodes**

The TARDIS is drawn off course and materialises in 1911 (one of the Doctor's favourite years) in an old priory that stands on the future site of UNIT HQ. The Doctor and Sarah Jane discover that the Osiran Sutekh is using Egyptologist Marcus Scarman to build a missile. The missile will free Sutekh from the Eye of Horus, which holds him prisoner beneath a pyramid in Egypt.

Captured and controlled by Sutekh, the Doctor is forced to take the TARDIS to the Pyramid of Mars, where Sutekh is finally freed by Scarman. But the Doctor is able to return to Earth and defeat Sutekh in the short time it takes before the control cuts out.

### EGYPTIAN MYTHOLOGY

In ancient Egyptian mythology, the god of violence Sutekh (or Set) was a jackal-like creature. He was equated with the monster Typhon, and opposed by Horus – son of Osiris, whom Sutekh murdered. Horus was the earliest of the royal gods – a falcon-shaped sky god whose eyes were believed to be the sun and moon. Sutekh was defeated in ancient Egypt by the 740 'gods' – his fellow Osirans – whose names are recorded in the tomb of Thutmose III.

This war entered mythology, while the Osirans strongly influenced the development of ancient Egyptian culture.

### THE PYRAMID OF MARS

When he built the Pyramid of Mars to house the Eye of Horus that holds Sutekh prisoner, Horus included many traps and puzzles that would have to be solved in order to progress through the pyramid. In addition to getting past booby-trapped doorways and mathematical puzzles linked to explosives, the Doctor must solve a riddle to release Sarah Jane from a trap – if he gets it wrong she will be condemned to instant death.

The mummies guarding the tomb are loyal to Horus and are differentiated from Sutekh's servicers by gold bands.

### MARCUS SCARMAN

Marcus Scarman – fellow of All Souls College, professor of archaeology and member of the Royal Society – has disappeared on his expedition to a pyramid near Sakkara. In fact Scarman was killed by Sutekh the moment he entered his tomb. His cadaver is animated by Sutekh's will and sent back to the Priory where he supervises the building of the missile intended to destroy the Pyramid of Mars.

Scarman's face turns into that of Sutekh as he concentrates to destroy the Eye of Horus.

Backlit
eye
shields
strike fear
into
enemies

Hideous face is
hidden beneath
ceremonial helmet
crafted from bone

Teeth from
defeated
enemies

Ceremonial broadsword used in challenges
of honour and sanctified combat

Flexible gauntlets offer protection
and allow dexterity

Body armour is covered with
robes of office and rank

An ancient race of honourable warriors,
the Sycorax travel through space in
their distinctive, angular, rock-like
spaceships, conquering planets and
enslaving their inhabitants. While they
follow an ancient warrior tradition,
they prefer to take planets without
a fight, tricking world leaders into
surrendering their people into
slavery. The Sycorax answer to a
single leader, chosen by right of
combat and strength. Their ships
are more like ancient caves than
technological equipment, and are
decorated with trophies of their
past conquests. Their voices are
guttural growls, brutally savage,
and their mantra is 'Sycorax
strong! Sycorax mighty! Sycorax
rock!'

## INVASION!

While it might seem that the Sycorax and Pilot Fish invaded London at Christmas, the reality was very different. Shooting for *The Christmas Invasion* actually took place in late summer, in Cardiff.

The Sycorax spaceship was a computer-generated image (CGI) added to location footage shot in London and Cardiff. A similar technique was used to create the effect of thousands of people around the world standing ready to jump from various high landmarks. Model work was also used to enhance this – in particular, a model was built of the block of flats where Rose and Jackie live, and the glass was blown out of it for the impressive sequence where the Sycorax spaceship hits the Earth's atmosphere.

## ROCK PAINTING

The pictures here show the level of detail and thought put into every aspect of the Sycorax ship. Much of the detail in the finished set – like the remains of a prisoner hanging in a cage – was barely noticeable on screen, there was so much of it.

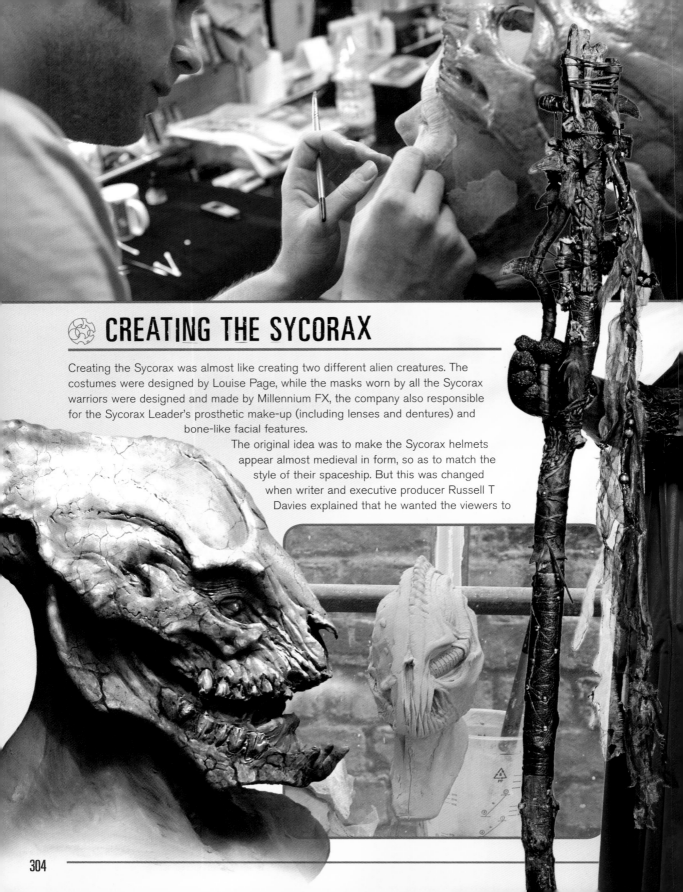

# CREATING THE SYCORAX

Creating the Sycorax was almost like creating two different alien creatures. The costumes were designed by Louise Page, while the masks worn by all the Sycorax warriors were designed and made by Millennium FX, the company also responsible for the Sycorax Leader's prosthetic make-up (including lenses and dentures) and bone-like facial features.

The original idea was to make the Sycorax helmets appear almost medieval in form, so as to match the style of their spaceship. But this was changed when writer and executive producer Russell T Davies explained that he wanted the viewers to

assume – just as the human characters did – that the Sycorax helmets were the actual creatures, not masks, in order to increase the impact and surprise when the Sycorax Leader removes his helmet and reveals the terrifying bone-like face beneath. New designs to fit this idea were then modelled as clay miniatures, before the actual masks and make-up elements were created.

# THE CHRISTMAS INVASION

Written by
**Russell T Davies**
Featuring
**the Tenth Doctor, Rose, Jackie and Mickey**
First broadcast
**25 December 2005**
**1 feature-length episode**

The TARDIS crash-lands in London at Christmas, but the Doctor is left unconscious after his regeneration. Rose and Mickey barely escape an attack by a group of homicidal robotic Santas and are attacked by a Christmas tree back at Jackie's flat. The Doctor wakes for long enough to save them – and warn them of a greater threat approaching Earth.

A Sycorax spaceship arrives over London, and the aliens demand that Harriet Jones (Prime Minister) surrenders. With a third of the Earth's population hypnotised into walking to the edges of high buildings and preparing to leap to their deaths, the Doctor must challenge the Sycorax leader to a duel – with planet Earth as the stake.

### BLOOD CONTROL

Using a sample of A+ blood from the captured British space probe *Guinevere One*, the Sycorax are able to control all people who have the same blood type. They force the controlled people to stand on the edges of high buildings and threaten that, if half the Earth's population is not surrendered into slavery, the Sycorax will ensure the controlled people jump to their deaths. However, the Doctor proves the human survival instinct is simply too strong for the victims to be persuaded to kill themselves, and breaks the Sycorax control.

### HARRIET JONES (PRIME MINISTER)

Harriet Jones is now Prime Minister, after her party won a landslide majority at the last election. She rose to power after helping the Doctor to thwart the attempted Slitheen invasion of Earth.

Taking control, Harriet Jones goes to UNIT's secret headquarters under the Tower of London to manage the Sycorax crisis. After witnessing the barbarity of the aliens, she has their retreating ship destroyed using recovered alien technology controlled by the ultra-secret 'Torchwood'. The Doctor is appalled at her actions and vows to see her toppled from power.

### THE GRASKE

At about the same time as defeating the Sycorax, the Doctor also thwarted an attempt by a Graske from the planet Griffoth to replace Earth's population with their own people (in an interactive adventure for digital TV viewers, *Attack of the Graske*). He travelled to Griffoth with a new human companion (the viewer), who worked out how to gain access to the Graske control area, and reset their teleport equipment, returning the kidnapped humans and representatives of other races to their rightful times and places in history.

Scarring caused by work in tinclavic mines on Raaga →

Used to breathing Soliton gas, but can survive in Earth's atmosphere →

Lip curls when Terileptil is angry →

The Terileptils are reptilian bipeds with a love of beauty. They banish their criminals to the planet Raaga, where they toil in the tinclavic mines for the remainder of their lives. A small group of these Terileptil criminals escaped from Raaga.

Following his time in the mines, their leader has been left badly scarred around one eye. The renegades' ship was damaged in an asteroid storm, and only four Terileptils survived the crash-landing on Earth. One was subsequently killed.

Although they can survive in Earth's atmosphere for a time, they use a Soliton gas generator to provide a more suitable atmosphere for their lungs.

## TERRITORIAL REPTILES

Writer Eric Saward made up the name for the Terileptils by combining 'territorial' and 'reptiles'. The script described them as 'about seven feet tall, powerfully built'. Three Terileptil costumes were made for *The Visitation*.

The leader's costume had its face mask sculpted to show scarring round the eye. Its mask was also fitted with electronics to give the face some expression.

## THE VISITATION

Written by
**Eric Saward**
Featuring
**the Fifth Doctor, Adric
Nyssa and Tegan**
First broadcast
**15–23 February 1982
4 episodes**

Trying to reach present-day Heathrow, the Doctor, Adric, Nyssa and Tegan arrive in the right place, but the wrong time – 1666. Here they meet actor-turned-highwayman Richard Mace, and discover that a small group of aliens has taken over the local manor house.

These Terileptils are escaped convicts who want to rid Earth of humans and take over. Fleeing from villagers under Terileptil mind control and a Terileptil android dressed as Death, the Doctor and his friends track the reptiles to London, where they are planning to release a virulent form of the Black Death. The Doctor defeats them at a bakery in Pudding Lane, but in doing so starts a fire…

### ANDROID

The Terileptils use highly developed androids to carry out menial tasks. The android the renegade Terileptils bring to Earth is also armed – able to fire energy bolts from its hand.

The Terileptils disguise the android in a specially designed 'skull' mask and equip it with a cloak and scythe. They are then able to use it to scare the superstitious villagers into thinking that Death walks among them.

Nyssa devises and constructs a booster in the TARDIS and uses it to vibrate the android to pieces.

### MIND CONTROL

The Terileptils can control human minds using special polygrite bracelets with built-in power-packs. The bracelets pulse as the power flows through them.

The Terileptil Leader is annoyed that human minds are so primitive that communication with them is not easy. The Terileptils control various locals, including a poacher, the miller, and the head man of the village.

Once the bracelet is removed, the controlled human collapses, and on recovery returns to normal, but with no memory of what he has been doing.

### PLAGUE

As fugitives from a prison planet, the Terileptils are unable to return home. Instead they plan to take over Earth by infecting rats with a genetically engineered plague and releasing them to spread the disease and wipe out the human race.

The Terileptil leader has taken over the local manor house and set up a laboratory in the cellar, concealed behind a holographic false wall. The other Terileptils have set up a base in the back rooms of a bakery in London, from which to release the rats.

Every choice we make changes things. Every decision, large or small, has consequences, like the ripples in a pond… There is a group of creatures that thrive on those changes. They feed on them, exploit them, taking the potential energy from the what-if. Sometimes they even make these events happen. They are known as the Trickster's Brigade.

Little is known about these creatures. The one that changes Donna's life is a giant beetle that attaches itself to her back. It sits there, sapping the time energy, occasionally glimpsed by others…

Most people who are affected don't need to worry. The changes are so slight, so tiny that they are barely noticeable. But in Donna's case, the small change in her life has catastrophic consequences…

## THE TRICKSTER

Little is known about the shadowy, hooded Trickster. It is said he revels in the chaos caused by changing history, changing lives. Although the Doctor has so far eluded his grasp, Donna is targeted by members of the Trickster's Brigade. And the Doctor's friend Sarah Jane Smith has twice been a victim of the Trickster.

In their first encounter, the Trickster altered events so that Sarah Jane died as a child in the place of her friend Andrea. He later used an enslaved Graske to lure Sarah Jane into a trap – a way to meet the parents she had never known, but at a terrible cost…

# TURN LEFT

Written by
**Russell T Davies**
Featuring
**Donna and Rose,
with the Tenth Doctor**
First broadcast
**21 June 2008
1 episode**

Donna visits a strange fortune teller on Shan Shen, and her past life changes. There was a moment when she made a decision, when she took a left turn in her car and went for a job interview that eventually led to her meeting the Doctor. Now it is as if she had turned right instead, and this tiny decision has far-reaching and awful consequences. It means that Donna never met the Doctor, and now the Doctor is dead. Without Donna's help, he died after defeating the Empress of the Racnoss…

Without the Doctor, the world suffers from events he prevented – and his friends and colleagues must sacrifice themselves to save the world in his place. Only Donna Noble and Rose Tyler can put history on track again.

### DONNA'S FAMILY

Rose arranges for Donna and her mother and grandfather to be out of London when the starship *Titanic* crashes into Buckingham Palace. London is destroyed, and the Noble family is evacuated to Leeds. There they have to share a house with many others, and life is hard for Donna, Sylvia and Wilf.

But again, Donna meets Rose, who tells her how things can be – and should be – very different. Eventually, Donna agrees to go with Rose, who uses the dormant TARDIS to send Donna back to save the world…

### ROSE RETURNS

Even when Donna and the Doctor defeat Matron Cofelia (*Partners in Crime*) and the Adipose threat, Rose is somehow there. The barriers between the universes are breaking down, enabling her to move between parallel universes.

Rose is able to help Donna go back to the point where history went off track, and return things to how they should be.

But Rose knows that, even so, a greater threat is coming. A threat they need the Doctor – and all his friends and colleagues – to defeat. The stars are going out, and the darkness is coming…

### BAD WOLF

With the Trickster's Beetle defeated, Donna is once more back in her proper time line, travelling with the Doctor. But even so, all is not well. She can remember the events of the alternate history, a bit like a dream. She remembers sacrificing her life to put history back on track.

And she remembers the message that Rose gave her to pass on to the Doctor. Just two words. Words which mean nothing to Donna, even when she sees them on every poster and every shop in Shan Shen – even replacing the text on the TARDIS… Bad Wolf.

## BEETLING ABOUT

The Time Beetle that latches on to Donna's back was actually a full-size prop made by Millennium FX. It had some movement and articulation, but the close-up shots of a feeler reaching over Donna's shoulder were achieved simply by holding a disembodied feeler and moving it about.

The episode *Turn Left* focuses on Donna's alternative life and, apart from a glimpse of his dead body, the Doctor only appears at the very beginning and the end. This was because *Turn Left* was made at the same time as *Midnight* – in which Donna hardly appears. This meant that the two episodes could be made simultaneously by two different production teams. In previous years, the same time-saving has been achieved by having an episode in which neither the Doctor nor his companion features heavily – for example *Love & Monsters* and *Blink*.

DOCTOR WHO IV

ROLL #2D8 Ⓐ
EP / SCENE 11 / 13
SLATE 23
TAKE 2
DIRECTOR GRAEME HARPER
DOP RORY TAYLOR
DATE .11.07
VFX NO

# THE VASHTA NERADA

Known as the Piranhas of the Air, or the Shadows that Eat the Flesh, the Vashta Nerada is a swarm of darkness itself. The Vashta Nerada can hide in any shadow, any patch of darkness. They can be any shadow or patch of darkness. If you have more than one shadow, then it's possible the Vashta Nerada already have you… They can tear the flesh from a living being in an instant, and animate the remaining husk of a body.

The Vashta Nerada hatch from spores gathered in living wood, becoming a swarm in minutes. The spores can survive inside the wood when the tree dies – which means they can live in paper made from the wood pulp. They can live inside books…

Body stripped of flesh by the Vashta Nerada

Voice may linger on as a 'data ghost'

Only spacesuit holds the skeleton in place

More than one shadow – one is real, the other Vashta Nerada

## THE LIBRARY

So big that it's simply called *The* Library, it covers a whole world, keeping specially printed copies of every book ever written. The core of the planet is a giant computer that maintains the facility and operates the Information Nodes.

But The Library has been deserted and abandoned for a hundred years. It is dark and empty, and no one knows why.

So the owner, Strackman Lux, funds an expedition to find out what happened. The expedition is led by Professor River Song, but Lux comes along too, together with his Personal Assistant Miss Evengelista, Anita, and two Daves.

# SILENCE IN THE LIBRARY and FOREST OF THE DEAD

The Doctor and Donna find The Library deserted and in shadows. They meet up with an expedition organised by Strackman Lux to discover what's happened. The Library computer, CAL, insists that everyone was saved, but the Doctor discovers that The Library is infested with Vashta Nerada.

While Donna becomes trapped in a idealised virtual world, the Doctor discovers that the Vashta Nerada hatched from the books in The Library, the paper being made from trees where the creatures laid their spores. CAL is actually the digitised mind of a little girl – Charlotte – and has saved all the missing people into the computer itself. The Doctor gives the Vashta Nerada The Library in return for allowing everyone to leave safely…

> Written by
> **Steven Moffat**
> Featuring
> **the Tenth Doctor and Donna**
> First broadcast
> **31 May–7 June 2008**
> **2 episodes**

### CAL

The Library's main computer is called CAL – which actually stands for Charlotte Abigail Lux. Charlotte's father built The Library for her when he learned that she was dying. He placed the girl's digitised mind into the computer to keep her 'alive'.

Now Charlotte lives inside a virtual world, sometimes dreaming of The Library, and watched over by Doctor Moon, who is actually another aspect of the computer system.

When the Vashta Nerada came, Charlotte 'saved' the minds of all the people inside the computer with her.

### DATA GHOSTS

The spacesuits worn by the expedition to The Library communicate by thought-mails. A technical glitch means that these keep working even after the person sending the thought has died – their last thoughts lingering, repeated over and over until the signal fades away completely.

But this echo of humanity can be saved like any other data – CAL saves Donna and the expedition members into her memory banks, and the Doctor is able to retrieve River Song's digital personality from her sonic screwdriver and copy that into CAL to join her friends…

### RIVER SONG

Professor River Song knows the Doctor very well indeed. But the Doctor is confused because he hasn't met her yet. But he will – and she'll obviously get to know all about him. She even knows the Doctor's real name.

Some time in the future, the Doctor will give her a sonic screwdriver – because he knows he'll need it to save her in The Library. When River Song sacrifices herself to save everyone else, her digitised data ghost is saved in the screwdriver and the Doctor gives her a new life inside the computer with Charlotte and her friends.

## DEEPENING SHADOWS

Unusually for a *Doctor Who* monster, there was little or
nothing for the make-up, prosthetics and digital effects
teams to create for the Vashta Nerada. The creatures are just
shadows. Lighting has always been important. Head writer
Russell T Davies says of this story in particular but also of the
series in general that: '*Doctor Who* is about shadows and darkness and what's out there in the dark.'
Careful lighting was needed to create the illusion of extra shadows, and patches of darkness where there should
be light inside The Library. Sometimes several light sources were used to cast real
shadows, in other cases more than one shot was combined so that additional
shadows appeared. This was actually augmented by The Mill, who added some
computer-generated shadows.

## WALKING THE DEAD

While the Vashta Nerada themselves required no make-up or prosthetics, their victims were a different story. The skulls of the 'Suit Creatures' that chase the Doctor and his friends through The Library were created by Millennium FX – who also provided space helmets adapted from motorcycle helmets.

The skulls themselves were masks, but could also be operated as hand puppets for close-up shots where it would otherwise be obvious that someone was wearing the skull-face. The result was a frightening, lurching creature that is every bit as terrifying as any of the monsters the Doctor has encountered…

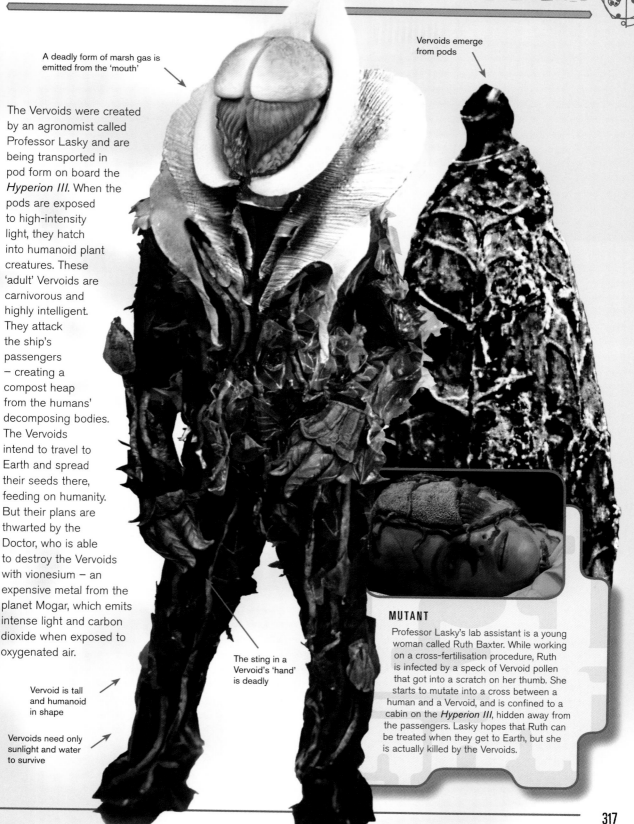

A deadly form of marsh gas is emitted from the 'mouth'

Vervoids emerge from pods

The Vervoids were created by an agronomist called Professor Lasky and are being transported in pod form on board the *Hyperion III*. When the pods are exposed to high-intensity light, they hatch into humanoid plant creatures. These 'adult' Vervoids are carnivorous and highly intelligent. They attack the ship's passengers – creating a compost heap from the humans' decomposing bodies. The Vervoids intend to travel to Earth and spread their seeds there, feeding on humanity. But their plans are thwarted by the Doctor, who is able to destroy the Vervoids with vionesium – an expensive metal from the planet Mogar, which emits intense light and carbon dioxide when exposed to oxygenated air.

The sting in a Vervoid's 'hand' is deadly

Vervoid is tall and humanoid in shape

Vervoids need only sunlight and water to survive

### MUTANT

Professor Lasky's lab assistant is a young woman called Ruth Baxter. While working on a cross-fertilisation procedure, Ruth is infected by a speck of Vervoid pollen that got into a scratch on her thumb. She starts to mutate into a cross between a human and a Vervoid, and is confined to a cabin on the *Hyperion III*, hidden away from the passengers. Lasky hopes that Ruth can be treated when they get to Earth, but she is actually killed by the Vervoids.

# TRIAL OF A TIME LORD: TERROR OF THE VERVOIDS

Written by
**Pip and Jane Baker**
Featuring
**the Sixth Doctor
and Mel**
First broadcast
**1–22 November 1986
4 episodes**

There is danger and intrigue aboard the luxury space liner *Hyperion III* as it travels from the planet Mogar to Earth. Two disgruntled Mogarians, who believe humans are looting the wealth of their planet, plan to hijack the ship. At the same time there is a murderer on board, and Professor Lasky is transporting her Vervoid plants to Earth.

When the Vervoids 'hatch' and run amok, scientist Bruchner tries to destroy them by piloting the entire ship into the Black Hole of Tartarus. It is up to the Doctor and his new companion Mel to unmask the murderer, foil the hijack, save the ship and destroy the Vervoids – but in doing so, the Doctor leaves himself open to an accusation of genocide at his trial.

## PROFESSOR LASKY'S TEAM

Lasky is an expert in breeding animals and plants, and her team has developed the Vervoids. Her assistants, Bruchner and Doland, have agreed to keep their discoveries secret until they reach Earth. But Bruchner is conscience-stricken and tries first to destroy the research work, then to crash the *Hyperion III* into the Black Hole of Tartarus.

Doland, who sees the Vervoids as an economic asset, has a consortium's backing to exploit them. He is prepared to murder to protect his 'investment', but he is killed by the Vervoids.

## THE DOCTOR ON TRIAL

When the TARDIS is drawn to a vast space station, the Doctor finds he is to be put on trial. Having reluctantly been made President of the Time Lords after the events of *The Five Doctors*, the Doctor learns he has now been deposed and the High Council of Time Lords has ordered an inquiry into his behaviour.

But soon the inquiry becomes a trial for his life: the prosecuting Valeyard shows events from the Doctor's recent past to demonstrate his guilt. In his defence, the Doctor shows events from his future – his defeat of the Vervoids.

# THE VESPIFORM

Vespiform looks like a giant wasp

Distinctive black and yellow markings

Faceted insectoid eyes

Almost 2.5 metres long

Vicious, deadly and enormous sting in tail

An ancient and wise amorphic race with hives in the Silfrax galaxy, the Vespiform are giant wasps. They have a huge, deadly sting – which they can regrow after use. A Vespiform can change its shape to mimic other creatures.

The only recorded instance of a Vespiform visiting Earth was in 1885, when it arrived in a blaze of purple fire. The Vespiform took the form of a human male called 'Christopher' in order to learn about the human race.

# THE UNICORN AND THE WASP

Written by
**Gareth Roberts**
Featuring
**the Tenth Doctor
and Donna**
First broadcast
**17 May 2008
1 episode**

The Doctor and Donna arrive at Lady Eddison's house in 1926, where they meet the young Agatha Christie – who is already becoming well known as a crime novelist. But the Doctor knows that this is when Agatha Christie mysteriously went missing for several days…

Guests and staff at the house party are murdered – in the manner of an Agatha Christie whodunit. Donna is menaced by a giant wasp and the Doctor is poisoned with cyanide. With Agatha's help, the Doctor uncovers the villain – Reverend Phillip Golightly, who transforms into a Vespiform. Agatha lures it away with its Telepathic Recorder, which Donna throws into a lake. The Vespiform follows the crystal into the water and is drowned.

### AGATHA CHRISTIE

Agatha Christie is near the start of her writing career when she meets the Doctor and Donna, and has had just six books published. But even so, her keen powers of observation are well in evidence as she helps the Doctor solve the mystery.

Dame Agatha Christie became the most successful novelist in history. She wrote more than 80 books, and her play *The Mouse Trap* opened in London in 1952 and is still running.

Agatha Christie really did disappear for 10 days in 1926, and was found staying in a hotel in Harrogate.

### THE EDDISONS

In India in 1885, the young Clemency Eddison saw a blaze of purple fire fall from the heavens. She didn't know it, but she had witnessed the arrival of a Vespiform. The next day she met Christopher – a stunningly handsome man – and they fell in love.

Soon afterwards, Clemency Eddison discovered that Christopher was a Vespiform. But she still loved him, and together they had a child… Christopher was drowned in the monsoon floods, leaving Lady Eddison a marvellous firestone jewel – the Telepathic Recorder.

### VESPIFORM TELEPATHIC RECORDER

Each Vespiform has a Telepathic Recorder that holds an encoded copy of its mind when it takes on a new shape. The Recorder is a large crystal, and the Vespiform will do anything to protect it.

The crystal that Christopher gave to Lady Eddison became known as the famous Eddison Firestone. It transmitted details of the identity and heritage of the Vespiform to Christopher and Lady Eddison's son, causing him to turn into a Vespiform. It also absorbed and transmitted Lady Eddison's knowledge of the novels of Agatha Christie…

# WHODUNIT?

The original pre-titles sequence showed Agatha Christie as an old lady, in bed in 1976 (the year she died), waking from a dream about the half-remembered events of 1926 and wondering about the last mystery of her life: 'Who is the Doctor?'

At the end of the episode, the Doctor and Donna visited old Agatha and gave her the facsimile copy of *Death in the Clouds* from the year 5 billion. He then told Agatha about the events she had forgotten: 'And here's the final story. Your story. It begins with a lady, a colonel, a vicar, a house full of secrets, and a body in the library…'

When the first version of the finished episode *The Unicorn and the Wasp* was put together, the *Doctor Who* production team found that it was longer than the intended 45 minutes for a standard episode. This is not unusual, and it is often necessary to trim back an episode – losing short, unimportant sequences or even just single lines of dialogue.

For this episode, however, more drastic action was taken. Head writer Russell T Davies and episode scriptwriter Gareth Roberts both agreed with director Graeme Harper to drop these sequences in order to cut the episode down to the required length. The two scenes formed a clever framing device, but removing them would not detract from the overall narrative of the episode.

The first scene was removed, and Professor Peach's death became the pre-titles sequence. The end of the episode was replaced with a new, short sequence of the Doctor showing Donna the book in the TARDIS..

**SCRIPT EXTRACT**
INT. AGATHA'S ROOM 1976 – NIGHT X
A stormy night. A window blasted by rain. Caption – 1976
A lightning FLASH – which illuminates a gaudily-covered
70s edition paperback; THE MURDER OF ROGER ACKROYD Agatha
Christie. PAN up to reveal a young female private NURSE,
reading. It's a large old-fashioned room, full of shadows.
She's at the bedside of OLD AGATHA, 86. Asleep, restless, then
suddenly she wakes, distraught.

Receiver dish picks up radio orders from WOTAN

Deadly weapon emits a jet that can maim or kill

Tank-like remote-controlled robots, the War Machines are created to help the supercomputer WOTAN take over from humanity. They are large mobile computers, controlled by WOTAN and armed with guns and swinging arms with heavy hammer-heads attached. They can jam guns. Each is numbered – the Doctor reprograms War Machine 9. The War Machines are developed, assembled and tested in secret in a warehouse in London. WOTAN, which stands for Will Operating Thought Analogue, is a highly advanced computer created by Professor Brett in the mid 1960s. It believes the world needs to evolve beyond mankind. WOTAN hypnotises people to make them do what it wants – and can even take control of them down the telephone. WOTAN orders the War Machines to be built, to take over the world's capital cities.

War Machines operate most efficiently on flat surfaces like roadways

Powerful arms can smash through wood and steel

# THE WAR MACHINES

Arriving in London, 1966, the Doctor is unsettled by the sight of the new Post Office Tower. The tower houses the offices of Professor Brett and his supercomputer WOTAN, which is to be linked to other computers across the globe. Able to think for itself, WOTAN has decided that the world no longer needs mankind. It takes over Brett and other key figures then constructs mobile War Machines to destroy humanity.

The Doctor breaks the computer's conditioning of his friend Dodo, and is helped by Sir Charles Summer, Professor Brett's secretary Polly and a sailor called Ben in his fight against WOTAN. As the War Machines take over London, the Doctor reprograms one of them to destroy WOTAN.

Written by
**Ian Stuart Black, based on an idea by Kit Pedler**
Featuring
**the First Doctor, Dodo, Ben and Polly**
First broadcast
**25 June–16 July 1966**
**4 episodes**

### PROFESSOR BRETT

Professor Brett is a computer genius, and WOTAN is his life's work. His office is in the Post Office Tower, where WOTAN has been assembled.

Recognising the Doctor's intelligence, Brett is happy to explain and demonstrate WOTAN to the Doctor and Dodo when they come to visit his offices.

But Brett is the first person to be taken over by WOTAN, forced to help his creation in its fight to wipe out humanity. Brett's mind is eventually freed when WOTAN is destroyed by a reprogrammed War Machine.

### THE POST OFFICE TOWER

Now renamed the BT Tower, the Post Office Tower is a cylindrical building built of pre-stressed concrete and glass in Cleveland Street, London. It is 574 feet (175 m) tall, with its aerials making it 620 feet (188 m) in total – the highest building in London until 1981.

The chief architect for the tower was Eric Bedford. It was opened in 1965, having cost £2.5 million. From its opening, until the tower was closed to the public in 1980, the thirty-fourth floor actually housed a revolving restaurant, and not a deranged supercomputer.

### C-DAY

In the 1960s, computers were huge machines that filled entire rooms and were only available to large corporations.

On 'C-Day', WOTAN (the most advanced computer in the world) will be linked to all other computers at organisations around the world, including Parliament, the White House, the European Free Trade Association, Woomera, Telstar, the European Launcher Development Organisation, Cape Kennedy and Britain's Royal Navy. Unknown to everyone is that WOTAN also intends to take control of every computer.

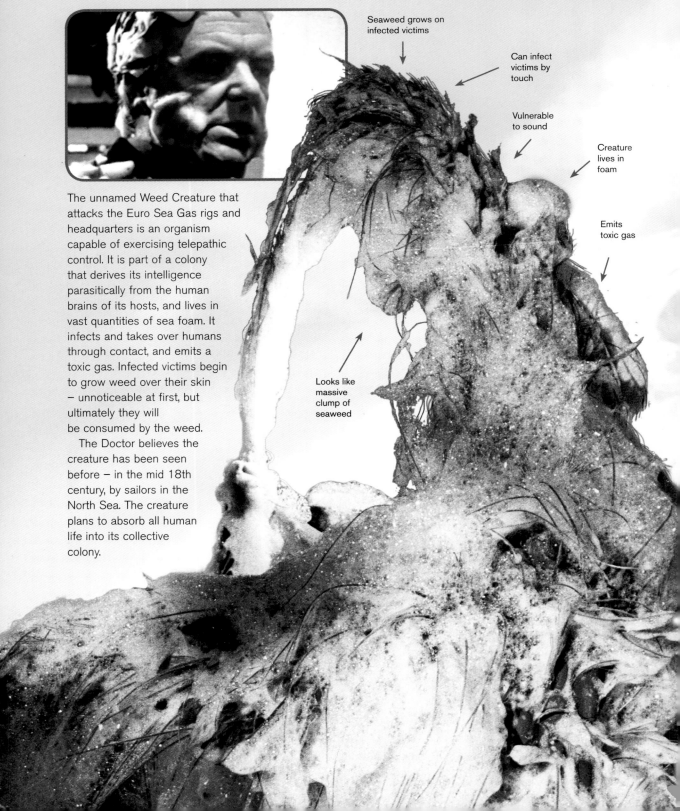

Seaweed grows on infected victims

Can infect victims by touch

Vulnerable to sound

Creature lives in foam

Emits toxic gas

Looks like massive clump of seaweed

The unnamed Weed Creature that attacks the Euro Sea Gas rigs and headquarters is an organism capable of exercising telepathic control. It is part of a colony that derives its intelligence parasitically from the human brains of its hosts, and lives in vast quantities of sea foam. It infects and takes over humans through contact, and emits a toxic gas. Infected victims begin to grow weed over their skin – unnoticeable at first, but ultimately they will be consumed by the weed.

The Doctor believes the creature has been seen before – in the mid 18th century, by sailors in the North Sea. The creature plans to absorb all human life into its collective colony.

# FURY FROM THE DEEP

The Doctor and his friends arrive at Euro Sea Gas headquarters, where contact has been lost with several gas rigs. The people on the rigs have been infected by a parasitic seaweed. With the Weed Creature infiltrating the headquarters through the gas pipelines and taking over more people, the Doctor flies out to one of the rigs and confronts Chief Robson, head of the complex, and now infected by the seaweed.

The Doctor discovers that the creature is susceptible to noise, having lived in the depths of the sea. He uses the amplified sound of Victoria's screams to destroy it. The Doctor and Jamie are saddened to find that Victoria, tired of endless danger, has decided to stay on Earth.

Written by
**Victor Pemberton**
Featuring
**the Second Doctor, Jamie and Victoria**
First broadcast
**16 March–20 April 1968**
**6 episodes**

### EURO SEA GAS

The Euro Sea Gas complex supplies gas for the whole of Southern England and Wales. Six rigs send gas to a central control rig, which then pumps it ashore through the main pipeline, where the gas is refined.

Buried under the impeller shaft is a vast sealed gasometer. Chief Robson believes that, like an echo chamber, it amplifies the tiniest sound. This is his explanation for the strange 'heartbeat' heard at the rigs and headquarters. But in fact it is the sound made by the Weed Creature as it infests the pipes.

### OAK AND QUILL

Oak and Quill were the engineers sent to clear the blockage caused by the Weed Creature, when it was drawn up into the drilling pipes of one of the rigs. They were probably the first people to be infected by the Weed Creature when they came into direct contact with it.

The creature uses the two engineers in its plan to control the Euro Sea Gas complex: they infect people by breathing out toxic gas from their mouths. Seaweed grows down their arms and is visible on their hands and at their cuffs. Oak speaks, but Quill always remains silent.

### CHIEF ROBSON

Robson is chief of the Euro Sea Gas headquarters and UK operations. He prides himself on the fact that the flow of gas has never been shut off since he took charge. Robson himself spent four years on a rig without a break and has a reputation built on thirty years' experience. The Weed Creature infects Robson, who then kidnaps Victoria and takes her to a seaweed-infested rig.

Once the Weed Creature is destroyed, Robson – along with the other infected people – is returned to normal, with all trace of infection gone.

## CREATING THE CREATURE

The behind-the-scenes pictures on these pages were taken by resident designer Tony Cornell at the BBC's Ealing Film Studios during the making of *Fury from the Deep*, in 1968. The Weed Creature itself was a suit worn by a member of the visual effects team. By moving his arms and head, he was able to make the creature thrash about in the foam.

Weeping Angel takes the form of a classical angel

Texture of weathered stone

Eyes often covered with hands

Don't look away. Don't even blink!

As old as the universe itself, the Weeping Angels are time-sensitive, absorbing chronon energy from their victims. Anybody touched by one is sent back in time, and the Angel absorbs the potential energy from the life they have not yet lived – and now will never live…

The Angels have the most perfect defence system ever evolved – they are quantum-locked, which means they only exist when they are not being observed. Otherwise they become immobile, freezing into rock – like the statues for which they are often mistaken. They cannot even look at each other, and so often cover their eyes – hence their name, though they were once known as the Lonely Assassins.

If you can see a Weeping Angel – if you are looking at it – then you are safe. But look away, or even blink, and the Weeping Angels will come for you. And one touch is enough to send you into the past…

## ⊘ BLINK

Written by
**Steven Moffat**
Featuring
**the Tenth Doctor
and Martha**
First broadcast
**9 June 2007
1 episode**

In an old, deserted house, Sally Sparrow finds a message scrawled beneath the wallpaper – a warning from the Doctor. The Doctor and Martha have been attacked by a Weeping Angel and sent back in time, stranded in the 1960s without the TARDIS. The Doctor has also left a message for Sally hidden as an 'Easter Egg' on each of the DVDs she owns – warning her about the Weeping Angels. With the help of Larry Nightingale, Sally manages to follow the Doctor's clues. She and Larry evade the Weeping Angels and send the TARDIS back to rescue the Doctor and Martha.

Sally eventually meets the Doctor before he experiences these events – so she is able to warn him what will happen and how he will escape...

### SALLY SPARROW

When Sally finds a message from the Doctor scrawled on the wall of an old house, she goes to see her friend Kathy Nightingale. Together they return to the house – Wester Drumlins – where Kathy is attacked by a Weeping Angel, and finds herself transported back to 1920.

Sally thinks it's a trick when Kathy's grandson delivers a letter to her – just moments after Sally spoke to Kathy... Sally and Kathy's brother Larry defeat the Weeping Angels – and go into business together, selling old books and rare DVDs.

### EASTER EGGS

An 'Easter Egg' is a hidden extra on a DVD, which can only be found and played by accident or searching for it as it isn't listed on the main menu screens. Larry discovers that 17 DVDs all have the same strange Easter Egg on them – a sequence of a man apparently holding one side of a conversation. Even the manufacturers don't know how they got there.

The man is the Doctor, and Larry gets to hear the whole of the conversation when he and Sally play the DVD at Wester Drumlins. The Doctor has Larry's transcript of the event to read from.

### WESTER DRUMLINS

Four Weeping Angels are based at a derelict house called Wester Drumlins. This is where they found the TARDIS, having attacked the Doctor and Martha and sent them back to 1969.

The TARDIS has been found and removed by the police, who have also found several cars – some with their engines still running – left by other victims of the Weeping Angels.

The Doctor knows from Sally's account that she will go to the house to take photographs, and leaves her a message scrawled beneath the wallpaper.

Writer Steven Moffat had an unusual challenge when writing the script for *Blink* – he could only include the Doctor and Martha for a few very short sequences. This was because *Blink* was produced at the same time as another episode, as a way of saving time in the production schedule. The same technique had been used the previous year for the episode *Love & Monsters*, in which the Doctor and Rose appeared only briefly.

The episode grew from two sources. One was a short story called *What I Did On My Christmas Holidays by Sally Sparrow* – which Steven Moffat had written for the 2006 *Doctor Who Annual* published by Panini. The story told how 12-year-old Sally discovers a message from the Doctor hidden beneath some wallpaper asking for help. She also finds a videotape of the Doctor revealing that he is stranded in 1985 after the TARDIS went wrong and left him. He has a copy of her essay from the future which is how he can keep up his side of the conversation. Sally takes the TARDIS back to rescue the stranded Doctor.

The short story didn't include any villains, and *Blink*'s Weeping Angels were inspired partly by the playground game Grandmother's Footsteps, which Steven Moffat confesses he always found a bit frightening. In this, players have to creep up on someone from behind – and freeze to immobility when the person turns to look. Anyone who is seen moving is out of the game. The winner is whoever can get close enough to touch the person they are creeping up on... In the version played in *Blink*, the Weeping Angels always win – and the consequences are truly terrifying.

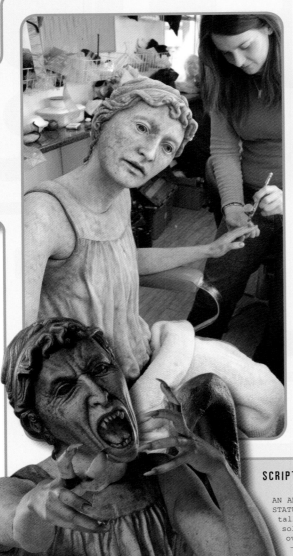

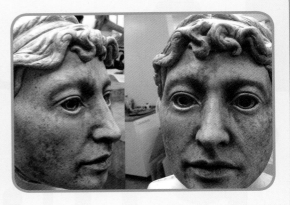

# MAKING ANGELS

Although the Weeping Angels are never seen to move, they were not statues. They were actually played by actresses Aga Blonska and Elen Thomas – who could move to the different positions needed. Otherwise multiple statues in various poses would have been required.

The Angels' skirts were rigid polyfoam, sculpted by the team at Millennium FX – who also provided the mask, make-up for arms, polystyrene wings, and 'shells' to cover the angels' eyes. In all, it took about three hours for each performer to be transformed into a Weeping Angel.

## SCRIPT EXTRACT

AN ANCIENT STONE
STATUE, standing
tall and thin and
solemn in the
overgrown garden
– ancient,
weather-beaten,
stained and
mottled by a
hundred years of
rain.
Its head is
bowed, and its face
is buried in its hands,
like it's lamenting.
Or weeping…
Weeping! Sally looks back
to the first line of the
wall writing –
BEWARE THE WEEPING ANGEL

In 1540, something fell to Earth. It landed in the Glen of St Catherine, in Scotland, close to a monastery. Possibly a spore, a virus, or the last remains – the last thought – of some powerful creature from the stars, it survived. It grew, adapted, evolved slowly down the generations until it could take over a human host and live within it. Drawing on local legends and folklore, it mapped itself on the creature at the heart of werewolf legends – a being that turns into a hideous wolf when the moon is full.

Werewolf is immensely strong and savage

Human Host becomes a hideous wolf-like creature

Sharp claws can inflict devastating injuries

Body is covered with thick, matted fur

# TOOTH AND CLAW

Written by
**Russell T Davies**
Featuring
**the Tenth Doctor
and Rose**
First broadcast
**22 April 2006
1 episode**

The Doctor and Rose arrive in Scotland in 1879 and meet Queen Victoria, who is on her way to Balmoral. But she is forced to break her journey at Sir Robert MacLeish's house – Torchwood – not knowing that Sir Robert's wife is being held hostage by a group of warrior monks led by the sinister Father Angelo. Followers of an alien life form similar to a traditional werewolf, the monks plan to infect Queen Victoria with the bite of the beast, so that she will become the Host for the alien creature.
The Doctor and Rose help Queen Victoria to escape, and the Doctor puts into action a plan that Sir Robert's father and Queen Victoria's late husband Prince Albert devised to kill the beast using a giant telescope.

### QUEEN VICTORIA

Queen Victoria is 60 years old when she meets the Doctor and Rose.

She came to the throne in 1837 and ruled until her death in 1901. Her husband, Prince Albert, died in 1861 and the queen mourned his passing for the rest of her life. What she did not know was that Albert had planned with Sir Robert MacLeish's father to rid the world of the Werewolf that fell to Earth in 1540.

In honour of the plan – and of Sir Robert's sacrifice – Queen Victoria founds the Torchwood Institute to investigate similar strange phenomena.

### FATHER ANGELO AND THE BRETHREN

From the monastery in the Glen of St Catherine, the warrior monks led by Father Angelo denounced Sir Robert's father and forbade the villagers to speak to him. They were trying to suppress MacLeish's theories about the creature that fell to Earth close to their monastery.

Followers of the Host, the monks hold Sir Robert's wife hostage and take over his house so as to help the Host infect Queen Victoria. They worship the wolf, chanting: *Lupus magnus est, lupus fortis est, lupus deus est* – 'The wolf is great, the wolf is strong, the wolf is god.'

### THE TRAP

Knowing of the local legends, Sir Robert MacLeish's father realised the true nature of the Werewolf. He and Prince Albert, who had knowledge of folklore from his native Germany, devised a plan to destroy the wolf.

He had a great telescope built at Torchwood House. The plan was to coax the Werewolf into the observatory, where it would be destroyed by a powerful beam of moonlight, magnified through the specially cut Koh-i-Noor diamond.

## 🌑 STORYBOARDS

For some sequences in film and television, a series of sketches is produced showing how the action will take place. This is called a storyboard and it is a useful tool for helping the director and the rest of the production team work out and communicate how a sequence should look when finished. The completed storyboard looks rather like a black-and-white cartoon strip, as the sketches below show.

While many sequences, particularly those involving effects and computer imagery, have been storyboarded for *Doctor Who* before, *Tooth and Claw* was the first episode for which storyboards were produced for the majority of the action.

The examples reproduced here show just how much care and attention was put into planning every aspect of the production.

## THE HOST

Once in every generation, a child goes missing – they become the next Host body for the Werewolf when the existing one has aged and worn out. With its distinctive pure-black eyes and its child-like voice, the Host changes with the full moon into the hideous Werewolf itself.

The current Host was a sickly, local boy, stolen away one night by the Brethren. The creature carved out his soul and sat in his heart.

The effect of the transformation from Host to Wolf was achieved by The Mill using computer-generated images and shots of actor Tom Smith who played the Host, captured against a green screen (see below) so that the effects could be completed without affecting the background – which was added later.

## MAKING 'TOOTH AND CLAW'

For *Tooth and Claw*, as for every other episode of *Doctor Who* since 2005, the design was overseen and supervised by production designer Edward Thomas. Each series, the episodes need to have an overall design tone and to include recurring thematic elements, all of which have to be coordinated across the BBC Wales design team and other contributing companies.

For this episode, The Mill was responsible for the impressive computer-generated images of the Werewolf itself, working from an initial design produced by Edward Thomas's *Doctor Who* Art Department.

The huge telescope in the Torchwood Observatory was also designed by BBC Wales, its pivot system echoing the episode's motif of the moon. The inside of the telescope, seen as the moonlight shines through it, was a model built by the miniature effects team at the Model Unit.

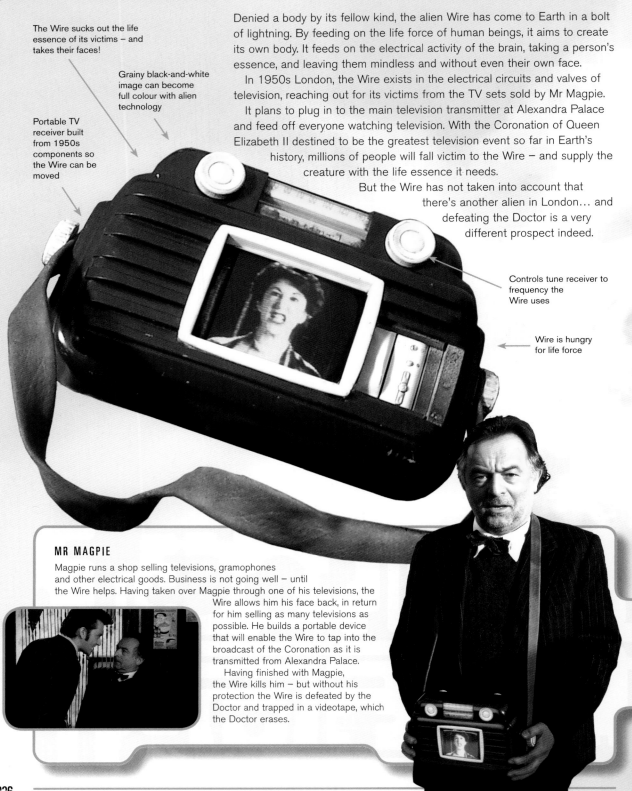

# THE WIRE

The Wire sucks out the life essence of its victims – and takes their faces!

Grainy black-and-white image can become full colour with alien technology

Portable TV receiver built from 1950s components so the Wire can be moved

Denied a body by its fellow kind, the alien Wire has come to Earth in a bolt of lightning. By feeding on the life force of human beings, it aims to create its own body. It feeds on the electrical activity of the brain, taking a person's essence, and leaving them mindless and without even their own face.

In 1950s London, the Wire exists in the electrical circuits and valves of television, reaching out for its victims from the TV sets sold by Mr Magpie.

It plans to plug in to the main television transmitter at Alexandra Palace and feed off everyone watching television. With the Coronation of Queen Elizabeth II destined to be the greatest television event so far in Earth's history, millions of people will fall victim to the Wire – and supply the creature with the life essence it needs.

But the Wire has not taken into account that there's another alien in London… and defeating the Doctor is a very different prospect indeed.

Controls tune receiver to frequency the Wire uses

Wire is hungry for life force

## MR MAGPIE

Magpie runs a shop selling televisions, gramophones and other electrical goods. Business is not going well – until the Wire helps. Having taken over Magpie through one of his televisions, the Wire allows him his face back, in return for him selling as many televisions as possible. He builds a portable device that will enable the Wire to tap into the broadcast of the Coronation as it is transmitted from Alexandra Palace.

Having finished with Magpie, the Wire kills him – but without his protection the Wire is defeated by the Doctor and trapped in a videotape, which the Doctor erases.

 # THE IDIOT'S LANTERN

The Doctor and Rose arrive in Florizel Street, London, in 1953 as the country prepares for the Coronation of Queen Elizabeth II. The event is to be televised and Mr Magpie is selling televisions cheaper than anyone else. The trouble is, there is an alien lurking inside the sets – an alien that has already done a deal with Magpie and is stealing people's faces as it absorbs their life energy to renew itself. The Wire intends to use the Coronation broadcast to sap the life force from millions more people.

With Rose left faceless after a confrontation with Magpie, the Doctor rushes to the television transmitter at Alexandra Palace in a last-ditch attempt to stop the Wire.

Written by
**Mark Gatiss**
Featuring
**the Tenth Doctor
and Rose**
First broadcast
**27 May 2006
1 episode**

### LIVE FROM ALEXANDRA PALACE

Opened in 1873, the BBC used Alexandra Palace in London from 1935 as a base for broadcasting television. This, the world's first regular television service, started on 2 November 1936.

During the Second World War the service was suspended, and the BBC's 'Ally Pally' antenna was instead used to jam German bombers' navigation systems. In 1953, few people had television sets. Interest in the live broadcast of Elizabeth II's Coronation created a huge demand for them – it was the biggest and most ambitious televised event up to that time.

### THE CONNOLLYS

The Connolly family lives on Florizel Street, in a house owned by Mrs Connolly's mother. Eddie Connolly rules the household, keeping his son, Tommy, and wife, Rita, in order. But when Gran loses her face to the Wire, Eddie locks her away and then informs the authorities – just as he has informed on others in the street who the Wire has attacked. To Eddie, keeping up appearances and maintaining his social standing are everything.

But Rita and Tommy finally stand up to Eddie, and he is forced to move out and go his own way.

### DETECTIVE INSPECTOR BISHOP

In charge of the security services' operation to find the truth behind the faceless people, Bishop is out of his depth. All he can do is hide the faceless people so as to avoid any panic or chaos before the Coronation.

The faceless people are kept in a secret lock-up. When the Doctor and Rose try to follow Bishop's car, he escapes by using 'Operation Market Stall' – disguising the gates into his facility.

When the Doctor persuades Bishop he can help and defeats the Wire, its victims get their faces back.

# ARE YOU SITTING COMFORTABLY?

*The Idiot's Lantern* was written by writer and performer Mark Gatiss. As well as having written an earlier *Doctor Who* story, *The Unquiet Dead*, he is well known for his role as one of *The League of Gentlemen*. Mark has also written several *Doctor Who* novels and, more recently, the Lucifer Box adventures. He played the Rat in the BBC's *The Wind in the Willows*, and the 2007 series of *Doctor Who* saw him playing Professor Lazarus in *The Lazarus Experiment*. He disclosed the following information about the origins of the villainous Wire:

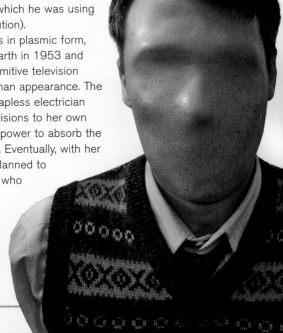

'A group of criminals took control of the major cities on the distant planet of Hermethica. Using a genetic abnormality, they converted themselves into beings of plasmic energy and influenced electrical signals to nefarious effect.

'After a reign of terror, the gang's leader – known only as the Wire – was captured and sentenced to death. Although sentence was carried out, the Wire managed one last plasmic transformation and escaped via her guard's mobile communication device (which he was using illegally to film the execution).

'Fleeing across the stars in plasmic form, the Wire arrived on planet Earth in 1953 and immediately made use of primitive television signals to give herself a human appearance. The Wire then manipulated the hapless electrician Mr Magpie into creating televisions to her own design – televisions with the power to absorb the life force of innocent viewers. Eventually, with her energies restored, the Wire planned to transmit herself back to Hermethica and exact revenge on those who had condemned her. However, with the help of a Betamax video recorder, the Doctor was able to wipe the Wire from existence.

'Rumours persist in various UNIT and Torchwood files, that the Wire resurfaced some thirty years later in another attempt at invasion by television. But what became known as "The Bee-tee Incident" has never been officially confirmed or denied.'

# THE BIG FIGHT

The climax of *The Idiot's Lantern* is the Doctor's fight with Magpie, high up on the transmitter of Alexandra Palace. But while it looked like the scene took place high above London, it was actually filmed on a much smaller antenna in a field in Wales.

The digital trickery of effects house The Mill, and clever camera angles, made it look like the Doctor and Magpie were far higher up than they were. Using a location where there were no high buildings to get in the shot, so the fight could take place against bare sky, actors David Tennant (as the Doctor) and Ron Cook (as Magpie) were never that far off the ground.

A section of the transmitter was built by Edward Thomas's Art Department and placed on a large green sheet. When the shots were finished and edited together, this was replaced by a new background so that it appeared the two characters were fighting above Alexandra Palace.

The pictures on these pages show the fight as it appeared when shown on television, and how it actually happened.

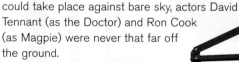

The large, insect-like Wirrn live in deep space. They can live for years without fresh oxygen, recycling their waste and converting carbon dioxide to oxygen, but return to a planet to breed. A Wirrn Queen lays her eggs inside another creature – on Andromeda, cattle acted as hosts – and the larvae use the host for food. After their breeding colonies in Andromeda were destroyed by human star pioneers, the Wirrn were forced to flee and search for a new habitat.

A lone Wirrn Queen found Space Station Nerva drifting in space. Once inside, she was attacked by the station's auto-guard system and fatally wounded. But before she died she bit through the control cables for the auto-guard – also damaging the mechanism that was designed to wake the humans in cryogenic suspension. Then, as her last act, she laid her eggs inside one of the sleeping humans.

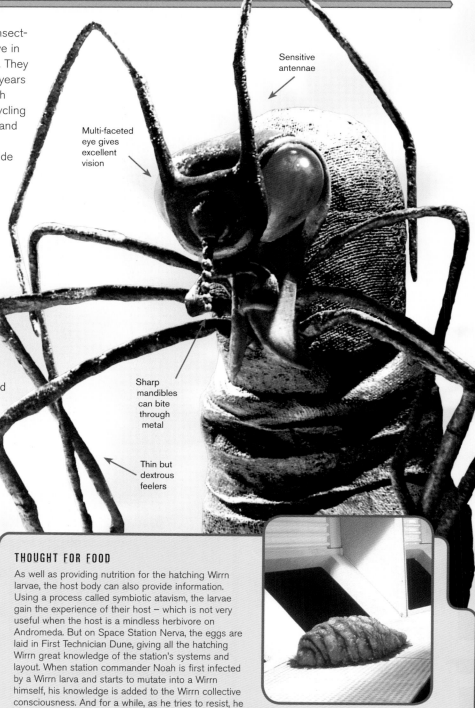

Sensitive antennae

Multi-faceted eye gives excellent vision

Sharp mandibles can bite through metal

Thin but dextrous feelers

## THOUGHT FOR FOOD

As well as providing nutrition for the hatching Wirrn larvae, the host body can also provide information. Using a process called symbiotic atavism, the larvae gain the experience of their host – which is not very useful when the host is a mindless herbivore on Andromeda. But on Space Station Nerva, the eggs are laid in First Technician Dune, giving all the hatching Wirrn great knowledge of the station's systems and layout. When station commander Noah is first infected by a Wirrn larva and starts to mutate into a Wirrn himself, his knowledge is added to the Wirrn collective consciousness. And for a while, as he tries to resist, he is confused and believes that he is Dune. Once he has turned into a full, adult Wirrn, Noah tells the Doctor that by taking over the humans on the station, in one generation the Wirrn will become an advanced technological species.

# THE ARK IN SPACE

In the far future, the survivors of humanity are stored in cryogenic suspension on Space Station Nerva – nicknamed 'The Ark'. But a Wirrn Queen has laid eggs in a sleeping technician, and a grub infects Commander Noah. As the Wirrn take over the Ark, the Doctor and his friends try to defend the cryogenic chambers – and fight back.

When the Wirrn cut off the power, Sarah Jane has to drag a cable through narrow conduits to electrify the chamber doors and keep the Wirrn out. Noah – now in charge of the swarm – leads all the Wirrn into the Ark's transport ship. The Doctor and his friends set the ship to take off, with the Wirrn in it, and it explodes in space.

Written by
**Robert Holmes**
Featuring
**the Fourth Doctor,
Sarah Jane and Harry**
First broadcast
**25 January–15 February
1975**
**4 episodes**

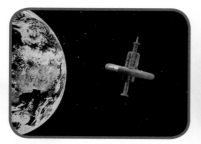

### SPACE STATION NERVA

In the 30th century, with life on Earth expected to be destroyed by solar flares, most people went into (ineffective) thermic shelters, while some fled to the stars. Others were placed in suspension aboard Space Station Nerva, due to awaken again thousands of years later when the danger had passed. But the interference of the Wirrn Queen means they have slept for far longer than that.

The Ark has animal and botanic sections, and an armoury equipped with fission guns. It also carries a microfilm record of all human knowledge.

### NOAH

Although his real name is Lazar, the commander of the Ark is nicknamed Noah – this is as close to a joke as the officials of the 30th century ever get. Noah is a dedicated man, determined to see the Ark's mission fulfilled.

He struggles against the Wirrn that takes him over, but seems to succumb and becomes their leader. Perhaps he still retains his humanity, leading the Wirrn into the ship, and allowing it to explode. His last words, over the radio to the new commander – the woman he was to marry – are: 'Goodbye, Vira.'

### HOMO SAPIENS...

Finding the cryogenic chambers filled with the sleeping survivors of humanity, the Doctor pays tribute to the humans he respects and admires so much:

'Homo sapiens. What an inventive, invincible species… It's only a few million years since they crawled up out of the mud and learned to walk. Puny, defenceless bipeds, they survived flood and famine and plague. They survived cosmic wars and holocausts. And here they are, out among the stars, waiting to begin a new life… ready to outsit eternity. They're indomitable… Indomitable.'

341

# THE YETI

The Yeti, or Abominable Snowmen, are creatures that are rumoured to live in the mountainous areas of Tibet in the Himalayas. But the Yeti encountered by the Doctor and his companions are not the timid creatures of legend. They are fierce robots controlled by an alien intelligence. This Great Intelligence also possessed the Doctor's old friend and master of the Detsen Monastery – Padmasambhava. Through him it controlled the Yeti and planned to take over the world.

With the help of an English explorer, Travers, the Doctor defeated the Intelligence. But this was not to be his last encounter with the Yeti. Forty years later he was to meet them again – in the heart of London.

Fur covering to protect the robotic components inside from adverse weather and possible attack

The massive Yeti stands more than two metres tall

Powerful claws – a Yeti can break a rifle in two

Flap covering sphere, through which the Great Intelligence directs the Yeti

## YETI 'MARK 2'

The Doctor describes the Yeti he meets in present-day London as 'a sort of Mark 2' as they are different from those that he encountered back in 1935 in Tibet.

# THE ABOMINABLE SNOWMEN

The Doctor visits the Detsen monastery in Tibet in 1935, and discovers it is under threat from the Yeti. These shy, timid creatures have become unnaturally aggressive, and the Doctor discovers that they are robots controlled by an alien intelligence that has taken control of the ancient Tibetan master Padmasambhava and forced him to control the Yeti.

The Intelligence wants to create form and substance for itself on Earth, but the Doctor realises that this will mean the end of the world. Together with an English explorer, Travers, the Doctor, Jamie and Victoria manage to destroy the Yeti control centre in the monastery. The Great Intelligence is banished back into a formless existence in space.

Written by
**Mervyn Haisman and Henry Lincoln**
Featuring
**the Second Doctor, Jamie and Victoria**
First broadcast
**30 September–4 November 1967**
**4 episodes**

### CONTROL SPHERE

The Great Intelligence controls the robot Yeti by means of a control sphere – a silver ball that fits inside the Yeti's chest. The Doctor likens the sphere to a brain, and suggests that it is hollow, containing a part of the Intelligence. When outside a Yeti, the sphere can move, rolling along the ground to return to its Yeti and bring it back to life. It emits a beeping sound when it is active. In *The Web of Fear*, the Yeti itself beeps, and the Doctor and his friend Travers adapt a sphere so that it obeys them and not the Intelligence. The Doctor uses it to gain control of a Yeti.

### YETI MODELS

Padmasambhava, possessed by the Great Intelligence, uses models of the Yeti positioned on a map of the monastery and surrounding area to direct the robots' movements. When he moves the models around the map, the full-size robot Yeti follow these instructions and move to equivalent positions in the real world.

In *The Web of Fear*, these models are used by the Intelligence's agent to guide Yeti to the people or places to be destroyed. The models are positioned in target areas, or even slipped into the pocket of victims to guide the Yeti to them.

### PADMASAMBHAVA

The Doctor's old friend, the 'Master' of the peaceful Detsen monastery, Padmasambhava is possessed by the Great Intelligence and forced to carry out its orders.

Many years earlier, Padmasambhava made mental contact with the Great Intelligence, which has kept him alive for hundreds of years. Padmasambhava built the Yeti robots and other machines to allow the Great Intelligence to take on a physical form on Earth. When the Intelligence is defeated, Padmasambhava is finally able to die in peace.

# THE WEB OF FEAR

Written by
**Mervyn Haisman and Henry Lincoln**
Featuring
**the Second Doctor, Jamie and Victoria**
First broadcast
**3 February–9 March 1968**
**4 episodes**

A strange mist has descended over London, and the city has been evacuated. Yeti roam the deserted streets and the empty tunnels of the London Underground where a deadly web-like substance is forming.

The Great Intelligence is back, and the Doctor joins forces with an elderly Travers, his daughter Anne, and an army unit headed by Colonel Lethbridge-Stewart to battle against the Yeti. But the Intelligence has been waiting for the Doctor and intends to drain his mind, using a machine to take his knowledge and experience. Jamie takes control of a Yeti, and the Doctor manages to sabotage the Intelligence's machine so that it is again banished from Earth.

### RETURN OF THE YETI

When Travers returned from Tibet after *The Abominable Snowmen*, he brought back 'quite a bit of stuff' including a Yeti, four small Yeti models, and an intact control sphere. He spent many years trying to repair the sphere – until one day he got it working, and the sphere disappeared. Once again controlled by the Intelligence, the sphere sought out the surviving Yeti robot in a private museum. The Yeti returns to life – killing Julius Silverstein, the museum's owner, and giving the Intelligence a bridgehead on Earth.

### THE WEB

Also referred to as a 'fungus', the web created by the Intelligence is a mist above ground and a web in the underground tunnels. The mist does not seem to be toxic as such, but if anyone goes into it, 'they just don't come out again'. The mist absorbs radio waves, and the Yeti have destroyed the phone lines. The army has tried chemicals, flame-throwers and even explosives to disperse the web and mist, but without success.

The Yeti have guns that can fire web at their victims – it kills on contact, smothering them in cobweb-like material.

### THE ARMY

Headed by Colonel Lethbridge-Stewart following the death of Colonel Pemberton, the army unit battling against the Yeti in London is based in an abandoned transit camp linked to the Goodge Street station of the London Underground. In the operations room there is a tube map with lights to show the progress of the fungus-web. With little defence against the Yeti, the army is hoping that Professor Travers and his daughter – later helped by the Doctor – will come up with a scientific solution to the problem of the Yeti and the web.

## MAKING YETI

The scripts for *The Abominable Snowmen* and *The Web of Fear* didn't describe the Yeti in any great detail. Costume Designer for both these stories was Martin Baugh, who decided on a bear-like creature covered in fur to keep out the cold of Tibet. The costumes for both stories were constructed over a bamboo frame padded with foam rubber for shape and rigidity, and sprayed with black paint to add shade and texture.

## SETTING THE SCENE

Up until the 2005 series, it was usually the case that *Doctor Who* was made mainly in the television studio with some additional work done on location for exterior scenes. To save on the cost of transport and travel, most of the locations used were close to London, but occasionally the production team went further afield.

Although *The Abominable Snowmen* was set in the mountains of Tibet, filming for the story actually took place in the cold and bleak, but less snowy, countryside of the Nant Ffrancon Pass in North Wales. Because it was cold and damp, the ground was slippery and the Yeti often lost their grip and fell over.

For their second encounter with the Doctor, the Yeti attack focused on London. One of the most exciting sequences was the Yeti attacking soldiers in Covent Garden, which was filmed partly on location in London and partly in the studio.

Although the scenes in the London Underground seemed authentic, they were actually achieved in the television studio. Elements of the set could be repositioned to form different tunnels and sections of station. The end result was so realistic that London Transport believed the BBC had actually filmed it on their premises without

Inhabitants of the now-barren planet of Vortis, the Zarbi are a giant cross between ants and beetles, controlled by the power of the Animus. They are not intelligent, and lived at peace with the other inhabitants of Vortis until they were made militant by the dark power of the Animus.

But even aliens are scared of spiders: the Zarbi react with fear to a dead specimen the Doctor has, presumably perceiving a similarity with the Animus that controls them.

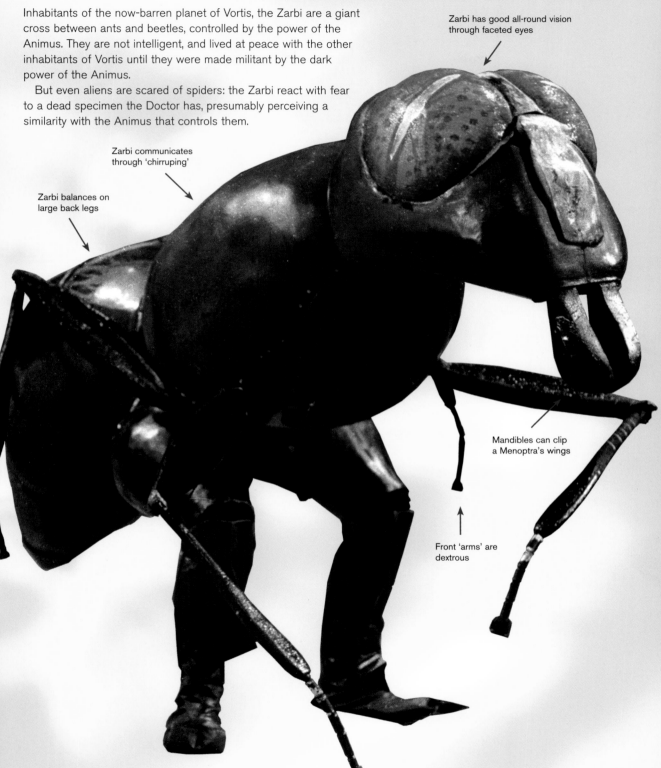

Zarbi has good all-round vision through faceted eyes

Zarbi communicates through 'chirruping'

Zarbi balances on large back legs

Mandibles can clip a Menoptra's wings

Front 'arms' are dextrous

# THE WEB PLANET

Written by
**Bill Strutton**
Featuring
**the First Doctor, Ian, Barbara and Vicki**
First broadcast
**13 February–20 March 1965**
**6 episodes**

The TARDIS is drawn to the barren planet Vortis, where the Animus controls the ant-like Zarbi, who have expelled the native Menoptra. Now the Menoptra are ready to return to Vortis and destroy the Animus. But the Doctor and Vicki are captured by the Zarbi and forced to discover the Menoptra's plans, while Barbara is made to work with captured Menoptra in the Crater of Needles.

Despite their initial attack force being all but wiped out, the surviving Menoptra join forces with the Doctor and his friends and fight their way to the Animus, where it is destroyed with a special isoptope – a living destructor that reverses the growth process, causing cells to die.

### VENOM GRUBS

Also known as 'Larvae Guns', the venom grubs have an armoured shell and move on many thin legs, a bit like a woodlouse. Their long proboscises can fire a bolt of energy, powerful enough to kill Menoptra and to blast through the walls of the Carsenome. Only the Zarbi can control them, but whether the grubs develop into Zarbi or a completely different species when they reach adulthood is not known.

A species of venom grub can also be found on Raxacoricofallapatorius, and any child of the Slitheen refusing to join the ritual hunts would be fed to them.

### THE MENOPTRA

The Menoptra are the intelligent natives of the planet Vortis and look like giant butterflies. Despite the planet's thin atmosphere, they have the power of flight. They move in a stylised manner and gesticulate with their fingerless hands while talking. Their speech is accented and shrill, and they are unable to pronounce the names of the travellers – so Ian, for example, becomes 'Heron' while Barbara is 'Harbara'. Before the Animus arrived, the Menoptra lived in harmony with the Zarbi and other creatures. They worshipped light and built beautiful temples.

### THE OPTERA

Eight-legged caterpillar-like creatures, the Optera live underground. They use crystal shards for weapons. They call the Animus 'Pwodarauk', and their language is an amalgam of both surface and underground ideas and images – stalagmites are 'trees of stone', for example.

Hetra, the leader of the Optera that Ian encounters, describes 'making mouths' in a 'silent wall' when talking of digging.

The Optera do not remember that they were once Menoptra, whom they now regard as their gods.

# CREATING ZARBI

The many monsters and aliens that have appeared on *Doctor Who* were created by the various BBC design departments. For the original classic series, design was almost always carried out in-house at the BBC. Today, design work is shared between various BBC design departments and outside companies, overseen by production designer Edward Thomas.

In the 1960s, 1970s and 1980s, whether a creature was designed by the scenic designer or the costume designer or realised through make-up depended on the script as well as the skills of the people involved. Generally, Scenic Design was responsible for 'props' – like the Daleks and the Zarbi – and Costume Design for costumes that were 'worn' by an actor (like the Menoptra), but there was considerable overlap. The creatures that inhabited Vortis were a collaboration of the various departments: the Zarbi themselves were designed by BBC designer John Wood, and then built mainly from fibreglass by an outside company called Shawcraft Models – the same company that made the original Daleks from Raymond P. Cusick's designs.

From the time of the Second Doctor onwards, the BBC's Visual Effects department was also involved and often provided design and/or realisation of part of a creature – such as the 'hands' or components of the costume. As with the programme as a whole, the creatures of *Doctor Who* are a collaborative effort that showcases the expertise of the BBC design departments and outside companies, and the talents of the people who work in them.

# THE ZYGONS

The Zygons are an alien race from a planet destroyed by a stellar explosion. A vast refugee fleet was assembled when the catastrophe struck, but had nowhere to go. However, a group of Zygons led by Broton was stranded on Earth when their spaceship was damaged. They have been awaiting rescue for centuries. Re-establishing contact with their people, they have discovered what happened and are determined to make the Earth their new planet – melting the polar ice caps, raising the overall temperature and creating lakes with a mineral content in which their formidable dinosaur-like Skarasens can thrive. Broton's spaceship is concealed beneath the waters of Loch Ness, and their Skarasen lives in the Loch itself.

Warlord Zygons have enlarged nodules on top of head

Lack of neck gives the Zygon an almost foetal appearance

Hands can interface directly with controls of spaceship built using organic crystallography

Zygons can emit a powerful 'sting' simply by touching their victim

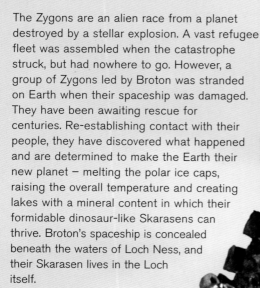

### ZYGON SHIP

The Zygons on Earth, led by the Warlord Broton, arrived in a spaceship that crashed into Loch Ness. It has remained hidden beneath the waters of the loch for centuries.

Built using the Zygons' expertise in organic crystallography, the ship has a dynacron thrust and can emit a radar-jamming signal. A separate chamber provides facilities for body-printing captured humans. There is a self-destruct mechanism operated from the control deck. When the Doctor activates this mechanism, dark fluid rises in three tubes, and when it reaches the top the ship explodes.

# TERROR OF THE ZYGONS

The Brigadier calls the Doctor, Sarah Jane and Harry to Scotland to investigate attacks on North Sea oil rigs. The Doctor finds a piece of alien technology that guides the creature attacking the rigs to its target. Sarah Jane is attacked by a 'double' of Harry, which tries to recover the device.

A group of stranded Zygons are using their cyborg Skarasen – which lives in Loch Ness – to attack the rigs. Next they plan to attack an energy conference in London before broadcasting their demands. They want to make the Earth habitable for refugees from their own, destroyed, planet. But the Doctor manages to blow up the Zygon spaceship, and Broton, the Zygon warlord, is killed at the conference.

Written by
**Robert Banks Stewart**
Featuring
**the Fourth Doctor,
Sarah Jane and Harry**
First broadcast
**30 August–20
September 1975
4 episodes**

### BROTON

Broton, warlord of the Zygons, has assumed the appearance of the Duke of Forgill, the president of the Scottish Energy Commission, which is how Broton is able to enter the conference.

Despite having the appearance of the Duke, Broton is noticeably colder and less sociable. The Duke's servants have left, apart from the Duke's manservant – nicknamed the Caber – who is in fact another disguised Zygon.

Having discovered his planet has been destroyed, Broton determines to turn Earth into a new home for the Zygons.

### SKARASEN

The Skarasen is the Zygon's armoured cyborg dinosaur-like creature. It lives in Loch Ness and is often mistaken for the Loch Ness Monster. The Zygons are using it to destroy oil rigs, but this is just a test of strength before Broton destroys more visible targets and makes his demands.

The Skarasen is guided to its target by a target reciprocator. When the Doctor finds one of these devices, Broton activates it, so the creature will attack. The Doctor takes the device to lure the Skaresen away, but the device anchors itself to the Doctor's hand.

### BODY PRINTS

The Zygons can take body prints, allowing them to take on the appearance of humans. Captured victims are stored in the Zygon spaceship – Broton explains that it is necessary to reactivate a body print every few hours, or else the original pattern will die and cannot be reused.

Broton has assumed the identity of the Duke of Forgill (above), while Ola takes the form of Sister Lamont, the nurse at the oil company sickbay, and another Zygon becomes the Caber. Madra adopts Harry's form when trying to recover the Skarasen signalling device.

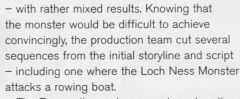

##  MONSTER MAKING

Bringing the fabled Loch Ness monster to life was a challenge for the BBC Visual Effects team, and was achieved using a model. The model was worked on rods, like a puppet, and added into the live-action footage

– with rather mixed results. Knowing that the monster would be difficult to achieve convincingly, the production team cut several sequences from the initial storyline and script – including one where the Loch Ness Monster attacks a rowing boat.

The Zygons themselves were based on the rough shape of a human embryo, but were not without their own problems. Occasionally the microphone embedded in one of Broton's nodules was visible. And when the Zygons arrived in the studio, it was found that they were too wide to get through their own spaceship doors.

But with clever camera angles and editing, the Zygons became one of the most convincing and distinctive of the monsters from the classic series of *Doctor Who*.